A SPOONFUL OF *grace*

A SPOONFUL OF *grace*

Mealtime Blessings in Bite-Sized Pieces

ANNETTE HUBBELL

A Spoonful of Grace

Published in the United States by Credo House Publishers,
a division of Credo Communications, LLC, Grand Rapids, Michigan
www.credohousepublishers.com

ISBN: 978-1-625860-66-8

Cover and interior design by Sharon VanLoozenoord
Editing by Donna Huisjen

Printed in the United States of America

First edition

Lovingly . . .

To daughter, Amy, who brought me to it.

To husband, Monte, who saw me through it.

To God be the glory and the reason for it.

Contents

parsley

Introduction

A Spoonful of Grace, a collection of 366 supercharged mealtime graces, is designed to provide honeyed little morsels—like manna—of meaningful exposure to prayer and the Bible at a most opportune time: the family meal. Like taking a daily vitamin—simple to swallow, yet big on benefits—these spiritual vitamins slip right into the day's busy schedule. They are unique, too, because each one is:

- Inspired by its companion Bible verse(s)
- Designed to be read in its entirety in two minutes or less
- Enhanced by a section called "Grace notes," which are discussion starters (with answers) to promote faith-filled conversations

What is your family's prayer-life like? Some have told me that they don't say grace, wished they did, and would if they had some structure. If you do say a daily grace, does the family look forward to it, or could you use a supplement to keep the exercise from becoming rote, meaningless, or—worse—something you discipline yourselves to get through? Using all 66 books of the Bible, these Scripture/grace duos are intended to restore the heartfelt warmth of prayer while at the same time steeping us in God's Word—one bite at a time. *A Spoonful of Grace* provides a means to develop prayerful habits and to savor the wisdom of the Bible in nourishing mouthfuls.

You'll find that each devotion provides fertile ground for conversation. Like adding vegetables to the spaghetti sauce, these graces nourish the mind and soul, inviting dialogue on faith and values—like sharing, honesty, friendship, and honorable conduct. Add food and—*voilà!*—you have a balanced meal!

If you're using these in the context of a family or other gathering, these readings are inviting, easily understood on various levels, and brief enough to hold the attention of hungry kids. I would venture to say that you're going to hear a certain amount of "*Wait.* It says *that* in the Bible?"

Don't forget to dig into the "Sunday Graces." These 52 readings are bigger spoonfuls—a bit longer— to allow for the suspenseful, engrossing retellings of such favorite stories as those of David and Goliath, Daniel in the lions' den, or Jonah and the big fish. There is also a "Special Graces" section for celebrations such as Easter, Thanksgiving, Christmas, and birthdays.

If you aren't accustomed to a grace-saying lifestyle, you're invited to start here. Whether shared together as a family or savored on your own, these insightful readings provide manna for the soul. If you need courage to say grace aloud in front of others, you'll find what you need here. If your prayer life is already rich, these devotions will add a nourishing tradition to the day.

I hope you enjoy *A Spoonful of Grace* and would love to hear your thoughts. Connecting with each other through a shared experience of devotional reading, discussion, and prayer is so important, and I would welcome stories of how daily grace enhances your life; you're welcome to share these on my website at www.spoonfulofgrace.com.

The combining of eating with prayer was such an important part of the Jewish culture in Jesus' time. Many of his parables were told in the context of eating and drinking, and prayer was an integral part of the daily meal. I can't help but smile when I think of that little boy as he watched Jesus feed 5,000 people with his meager meal of fives loaves and two fish. Give Jesus a little time at your meal and see what happens. You might just be amazed.

EVERYDAY
graces

Scripture

"Don't bargain with God. Be direct. Ask for what you need. This is not a cat-and-mouse, hide-and-seek game we're in. If your little boy asks for a serving of fish, do you scare him with a live snake on his plate? If your little girl asks for an egg, do you trick her with a spider? As bad as you are, you wouldn't think of such a thing—you're at least decent to your own children. And don't you think the Father who conceived you in love will give the Holy Spirit when you ask him?"—Luke 11:10–13 (MSG)

Grace

Dear Jesus, we thank you first, and then we eat! For the food that feeds our bodies and the blessings that feed our minds and souls, we say thanks. Lord, we're so excited about the plans you have for us! Stay by our side and help us grow into great people in your service. Show us that our wants become more like yours as we grow in you. Lord, you're amazing and all-knowing. Amen.

Grace notes

This is all about God giving you what you need, not necessarily what you want, for surely God loves you too much to say yes to prayers that would lead to harm. Look back at a time when, if you'd gotten what you asked for but didn't actually need, it would have been a disaster. Or how about a time when you wanted something so badly . . . but now say *What was I thinking?* Do you know the story of Midas, a greedy king who wished that everything he touched would turn to gold? That desire wasn't well thought out; he got his wish, all right: everything he touched turned to gold—even his food—and he starved to death. "Some of God's greatest gifts," pointed out the Country and Western singer Garth Brooks, "are unanswered prayers." Now *there's* something to think about!

mint

Scripture

"Listen with respect to the father who raised you, and when your mother grows old, don't neglect her. Buy truth—don't sell it for love or money; buy wisdom, buy education, buy insight. Parents rejoice when their children turn out well; wise children become proud parents. So make your father happy! Make your mother proud!"—Proverbs 23:22-25 (MSG)

Grace

Dear Father in heaven, please bless this food and those here with us. Please bless Mom and Dad; we want them to be happy. We know that when we learn the truth, tell the truth, and listen to the wise things they say, it makes them very, very happy. Let's not forget that they want us to be happy, too. And, Lord, when we're happy, they're happy—and that makes you happy! Yay! Everybody's happy. Happy, happy, happy! Amen.

Grace notes

Why do you think people say it's better to give than to receive? Ever notice how people clap their hands together when their happy? Ever notice how happy you feel when you're the cause of someone else's happiness? Think of surprising Grandma (or someone else's Grandma) with your latest drawing, cleaning your room without being asked, inviting a friend over to play with a new puppy, or giving someone a gift you've made. "If we try hard to bring happiness to others, we cannot stop it from coming to us also. To get joy, we must give it, and to keep joy, we must scatter it," said the British stock investor Sir John Marks Templeton, who made it a habit to be generous to others. He knew how to multiply his wealth!

Scripture

"The world of the generous gets larger and larger; the world of the stingy gets smaller and smaller."—Proverbs 11:24 (MSG)

Grace

Dear Father, we are grateful for this food, for our family, and for our time together. Give us generous hearts, Lord; teach us to be big-hearted, as you are. Remind us to do kind, giving things for others without even being asked. Help us see that our kindness might be someone else's only idea of what Jesus is like! Wow, that thought makes our *eyes* get big, too! And give us the desire to practice random acts of kindness—maybe helping someone feel like their world is a little less lonely, a little less cold. Wow, that makes the whole world feel bigger and brighter and happier and better! Yay, God. Amen.

Grace notes

Someone once said "Plant flowers in others' gardens and your life becomes a bouquet." That's another way of saying what fun it is to do nice things for others. So surprise your friend, a neighbor, or the person in line with you at the store with a little kindness. Maybe a smile, holding the door open, sharing your dessert, or letting someone cut in line. Careful—it could become a habit! Funny thing, though: *you're* the one who wins the prize. (What prize do you think this is?) Practicing random acts of kindness is like prayer in action. You can be sure God is smiling right along with you. "We make a living by what we get, but we make a life by what we give," said an unknown author.

bay

Scripture

"Friends love through all kinds of weather, and families stick together in all kinds of trouble."—Proverbs 17:17 (MSG)

Grace

Loving Father, thank you for your love and blessings, for this food, our family, and our friends. Remind us what a gift friendship is—and that includes family friendship. Remind us that to have a friend we have to be one, too. Encourage us to tell our friends how much they mean to us; our words might just change their world. Amen.

Grace notes

"Two persons cannot long be friends, if they cannot forgive each other's little failings," said a wise man named Jean de La Bruyere who lived 500 years ago. What qualities do you want most in a friend? Will you give them back the same qualities? Will you be as honest and kind to your friend as you want them to be to you? Do you have a brother or a sister? Are they your friend, too?

Scripture

"Do not judge, or you too will be judged."—Matthew 7:1 (NIV)

"Don't pick on people, jump on their failures, criticize their faults—unless, of course, you want the same treatment. That critical spirit has a way of boomeranging. It's easy to see a smudge on your neighbor's face and be oblivious to the ugly sneer on your own. Do you have the nerve to say, 'Let me wash your face for you,' when your own face is distorted by contempt? It's this whole traveling road-show mentality all over again, playing a holier-than-thou part instead of just living your part. Wipe that ugly sneer off your own face, and you might be fit to offer a washcloth to your neighbor."—Matthew 7:1–5 (MSG)

Grace

Dear Jesus, thank you for this food before us and for our friends and family. Thank you for helping us see that words like *don't judge* really mean *don't judge in a way you wouldn't want to be judged right back*. Help us see that sometimes what we criticize in others is the very thing we're guilty of doing ourselves. Show us, Lord, that this is really about examining our own lives, reminding us to take a good look in the mirror. Thanks, Jesus, for the washcloth. Amen.

Grace notes

We are more alike than we are different, and it's right to give everyone the benefit of the doubt, especially since we don't always know the whole story. Have you ever reacted badly to someone who seemed to be mean or crabby or unfriendly, only to find out later that they'd had a really bad day and were just miserable? Here's a tip: before you think or say something unkind about someone, imagine that someday they will be your best friend—or maybe your best friend's mother, father, or sister. When you look at it that way you're likely to be more understanding and forgiving. And that, in turn, says good things about *your* character. "When you judge others," said a man named Earl Nightingale, who had a radio show and wrote books, "you do not define them, you define yourself." What do you think he meant by that?

sage

Scripture

"You are the light of the world. A town built on a hill cannot be hidden. Neither do people light a lamp and put it under a bowl. Instead they put it on its stand, and it gives light to everyone in the house. In the same way, let your light shine before others, that they may see your good deeds and glorify your Father in heaven?"—Matthew 5:14–16 (NIV)

Grace

Dear Father, saying grace is one of the ways we praise you because it helps us remember where our food comes from: you. We give you thanks for our meal, for those with us, and for all your blessings today. Guide us to always be your light in this world, Lord, and give us ideas on how to do that. Encourage us to do kind things. When our friends see us doing good, what an example we will be! Food for thought, Lord. Amen.

Grace notes

Here's something you might want to do to shine *your* light: say grace, quietly together, in a restaurant! Not only are you thanking God, but others might see you do it and want to do it, too. (Why not include a blessing for the restaurant workers while you're at it?) Good manners in young people are always a delight (adults might even find it shocking!). What are some other ways you can show politeness? A famous man named Clarence Thomas said this: "Good manners will open doors that the best education cannot." You can be sure he knows what he's talking about—he's a United States Supreme Court Justice.

mint

Scripture

"God told Samuel, 'Looks aren't everything. Don't be impressed with his looks and stature. I've already eliminated him. God judges persons differently than humans do. Men and women look at the face; God looks into the heart.'"—1 Samuel 16:7 (MSG)

Grace

Heavenly Father, thank you for this food and for your blessing. May we come to see, Lord, that you are the *knower* of our hearts. Remind us that you chose the shepherd David—the youngest, least kingly-looking son of Jesse—to conquer the giant Goliath and become Israel's next king—because you knew the goodness in his heart. Thanks for the reminder that with you any of us can accomplish what seems to be impossible, and that if we believe in you you'll choose us to serve you, too. Amen.

Grace notes

This Scripture is about the prophet Samuel's experience in choosing Israel's next king. God refused Samuel's choices seven times before he got it right with David. Samuel thought that any of David's seven big, strong, brothers looked *more kingly* than David, the teenage shepherd. Samuel was looking at the brothers' handsome appearance—their wrapping paper, so to speak. But pretty wrapping doesn't always mean a pretty gift inside, does it? How often do we measure someone's worth—or lack of it—based on their clothes, looks, talents, or personality? Oops. How often do we do that to ourselves? Another oops. "Judgments prevent us from seeing the good that lies beyond appearances," said the author Wayne Dyer. Make a wrong judgment about someone else and both of you lose.

Scripture

"If you listen to me, you will know what is right, just, and fair. You will know what you should do. You will become wise, and your knowledge will give you pleasure."—Proverbs 2:9–10 (GNT)

Grace

Dear God, please bless our food, our family, and our friends. Help us to have happy talk at dinner. Inspire us to walk on the path marked "One Way," the one where we can see you and wave to you. What fun that will be! Teach us that a joyful life is all about having someone to love, someone to care for, something to do, and something to look forward to—that's the path to wisdom and happiness. Amen.

Grace notes

Mother Teresa, a Catholic nun who spent most of her life caring for homeless people in India, believed that God wants us to be faithful more than he cares about whether we're successful. That's because when you're faithful God will take care of all your needs. And he already knows your value. So hand over your burdens and worries to God. He loves you, has a perfect plan for you, and will make sure you're all right. Wisdom is one of the many gifts you'll receive when you listen to God. Not a bad deal, is it? Do you want to be a winner for God's kingdom? Then join God's team!

bay

Scripture

"Young people who obey the law are intelligent. Those who make friends with good-for-nothings are a disgrace to their parents."—Proverbs 28:7 (GNT)

Grace

Heavenly Father, we're grateful for friends who like to have fun while doing what's right. Keep us mindful that "good-for-nothings" can actually be very good at one thing: leading us into trouble. Help us see that we are known by the friends we hang out with. Encourage us to honor Mom and Dad by having friends who honor their own moms and dads. We ask your blessings on this food. Amen.

Grace notes

How can you tell which group of friends to hang with? Some kids form themselves into groups that like to tell you what to do. These in-groups want to control you, so they dare you to make yourself feel big by making others feel small—it's a kind of bullying. "Bullies want to abuse you," says a man named Nick Vujicic. "Instead of allowing that, you can use them as your personal motivators. Power up and let the bully eat your dust." Nick wants you to get strong and build up your "antibully antibodies." What do you think he means by that? Nick certainly has his challenges—he was born without arms or legs. Check out his Facebook page or read his book *Stand Strong: You Can Overcome Bullying (and Other Stuff That Keeps You Down)*.

Scripture

"Seek the Lord and his strength, seek his face continually. Remember his marvellous works that he hath done, his wonders, and the judgments of his mouth."—1 Chronicles 16:11–12 (KJV)

Grace

Almighty God, this is a time to give thanks. We depend on you for everything, including the food you set before us and the family who loves us. Even as we thank you, we remember those who are hungry and the lonely. Teach us that no life has to be lived without direction. Show us the special purpose you have in mind for us, Lord, and help us pay attention. Help us see that when you call us to do something, big or small, you prepare us for the task ahead. We can depend on it! Let's make that "We can depend on *you!*" Amen.

Grace notes

What does it mean to depend on the Lord? It's having someone to talk to, someone who understands you, someone who will give it to you straight up, someone you can go to for help. Does it also mean you can give up all responsibility—just sit back and let God take care of everything? No, of course not. (God didn't give you brains so you could leave them home. Would you want Dad to drive with his eyes closed, depending on God to steer and brake? Ha!) God is your partner; he's with you always. More than just a partner, actually—he's the one in charge. "If God is your co-pilot, then swap seats," said an unknown author.

sage

Scripture

"Let us not become tired of doing good; for if we do not give up, the time will come when we will reap the harvest. So then, as often as we have the chance, we should do good to everyone, and especially to those who belong to our family in the faith."—Galatians 6:9–10 (GNT)

Grace

Heavenly Father, thank you for your goodness—especially, right now, for the good food on our plates. Encourage us to be better people, Lord, because we're in this living thing together for the good of each other. Help us see that doing good is no chore when we're loving you—it'll be what we want to do. Remind us that doing things for others isn't about helping you directly (do you really need our help?). It's about how we help others, using strength borrowed from you. It's about standing by you so you can stand by us. Amen.

Grace notes

Are you happy because you're good, or good because you're happy? Now *there's* a question! "I have noticed, said President Abraham Lincoln, "that most people in this world are about as happy as they have made up their minds to be." Did you know that happiness doesn't just happen by itself, that there are things you can do to make yourself happier? Here's an easy one: get more sleep. It's really hard to be happy when you're cranky and dragging from lack of sleep. Eat at regular times. Stay connected to your parents. (Don't you love it when your mom and dad look right at you when you're talking? They love it just the same way when you make eye contact with them.) Do kind things for others. (It really isn't all about you.) And, of course, stay connected to God. What are some ways you can keep that connection strong?

Scripture

"Our Scriptures tell us that if you see your enemy hungry, go buy that person lunch, or if he's thirsty, get him a drink. Your generosity will surprise him with goodness. Don't let evil get the best of you; get the best of evil by doing good."—Romans 12:20–21 (MSG)

Grace

Merciful Father, we thank you for this time to eat and talk together; please bless our food and our fellowship. We thank you, too, for your generosity. Help us see that getting along better with other people could have everything to do with how *we* act toward *them*. Help us see that our gentle ways will open their eyes to better ways. Teach us that the way to *get the best of evil* is to become more like you. Amen.

Grace notes

Ever heard of WWJD? It stands for *What Would Jesus Do?* and was a popular reminder at one time. Kids would wear WWJD wristbands to remind them to ask themselves about the best way to act in a given situation. But because Jesus could do things we can't do—*ever* (miracles anyone?)—it may be that the question to ask instead is WWJS? (*What Would Jesus Say* for you to do?). That lets you off the hook for performing miracles, too! A wise Christian named Clement of Alexandria, a former unbeliever who lived about a hundred years after Jesus, said this about him: "The Lord ate from a common bowl, and asked the disciples to sit on the grass. He washed their feet, with a towel wrapped around His waist—He, who is the Lord of the universe!" Can you suggest some caring things Jesus would want you to do—like praying for or being kind to others? Don't you think that Jesus, who could have wiped out someone he didn't like with just a nod of his head, would tell you to trust his Word and not return evil with more evil?

Scripture

"Nothing is impossible with God."—Luke 1:37 (NLT)

Grace

Almighty God, thank you for loving us so much. Thank you for being big enough to pay attention to each of us—to all of us at the same time. Almighty God, we can't understand your mighty power, but we aren't meant to, right? Teach us to talk to you often in prayer, because that's how you want us to connect with you. And help us to never forget, Lord, that however you choose to answer our prayers, our relationship with you is way more important than those answers. Assure us that when we trust in you *anything* becomes possible. Please bless this food and bless our family. Amen.

Grace notes

We can do many things today that were once thought impossible; as technology and scientific understanding improve our minds are stretched. Our bodies are getting stretched, too. Just think about the accomplishments of today's athletes and of the records that keep getting broken. Roger Bannister, for example, was the first person to run the mile in less than four minutes. This was thought to be physically impossible until he did it on May 6, 1954. But once that record was broken and the world saw it could be done, it only took forty-six more days for someone else to run it faster. Forty-six days! Imagine that! "Never tell a young person that anything cannot be done," said the British historian G. M. Trevelyan. "God may have been waiting centuries for someone ignorant enough of the impossible to do that very thing." Do you think all this improvement has more to do with stronger and stronger bodies or with stronger and stronger will power and confidence? What can you do to s-t-r-e-t-c-h your faith?

bay

Scripture

"When I look at the sky, which you have made, at the moon and the stars, which you set in their places—what are human beings, that you think of them; mere mortals, that you care for them? Yet you made them inferior only to yourself; you crowned them with glory and honor. You appointed them rulers over everything you made; you placed them over all creation."—Psalm 8:3–6 (GNT)

Grace

El Olam, gracious Father, thank you for our food and family. May this food nourish our bodies and your love nourish our souls. Remind us, Lord, that you had us—each one of us—in mind before the creation. Encourage us to see ourselves as you see us so we can grow in confidence for the life you have prepared for us. Encourage us to use your name in a way that shows how mighty you are. You are Almighty God, who made heaven and earth. We love that you are also our loving Father, who calls on us to call on you. Anytime. Anyplace. Amen.

Grace notes

The Bible records at least 70 names for God. Here are just a few: *El Olam* (Everlasting God), *El Roi* (The God Who Sees Me), and *Abba* ("Daddy"). The Hebrew people used names to describe a certain feature about someone. God likes it when you use one of his names to match the desires of your prayer (like calling him *Abba* or Daddy when you want to feel close to him). What God doesn't like is when someone tosses off his name as a swear word, maybe to look cool or to express anger or disgust. Think about this: what you say reflects who you are, how you feel about someone, and what kind of relationship you have with them. You are God's ambassador—his representative on earth. So if you love God you hurt him and confuse other people if you abuse his name. Most importantly, God *commands* us not to do it. In fact, this is the first of his Ten Commandments. Because he's God, he gets to make the rules (and they're always good ones)—no argument there.

Scripture

"God is not a human being, and he will not lie. He is not a human, and he does not change his mind. What he says he will do, he does. What he promises, he makes come true."—Numbers 23:19 (NCV)

Grace

Almighty God, we ask your blessing on this food and on our family. Help us never to forget your greatness and your perfection. Help us understand that you, through the Holy Spirit, breathed life into the words of the Bible's authors. Direct our path, Lord, so that we may do what is right and live the life you have planned for us. Get the better of us, Lord. Then bring out, take, and use our best! Amen.

Grace notes

The Bible (its name comes from the Greek word *Byblos*) contains 66 books, written by 40 different authors over a period of 1600 years. Second Timothy 3:16 tells us that "all Scripture is given by God." If God could create the universe he could certainly direct the hearts, minds, and words of the 40 Bible authors, don't you think? God's Word is consistent and reliable; it's his truth. "A thorough knowledge of the Bible," said the American president Theodore Roosevelt, "is worth more than a college education." How blessed we are to have this textbook from God!

sage

Scripture

"'And so I tell you, keep on asking, and you will receive what you ask for. Keep on seeking, and you will find. Keep on knocking, and the door will be opened to you.'"—Luke 11:9 (NLT)

Grace

Lord Jesus, thank you for today, for our food, and for our family. Thank you for giving us an open door to seek you in prayer and for inviting us to be bold about it. Encourage us to talk to you a lot and to do what we can, with your Spirit's help, to make our thinking line up with yours. Remind us that your plans are greater than any ideas our minds can invent and that you have in your treasure trove everything we need. Direct our way, for your faithfulness is great. Amen.

Grace notes

If God already knows everything you need, why should you even have to ask? Well, God wants you to connect with him and to take time to think about what you need. He also gave you free will; that means that God will not *make* you do anything. He wants your faith to grow, and he wants you to be bold in asking—bold, but not greedy. These are powerful reasons God has given us for prayer. A famous Christian writer and preacher, Oswald Chambers, said, "God can do nothing for me until I recognize the limits of what is humanly possible, allowing him to do the impossible." What do you think he meant by that?

mint

17

Scripture

"If I give everything I own to the poor and even go to the stake to be burned as a martyr, but I don't love, I've gotten nowhere. So, no matter what I say, what I believe, and what I do, I'm bankrupt without love. Love never gives up. Love cares more for others than for self. Love doesn't want what it doesn't have. Love doesn't strut, doesn't have a swelled head, doesn't force itself on others, isn't always 'me first,' doesn't fly off the handle, doesn't keep score of the sins of others, doesn't revel when others grovel, takes pleasure in the flowering of truth, puts up with anything, trusts God always, always looks for the best, never looks back, but keeps going to the end."—1 Corinthians 13:3–7 (MSG)

Grace

Dear Jesus, thank you for this day, for our food, for our families, and most of all for you. Teach us that without love in our hearts every good word is wasted, every kind act is meaningless, and every good work is just . . . well, work. Thank you, Lord, that faith in you puts love into action. May we remember that you *are* love and that without you nothing else matters. We praise your holy name. Amen.

Grace notes

Meaning, value, purpose, work. None of it matters without love. The self-sacrificing Catholic nun Mother Teresa practiced what she said: "Love begins at home, and it is not how much we do . . . but how much love we put in that action." Love is faith in action, and the kind of love Paul talks about in Corinthians is what you should strive for. Try this: read today's verses again, substituting the name *Jesus* every time you come to the word *love* (where it makes sense, of course). You'll see that the love of Jesus is absolutely selfless; he's always thinking of you and others, and he wants nothing more than a loving relationship with you.

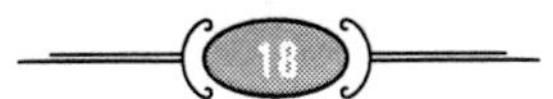

Scripture

"Depend on the LORD; trust him, and he will take care of you."
—Psalm 37:5 (NCV)

Grace

Dear Father, you are the one we trust. You are the one who is there for us. You are the one we can go to, knowing how much you love us. We love knowing and trusting that you will take care of us, but remind us that you're doing it your way, not our way. Remind us, too, that you are perfectly fair and perfectly just—and that the timing of everything is also yours, not ours. Teach us to ask for your help to get *through* troubles, not *out of* them. Teach us that you sometimes use troubles to help us grow up—that they are part of our life journey. Thank you, Lord, for blessing this meal and for blessing us with your presence at our table. Amen.

Grace notes

Whom or what do you trust? Your friends, parents, teachers? Do you trust, for example, that the sun will rise or the rain will come to water the gardens? That other drivers will stay (usually) within their lanes? You can count on these things, can't you? That's because predictable people and natural events have a track record with you. But even though God has a perfect track record, not everyone trusts him. Some may even believe in him but still not trust him. That makes no sense, does it? The author Corallie Buchanan said it well: "You say to God, 'I have never seen you provide for me.' God says to you, 'You have never trusted Me.'" Maybe some people don't trust God because they never made the effort to get to know him. What are you doing to know him better? Make that effort; it's the most worthwhile thing you'll ever do. Ever.

bay

Scripture

"People produce trouble as surely as sparks fly upward."—Job 5:7 (NCV)

Grace

Dear Father in heaven, bless our food and family; we look to you gratefully. Help us to be honest enough to admit that *we* are the cause of some of the problems that worry us, even though other troubles happen through no fault of our own. Guide us when friends go through hard times, reminding us that sometimes just being there, without saying anything at all, is the best support we can offer. Most of all, help us to remember that even through the worst of times you are close, working behind the scenes for our good. Inspire us to boldly trust your promise that you are with us and for us—because you love us so much. Amen.

Grace notes

Something happens and you don't understand why. Your friend snaps at you, or worse—was it something you did? Maybe, but maybe not. Or have you ever gotten in trouble for something you didn't do? Understanding the source of the problem is the first step in solving it. When trying to sort things out it's also important to remember that sometimes people aren't the problem at all; sometimes it's the problem that's the problem! "When God solves your problems you have faith in his abilities," said eleven-year-old Rashika Jain. She continued, "When God doesn't solve your problems He has faith in your abilities." Wow! Never underestimate the wisdom of a child.

Scripture

"Take a long, hard look. See how great [God] is—infinite, greater than anything you could ever imagine or figure out!"—Job 36:26 (MSG)

Grace

Almighty God, we're grateful that you invite us to be part of your family. Please bless our food. Please bless those who know you but especially those who don't yet know you, because they need you, too. Give us the wisdom to understand that you are ageless, that you have no limits, and that you love us faithfully. Encourage us to see and accept your love and goodness while respecting your power. Remind us how much you want to take care of us, and encourage us to ask for your guidance. Amen.

Grace notes

God is in all places at the same time. He has unlimited power, has no boundaries, and has perfect knowledge and endless love. What human can understand these things? You—or anyone—will never know enough to answer life's big questions. But God knows, and that should be enough for now. You don't need to understand everything about God to have a relationship with him; but you can trust that he'll give you new wisdom as you grow in his Word. A wise Bible scholar, teacher, and German spy during the dangerous days of World War II, Dietrich Bonhoeffer had this to say: "While it is good that we seek to know the Holy One, it is probably not so good to presume that we will ever complete the task."

Scripture

"My child, listen to your father's teaching and do not forget your mother's advice. Their teaching will be like flowers in your hair or a necklace around your neck."—Proverbs 1:8–9 (NCV)

Grace

Heavenly Father, thank you for this food, and thank you for Mom and Dad. Please bless them every day. Help us see that they want the best for us, that the twinkle in their eyes is there because they love us so much. Remind us that their job can be tough because we can be a handful. Encourage us to do good things without being asked—what a cool way of saying *I love you*! That's much better than a fistful of pretty flowers. Wonderful are your words, Lord. Amen.

Grace notes

Take a minute to go around the table and each describe every other person there, using one complimentary word or naming one thing you like about that person. Some of you might get some surprising answers. But wait—that was just a warm-up! Kids, pretend you're a newspaper writer. Ask Mom, Dad, or another close adult one question about a fun time in their childhood. "All grown-ups were once children," said Antoine de Saint-Exupéry, the author of *The Little Prince*, "but only a few of them remember it." Help them remember!

mint

Scripture

"Bless those who hurt you. Bless them, and do not call down curses on them. Be joyful with those who are joyful. Be sad with those who are sad. Agree with each other. Don't be proud. Be willing to be a friend of people who aren't considered important. Don't think that you are better than others."—Romans 12:14–16 (NIrV)

Grace

Dear Father, we are thankful for this food, for our families, and for our friends. May others see your goodness shining through us. Give us the desire to treat others the way we ourselves want to be treated—especially those others who are mean, sad, or hurting, because their hearts need healing, too. Lord, help us think of creative ways to be kind. Give us the courage to make a difference in someone else's life. Alleluia! Amen.

Grace notes

Think about a person you know, maybe someone who is shy or awkward or not the easiest to get along with. Then come up with a way to be kind to *that* person. For example, what if you decided at lunchtime to sit down next to someone who always eats alone? You may have to work up some courage, but you can do it. Say a little prayer right beforehand. As the author Brian Tracy reminds us, "Successful people are always looking for opportunities to help others. Unsuccessful people are always asking, 'What's in it for me?'"

Scripture

"I'm thanking you, God, from a full heart, I'm writing the book on your wonders. I'm whistling, laughing, and jumping for joy; I'm singing your song, High God."—Psalm 9:1–2 (MSG)

Grace

To the tune of *The Addams Family* TV show theme song:*

We thank you, God, for giving
The food we need for living.
For food and fun and friendship
We thank you, God—Amen!

Ah—men (snap, snap)
Ah—men (snap, snap)
Ah—men, Ah - men, Ah - men! (snap, snap)

So now we're going to eat it,
Because we really need it.
We praise you and adore you
We thank you, God—Amen!

Ah—men (snap, snap)
Ah—men (snap, snap)
Ah—men, Ah - men, Ah - men! (snap, snap)

*Music by Vic Mizzy

Grace notes

Psalm 98:4 calls on us to "make a joyful noise unto the Lord." It doesn't say sing sweetly, does it? It doesn't say murmur with an angel's sweet voice, does it? So what if your voice is goofy—do you think God cares? Sing out anyway—it'll make you feel good! "Laughter is God's blessing," reminded a pastor named Joseph Prince. And laughter goes well with praise, just as peanut butter goes well with jelly. Yum to both!

Scripture

"Son [and daughter], do what your father tells you and never forget what your mother taught you. Keep their words with you always, locked in your heart. Their teaching will lead you when you travel, protect you at night, and advise you during the day. Their instructions are a shining light; their correction can teach you how to live."—Proverbs 6:20–23 (GNT)

Grace

Heavenly Father, we love our mom, dad, and those others who take care of us, and we ask you to extra-special bless them. Help us pay attention to their advice because they were kids once too (*Really?*) and have had a lot of experience since then. Thank you for reminding us, Lord, to keep their words close to our hearts wherever we go, however far away. Help us to listen carefully to their words, because that's a way of saying "Thanks." We thank you for this food, Lord, and for making us a family. Amen.

Grace notes

Try to imagine what your parents (or any other grown-ups you may live with) were like as kids. Were they a lot like you? (Ask them!) Do you think they were as smart as you? Author Sean Covey (yes, he's a grown-up) understands this completely. He said, "It's especially hard to admit that you made a mistake to your parents, because, of course, you know so much more than they do." (You might begin to notice as you get a little older that your parents will start to get smarter. Funny how that works.)

Scripture

"Some people are wicked and no good. They go around telling lies, winking with their eyes, tapping with their feet, and making signs with their fingers. They make evil plans in their hearts and are always starting arguments. So trouble will strike them in an instant; suddenly they will be so hurt no one can help them."—Proverbs 6:12–15 (NCV)

Grace

Father God, we thank you for this food; please pour down your blessing on all of our family. We wish that every kid could have a mom and dad or other loving caregivers like we do. Bless those who don't know what a kind word is, because they need you more than they realize. Thank you for being our awesome friend and protector. Amen.

Grace notes

Sooner or later bullies get into big trouble. Don't ever encourage them or laugh at others along with them; just walk away. Get a buddy and be a buddy, not a bully (what a difference two little letters can make!). Jesus often protects us through others, so be sure to talk to Mom, Dad, or a teacher if someone seems to be out to get you or someone else. "Bullying is a horrible thing. It sticks with you forever. It poisons you. But only if you let it," said Heather Brewer, the author of *Dear Bully: Seventy Authors Tell Their Stories.*

Scripture

"I want you to treat others fairly. So let fair treatment roll on just as a river does! Always do what is right. Let right living flow along like a stream that never runs dry!"—Amos 5:24 (NIrV)

Grace

Thank you, Lord, for always being with us. Thank you for Mom and Dad and for the food they provide us. Help us to think about what it means to be fair, and inspire us to treat others well because it's the right thing to do and it's what you want from us. We are more than fairly certain that you love us—and that's the truth! You love all other people, too—the very same amount as you love us! Praise you for your Word, Lord. Amen.

Grace notes

Did you know that treating others fairly doesn't necessarily mean treating them equally? Imagine you had a pizza to divide between two people: three pieces each. That's treating them both equally, right? But then you learn that one is five years old and the other is fourteen. Now what would you say? Three pieces each wouldn't work so well, would it—too much for the little one and not enough for the teenager. Fair isn't always equal. Get it? Here's another example: think about bedtimes. Should they be the same for everyone in your family, no matter their age? Can you think of other examples? Of course, there's always the Calvin and Hobbs way of looking at things, as the cartoonist Bill Watterson tells us: "The world isn't fair, Calvin." "I know Dad, but why isn't it ever unfair in my favor?" Sometimes, it would seem, Calvin forgets to put himself in another person's shoes.

mint

Scripture

"Be wise in the way you act toward outsiders; make the most of every opportunity. Let your conversation be always full of grace, seasoned with salt, so that you may know how to answer everyone." —Colossians 4:5–7 (NIV)

Grace

Heavenly Father, please come to dinner, bless our family, and strengthen us with your grace and wisdom. Encourage us to be open and willing to talk about you with others. Give us eyes to see and ears to hear your Word. Remind us that there are wonderful examples of God's love in the Bible—some told with mystery, adventure, giants, or even talking animals! Today we say a blessing right out of your Word, Father: "I eat my fill of prime rib and gravy; I smack my lips."* We could also say it this way: "Good food, good meat; Good Lord, let's eat!" Amen.

*Psalm 63:5 (MSG)

Grace notes

To say we use words that are *seasoned with salt* is another way of saying we know something about what we're talking about. The best way to learn about God, so that you can feel comfortable talking to others about him, is by reading the Bible. There may be Bible classes at church, or you may get to go to a vacation Bible school, a Bible camp, or some other Bible group meeting. Christian books and videos can be a big help, too. Do you think Bible *learning* is all about boring, serious stuff? Maybe you should check out the stories about Daniel in the lion's den, David and the giant Goliath, Noah and the ark, or Balaam and his talking donkey, to name a few. Read about Shadrach, Meshach, and Abednego, and then search for Louie Armstrong singing about them on YouTube™. "I read novels," said the singer Johnny Cash. "but I also read the Bible. And study it, you know? And the more I learn, the more excited I get." How excited do you get about the Bible? How excited are you to share what you learn from it?

Scripture

"Words kill, words give life; they're either poison or fruit—you choose."—Proverbs 18:21 (MSG)

Grace

Dear God, thank you for our food, family, and friends; we like to get together at dinner and talk about things that matter. Lord, help us keep our mouths shut when we have nothing good to say, but make us brave when there is something we should say. Remind us to think about how our words would look plastered all over the internet. Would that make us happy? Would you be happy? Help us to think first and speak second. Amen.

Grace notes

Name some reasons that gossiping is bad. Let's face it, some words really sting. And know this: those who gossip *to you* will also gossip *about you* behind your back. And there's another side to gossip. Does gossip have to be false to hurt someone? Think of examples of something true that could still hurt someone's reputation if shared. When it comes to happy, helpful talk about someone that will build up that person's good name, be a role model with your friends. The poet Robert Service once said "Be sure your wisest words are those you do not say." Kids might say "Take that back!" but words can never really be taken back, can they?

Scripture

"Do not fret because of evil men or be envious of those who do wrong; for like the grass they will soon wither, like green plants they will soon die away."

"If the LORD delights in a man's way, he makes his steps firm; though he stumble, he will not fall, for the LORD upholds him with his hand." —Psalm 37:1, 23–24 (NIV)

Grace

Dear Father, we are happy that you are here with us. Thank you for our food, for each of those at this table, and for your ever-faithful love. Open our hearts to your ways and encourage us to trust you, knowing that you watch over us and will never steer us in a wrong direction. Remind us that you are perfectly fair and perfectly just to everyone. How comforting it is to know that though we fumble and stumble, you are always there to catch us. Take our hand, Lord. Amen.

Grace notes

Sometimes we see people doing wrong things and getting away with it. That doesn't seem fair, does it? You can be sure, though, that God takes note of every wrong action and every right one. When someone is sorry for a wrong act and asks for forgiveness, God forgives. He sees the person's heart as clean and pure, as though that sin had never happened. Until the person is sorry, though, watch out! "If your heart is a volcano," says the poet Kahlil Gibran, "how shall you expect flowers to bloom?"

Scripture

"My child, eat honey; it is good. And just as honey from the comb is sweet on your tongue, you may be sure that wisdom is good for the soul. Get wisdom and you have a bright future."—Proverbs 24:13–14 (GNT)

Grace

Praise to you, heavenly Father, and thank you for our food. Please bless it so that it will nourish our bodies. Help us to remember that life works best when we stick to your two greatest commandments: to love you more than anything or anyone else and to love others just as much as we love our own selves. You, Lord, are awesome and deserve our reverent respect. You're the Lord of heaven and earth, the Creator of all, the big Boss. Your Word is a treasure map with an arrow pointing right to the treasure. The Bible holds the keys to the kingdom of heaven, and you can't wait for us to find them. Amen.

Grace notes

The Bible holds the key to the most amazing treasure. It contains the secret to life, and you can find that key in this command from Jesus: love God more than anything or anyone else, and love other people just as much as you love yourself. Love God and others in this way, and you'll be on your way to wisdom that will be the greatest treasure you can imagine. "No man was ever wise by chance," said the ancient Roman thinker Seneca the Younger. Besides following Jesus' command to love, what are some ways you can gain wisdom?

sage

Scripture

"How well God must like you—you don't hang out at Sin Saloon, you don't slink along Dead-End Road, you don't go to Smart-Mouth College."—Psalm 1:1 (MSG)

Grace

Dear God, we thank you for the food and for the cook who cooked it. We thank you, too, for loving us; so true, so cool, so YOU! You love us and protect us—that's how the Good Book reads. In return we'll show you how clever we can be. We'll look for ways to be kind—just you wait—you'll see! We get it. We get it. We're smart! Smart! Smart! Amen.

Grace notes

What does it mean for someone to go to Smart-Mouth College? It's probably safe to say we've all attended classes there, isn't it? Swearing or trashy talk hurts God, because it dishonors his name and hurts his reputation. It's also smart-alecky, disrespectful, and mean. If you think using curse words or dirty words makes you look cool or grown-up, think again. "Swearing doesn't make your argument valid," said the writer Shannon L. Adler. "It just tells the other person you have lost your class and control."

Scripture

"Well-spoken words bring satisfaction; well-done work has its own reward."—Proverbs 12:14 (MSG)

"Speak without thinking, and your words can cut like a knife. Be wise, and your words can heal."—Proverbs 12:18 (ERV)

"Foolish people are easily upset. But wise people pay no attention to hurtful words."—Proverbs 12:16 (NIrV)

Grace

Heavenly Father, please bless this food. We believe in your great goodness and want to follow the example of your Son, Jesus. Help us remember how easily mean words can hurt—both your Spirit and other people. Open our eyes to this truth, Lord, and teach us to use our words in ways that heal and never harm. Help us remember, too, that you love every other person just as much as you love each of us. Cover us with your glory and wisdom. Amen.

Grace notes

Your words have the power to hurt—and the power to heal. Through your kind or encouraging speech, you can take others to the highest places, fuel their imaginations, and rock their worlds. But your unkind or thoughtless words can do just the opposite. Why not be the one who inspires and motivates others? Listen to these beautiful words from the hymn writer Frederick William Faber: "Kind words are the music of the world. They have a power which seems to be beyond natural causes, as if they were some angel's song, which had lost its way and come on Earth."

Scripture

"Never get a lazy person to do something for you; he will be as irritating as vinegar on your teeth or smoke in your eyes."—Proverbs 10:26 (GNT)

Grace

Dear Jesus, please bless our food, our family, and our friends. We thank you for Mom and Dad and for others who work hard to teach, help, and take care of us. Thank you for showing us that lending a helping hand is what friends do and that helpful attitudes and actions make friendships strong. Thanks for guiding us along our way, Lord. You're the greatest, and we pray that everyone may come to know your faithfulness and love for all. Amen.

Grace notes

Vinegar, bitter to the taste, was used in lots of ways in Bible times: as a preservative, medicine, detergent, or ingredient in recipes. Vinegar can be made from just about anything that you can pickle, such as dates, figs, grapes, beets, or rye. Like vinegar, a lazy person leaves a bitter taste in the mouths of the hardworking people around them. Can you see why? And can you see how being around a lazy person might make you lazy, too? Jules Renard, a writer who liked to use humor to make a point, said this: "Laziness is nothing more than the habit of resting before you get tired."

Scripture

"This is the Good News about Jesus Christ, the Son of God. It began as the prophet Isaiah had written: 'God said, "I will send my messenger ahead of you to open the way for you. Someone is shouting in the desert, get the road ready for the Lord; make a straight path for him to travel!"'

So John appeared in the desert, baptizing and preaching."—Mark 1:1–4(a) (GNT)

Grace

Glorious God, we are grateful for your blessing on this day and on our food. May we never forget that you are the Creator who loves us and has planned everything across time to make way for us to be with you in heaven. May we live with grace and confidence, knowing that you have a plan and purpose for each of us. Teach us that loving you because we want to—not because we have to—lets us share in your promise of wonderful, amazing things. God, you are awesome! Help us keep our faith in you. Amen.

Grace notes

The Gospels, written by Matthew, Mark, Luke, and John, are accounts of Jesus' life on earth. Did you know that the book of Isaiah is sometimes called the "fifth Gospel," even though it was written 700 years before Jesus was born? That's because Isaiah talked about Jesus as the Messiah, the Savior. Isn't it amazing how God's plan spans the ages of time? God wants us to share that Good News in our day too, even among our friends. Listen to the words of an unknown author (meaning that we don't know the person's name): "Preach the Gospel at all times. Use words if necessary." Can you think of a way to share the Good News of Jesus without words?

Scripture

"They dig a hole to trap others, but they will fall into it themselves."—Psalm 7:15 (NCV)

Grace

Merciful God, thank you for our food, our family, and our friends. The highest honor and glory belong to your name, for you alone are God. Remind us, Lord, to call out your name when we can't find our way out of that big, dark hole we've dug ourselves into. Remind us that you'll never stop loving us, and that no hole is too deep for you to pull us out. Plant our feet on solid ground, Lord. Hurray for you, God—you can fix anything. We promise to remember that. Amen.

Grace notes

So you've dug yourself into a hole? All that digging—the hole can get pretty deep, can't it? What to do? For starters, STOP digging! More sin won't fix the first sin. And here's something to always do: keep the promises you make. That alone will keep you out of a lot of holes. And when you do get out, look back and learn something from those holes. The inventor and scientist Philip Emeagwali probably learned many things the hard way. "The hardships that I encountered in the past will help me succeed in the future," he said. What do you think he meant by that?

sage

Scripture

"This is a record of the family line of Jesus Christ. He is the son of David. He is also the son of Abraham.

Abraham was the father of Isaac. Isaac was the father of Jacob. Jacob was the father of Judah and his brothers . . . [and after many generations] . . . Jesse was the father of King David.

David was the father of Solomon . . . [and after many generations] . . . Jacob was the father of Joseph. Joseph was the husband of Mary. And Mary gave birth to Jesus, who is called Christ."—Matthew 1:1–16 (NIrV)

Grace

Our everlasting Father, thank you for this food. Thank you for our family and for the joy of being together around this table. Thank you for our grandmas and grandpas; we pray for them, too. Matthew tells us that Abraham was the head of Jesus' family tree. Remind us that our own family tree connects all of us across time, too. Help us to see ways in which our actions might shape those who come after us. Inspire us to be good role models, and encourage us to imagine how we can make a difference in this world, now or later. We praise you, Lord. Amen.

Grace notes

How has your life been shaped by your parents and grandparents? What if Grandpa had made some other life choices? Could that have changed where you live and go to school, the friends you have, and even the beliefs you hold? Maybe, or maybe not. Jesus said that those believers who came after him would do greater things than he did.* How? Through the power of the Holy Spirit, we who bear Christ's name can accomplish amazing things. Pretty awesome thought, wouldn't you say? Baseball Hall of Famer Branch Rickey had something to say about what is truly important for a life well lived: "It is not the honor that you take with you, but the heritage you leave behind." What do you think about that?

*John 14:12

Scripture

"Wise son, glad father; stupid son, sad mother."—Proverbs 10:1 (MSG)

Grace

Dear Father, please bless our food and family. We know your heart is big for us. We hear this message loud and clear. It's meant for all of us girls and boys—for everyone. It's good and short. Amen, Amen, Amen!

Grace notes

Mark Twain once said "I didn't have time to write a short letter, so I wrote a long one instead." Get it? It can be much harder to get an idea across in fewer words. It's all right, though, to pray short prayers; God knows what's in your heart, and he can fill in the blanks.

Scripture

"The Bereans listened eagerly to Paul's message. They searched the Scriptures day after day to see if Paul and Silas were teaching the truth. As a result, many Jews believed, as did many of the prominent Greek women and men."—Acts 17:11(b)–12 (NLT)

Grace

Gracious Father, thank you for this food, which is good for us, and for your Word, which nourishes us in the most important way; make us hungry for more. *Bring on the questions*, you say, God, *because my Word is truth*. Remind us that you created our minds and hearts for us to learn all we can about you. Feed us your truth, Lord. Amen.

Grace notes

It seems as though everyone has an opinion, even if they don't know much about the subject, doesn't it? Take a cue from the Berean people. Ask lots of questions; dig deep. Grow with a wise and curious heart. "Science is the father of knowledge, but opinion breeds ignorance." Hippocrates said that way back in the year 370 B.C. (almost four hundred years before Jesus was born). Today, with all the social media available to influence people, imagine what he must think about all the opinions that are passed off as truth! Sad to say, it's easy to get taken in by what you find on the internet. Even more reason to dig deep. One thing you can be sure of, though: God's Word.

Scripture

"[Jesus] went on to tell a story to the guests around the table. Noticing how each had tried to elbow into the place of honor, he said, 'When someone invites you to dinner, don't take the place of honor. Somebody more important than you might have been invited by the host. Then he'll come and call out in front of everybody, 'You're in the wrong place. The place of honor belongs to this man.' Red-faced, you'll have to make your way to the very last table, the only place left. 'When you're invited to dinner, go and sit at the last place. Then when the host comes he may very well say, 'Friend, come up to the front.' That will give the dinner guests something to talk about! What I'm saying is, if you walk around with your nose in the air, you're going to end up flat on your face. But if you're content to be simply yourself, you will become more than yourself.'"—Luke 14:7–11 (MSG)

Grace

Jesus, thank you for being with us. We ask your blessing on this food and on our family. We hear you, Lord, telling us to just be ourselves so we can continue to grow in you. Remind us that you made each of us on purpose, for a purpose. Encourage us not to show off but to show *you* off by being generous, kind, and a good example, as you were here on earth. Help us remember that by giving attention to others we ourselves grow closer to you. May we remember that you made us, that your love for us lasts forever, and that you value us more than we can imagine—just the way we are. Amen.

Grace notes

God doesn't want you to elbow or shove others out of the way, saying "pick me, pick me." Nor does he want you to shrink into the background, as though you don't count for anything. Be yourself, knowing that God loves you more than you can imagine, and through him and for his kingdom you'll become more than you were before. "Be Yourself, but always your better self," said the Utah educator Karl G. Maeser. How do you suppose you can be your better self?

Scripture

"Then [Jesus] turned to the host. 'The next time you put on a dinner, don't just invite your friends and family and rich neighbors, the kind of people who will return the favor. Invite some people who never get invited out, the misfits from the wrong side of the tracks. You'll be—and experience—a blessing. They won't be able to return the favor, but the favor will be returned—oh, how it will be returned!—at the resurrection of God's people.'"—Luke 14:12–14 (MSG)

Grace

Father of all, thank you for this food, our family, and our friends. The place of honor at our table is always reserved for you. Help us see that this parable is about the need to love people who may not get loved enough, and challenge us to surprise someone with an act of kindness. Help us recognize that doing things for others is part of the way we fit into your great plan. Show us that loving others shows the world our love for you. Amen.

Grace notes

What kinds of unexpected acts of kindness could you do for other people? You could start out small by saying "please" and "thank you" more often and to more people. (There's certainly room for more appreciation and politeness in this world.) Who doesn't usually get thanked for all they do? How about the lunchroom volunteers, the crossing guards, or your teachers? "No act of kindness," pointed out the Greek storyteller Aesop hundreds of years before Jesus was born, "no matter how small, is ever wasted."

Scripture

"Good people are careful about choosing their friends, but evil people always choose the wrong ones."—Proverbs 12:26 (ERV)

Grace

Heavenly Father, teach us to choose our friends carefully, knowing that their influence can either make us stronger and closer to you or weaker and farther away. Thank you for being our friend and protector—forever. Thank you for this food, our family, and our other friends, too. Amen.

Grace notes

Many people have tried to define friendship. The American writer Somerset Maugham had this to say: "When you choose your friends, don't be short-changed by choosing personality over character." *What does that mean?* Personality is about the personal traits a person is born with: they may be shy, funny, serious, confident, or quick to act or speak—traits like that. Character is more about the qualities a person develops by working at it (or not!)—qualities like honesty, kindness, and dependability—or their opposites. Can you see why character is more important than personality? How would your friends describe your personality? Your character? What words or phrases would you use to describe your friends' personalities and characters?

mint

Scripture

"I am God—yes, I Am. I haven't changed."—Malachi 3:6a (MSG)

Grace

Everlasting God, we praise you and glorify your holy name. Help us to honor you for who and what you are: unchanging, eternal, and almighty. May we come to see that even though there is no house big enough to hold you, you make your home in each of our hearts through the Holy Spirit. This is such a mystery, Lord. Thank you for blessing us today; we love the way you love us. Amen.

Grace notes

God never changes. Not his character, not his promises, not his plans, and not his love for us. God cannot lie. If he could, he wouldn't be God. Remember these things when you think about him. This will help when you find yourself asking all of those big *Why?* questions. It will help you when your day isn't going so well. Above all, trust God—and tell him you do! Think about what Pastor Colin S. Smith said: "He is the Creator and the sustainer of all things. . . . He is neither helped by our faith nor hindered by our unbelief." Something to think about, isn't it? What does that mean for you?

Scripture

"God's word is true, and everything he does is right. He loves what is right and fair; the LORD's love fills the earth. The sky was made at the LORD's command. By the breath from his mouth, he made all the stars. He gathered the water of the sea into a heap. He made the great ocean stay in its place. All the earth should worship the LORD; the whole world should fear him."—Psalm 33:4–8 (NCV)

Grace

Eternal God, our Father, thank you for this food. Thank you for our family and for the time we can spend together in worship. We cannot know or understand all your ways, Lord, but we trust in your almighty, changeless, loving goodness. Guide us, Lord, and show us who you want us to be. You are holy, holy, holy, and we are grateful for your love, for life, for breath, for Mom and Dad, and for all the blessings we can't begin to count. The earth is filled with your glory. Amen.

Grace notes

"The whole world should fear him," says Psalm 33:8. Really? *Fear* is an interesting word. Here it doesn't mean trembling with fright (although who wouldn't do a bit of that if God were to suddenly appear in all his glory?). It means to obey and serve God, to do his will, to deeply respect him, and to be in reverent awe of him and of his mighty power. Proverbs 9:10 tells us that fearing God in this way is the beginning of wisdom. You'll come to understand this connection better as you grow. Whether we're talking about respect for God or for our parents, teachers, or others in authority, this kind of "fear" is an important part of growing up. "I fear only God. I don't fear any human. When you have that kind of spirit, you can just do what you have to do. Let it roll," said the (grown-up) musician and songwriter Stevie Wonder. What do you think he meant by that?

bay

Scripture

"Praise the LORD. I will praise the LORD with all my heart. I will praise him where honest people gather for worship. The LORD has done great things. All who take delight in what he has done will spend time thinking about it. What he does shows his glory and majesty. He will always do what is right. The LORD causes his miracles to be remembered. He is kind and tender. He provides food for those who have respect for him."—Psalm 111:1–5 (NIrV)

Grace

God Most High, thank you for this meal that you've provided and for the people around this table. We learn of your greatness, and we wonder who we are that you love and value us so much—in fact, that you pay attention to us at all! Grant us a grateful heart that we may wisely use the gifts you give us. Teach us to depend on your greatness. May we always be thankful for your kindness and mercy. We give thanks to you, for you are the one we are hungry for. Amen.

Grace notes

Just why does God love us so much? That question has been asked throughout history, and no one really knows the answer—not even King David. In Psalm 8:4 he asked God: "Why are people so important to you? Why do you even think about them? Why do you care so much about humans? Why do you even notice them?" The famous preacher Billy Graham tells us this: "The Bible says that God has a reason for keeping us here; if He didn't, He would take us to Heaven far sooner." He's right: God wants us to be close to him, yes, but he's very patient and wants to give the rest of the world a chance to know and love Jesus, too.

Scripture

"While a large crowd was gathering and people were coming to Jesus from town after town, he told this parable: 'A farmer went out to sow his seed. As he was scattering the seed, some fell along the path; it was trampled on, and the birds of the air ate it up. Some fell on rock, and when it came up, the plants withered because they had no moisture. Other seed fell among thorns, which grew up with it and choked the plants. Still other seed fell on good soil. It came up and yielded a crop, a hundred times more than was sown.' When he said this, he called out, 'He who has ears to hear, let him hear.'"—Luke 8:4–8 (NIV)

Grace

Father God, please bless our food and those who prepared it. Give us a grateful heart for everything that others do for us. Help us to think about the kind of soil our faith is growing in. We know you don't expect us to be perfect, but please help us to remember that it makes a difference who we hang out with. Remind us that by spending time with you we will grow big and strong spiritually and be able to serve you better, a hundred times over. We grow strong from listening to you and taking your words to heart. Hallelujah, Lord! We are saints in training! Amen.

Grace notes

Life is full of choices, and you can choose the "soil" you spend your time in. What kind are you choosing—and how might those choices change as you continue to grow? The actor Michael J. Fox has had to answer the question many times about what to do with his life. He said, "I have no choice about whether or not I have Parkinson's [a serious disease]. I have nothing but choices about how I react to it. In those choices, there's freedom to do a lot of things in areas that I wouldn't have otherwise found myself in." These words sound a lot like those of the prophet Isaiah in Isaiah 40:29: "He gives power to the weak, and to those who have no might He increases strength." Describe in your own words what this might mean in your life?

sage

Scripture

"Don't have anything to do with foolish and stupid arguments, because you know they grow into quarrels."—2 Timothy 2:23 (NCV)

Grace

Father God, we thank you for being with us, for this food, and for the many blessings of this day. We pray for a good night and a good tomorrow. Give us the wisdom to walk away from those who just want to start arguments. Teach us your gentleness so that we may set a good example. Lord, you are the greatest teacher, and we love that you are in our life. We know that we are blessed, and we want others to benefit from that blessing by the way we treat them and the Christ-like example we show. Amen.

Grace notes

Some people's bad behavior has nothing to do with you; it's as though they lash out at anyone who might be in their way. Don't fall to their level. Sometimes, though (and probably more often than not) arguments come from misunderstandings. Francois de La Rochefoucauld, a French nobleman who understood well the way people behave, said these wise words: "Quarrels would not last long if the fault was only on one side." *Hmmm!* Think about your last argument. Who would you say was at fault? But was that person *totally* at fault? It takes two to tango, doesn't it? (Or maybe this old saying should be two to "tangle!")

Scripture

"Has anyone by fussing before the mirror ever gotten taller by so much as an inch?

"What I'm trying to do here is get you to relax, not be so preoccupied with getting so you can respond to God's giving. People who don't know God and the way he works fuss over these things, but you know both God and how he works. Steep yourself in God-reality, God-initiative, God-provisions.

"You'll find all your everyday human concerns will be met. Don't be afraid of missing out. You're my dearest friends! The Father wants to give you the very kingdom itself. Be generous. Give to the poor. . . . The place where your treasure is, is the place you will most want to be, and end up being."—Luke 12:25, 28–34 (MSG)

Grace

Loving Jesus, thank you for this food and for all your other blessings. Encourage us to think about the wonderful treasures life offers—or, we should say, the treasures *you* offer us in life—and to chill out over the small stuff. Encourage us to look for you, because you are surely there. May we listen to you and understand your promises of a life full of adventure and promise. And may we put our priorities in the right place, loving most the things that you love best! That's what you say, Jesus—and we hold you to it. You are our ever faithful Lord. Amen.

Grace notes

Ever notice that what you pay the most attention to becomes what's most important to you? Jesus is telling you in the verses above that he has cleared your way of what might otherwise get in your way. He has taken care of your everyday needs so you can focus on fulfilling the grander purpose he has planned for your life. Don't be scared to take some risks, because you know that God is providing. The great inventor and artist Leonardo da Vinci understood this well. Listen to his words: "It had long since come to my attention that people of accomplishment rarely sat back and let things happen to them. They went out and happened to things." How does the difference this great man noticed apply to your thoughts about your future?

thyme

Scripture

"One day Jesus said to his disciples, 'Let's go over to the other side of the lake.' So they got into a boat and set out. As they sailed, he fell asleep. A squall came down on the lake, so that the boat was being swamped, and they were in great danger. The disciples went and woke him, saying, 'Master, Master, we're going to drown!' He got up and rebuked the wind and the raging waters; the storm subsided, and all was calm. 'Where is your faith?' he asked his disciples. In fear and amazement they asked one another, 'Who is this? He commands even the winds and the water, and they obey him.'"—Luke 8:22–25 (NIV)

Grace

Dear Jesus, we ask your blessings on this food. We ask for the wisdom to understand what you want to teach us in your Word. Remind us, Lord, that you are really here with us—right here and right now. Help us to see that even though your promises never included a life free from trouble, you stand ready to help us with whatever comes our way, no matter the storm and no matter the circumstance. Teach us to depend on you and to trust you with an open heart, because you want us to live by believing and not always just by seeing.* Our joy is in you, Lord Jesus. We are amazed by you, and we pray in your name. Amen.

*2 Corinthians 5:7

Grace notes

Problems in your life often come because of mistakes you make or wrong things you do. A life without sin or trouble could happen for you only if God hadn't given you a free will (free will is the ability to choose your own actions). Is that a world you'd want to live in—full of people programmed like a bunch of robots? What if someone *had* to love you or you *had* to love someone? That's not love, and don't you think Jesus knows that? The mystery writer Agatha Christie agreed, saying, "There's too much tendency to attribute to God the evils that man does of his own free will." Can you think of an example of people criticizing God for a problem in the world that is really caused by human sin?

bay

Scripture

"To be wise you must first have reverence for the Lord. If you know the Holy One, you have understanding. Wisdom will add years to your life. You are the one who will profit if you have wisdom, and if you reject it, you are the one who will suffer."—Proverbs 9:10–12 (MSG)

Grace

Father, thank you for bringing us together to share this food. Lord, we praise you for your powerful words. Inspire us to want to know you; fill us with a desire to read and think about what you say because that's the only way to a life that pleases you. Teach us to watch those who are wise and good and then to act the way they do. Lord, direct us to a life of honoring you and seeking wisdom—a prize-winning recipe for a blessed life. Amen.

Grace notes

A person with wisdom is smart, but a smart person isn't always sensible or wise. Have you ever heard someone say *So and so needs some common sense*? They mean that although this person may have book learning, when it comes to everyday matters he or she doesn't have a clue. The book of Proverbs is important because it helps us live lives that are smart in the right way. Proverbs is a collection of wise sayings that include lots of great advice about common sense ways to live exciting and productive lives. The great Spanish writer Miguel de Cervantes says this about proverbs: "Proverbs are short sentences drawn from long experience." What do you think that means? What might it have to do with learning from other's mistakes?

Scripture

"But don't, dear friend, resent God's discipline; don't sulk under his loving correction. It's the child he loves that God corrects; a father's delight is behind all this."—Proverbs 3:11–12 (MSG)

Grace

Father God, we know we can call you *Abba*—that means Daddy!—because you love us as your own children. Please bless us, and this good food; we want strong and healthy bodies. Thank you, too, for all our other blessings. We love that you love us, Lord, but gosh, so many rules for good behavior! Thanks for reminding us that discipline and guidance come from those who love us—and that a little discipline now can keep us out of big trouble later on. Remind us that when Mom says "Behave yourself!" she's working with you to build our character. Amen.

Grace notes

What do you think your kid-life would look like if no one loved you? Here's another way of asking the same question: What do you think your kid-life would look like if no one made rules for you to obey? Those who care for you and love you have to be good role models. Someday it'll be your turn for that, so learn all you can now. "Your children will become what you are, said the Minnesota Congressman David Bly, "so be what you want them to be." Not only do they have to be role models; they have to help you grow up. Cesar Millan is a dog whisperer, but he understands the kind of training needed by all young things. "Many dogs grow," he said, "without rules or boundaries. They need exercise, discipline and affection—in that order." Wait a minute: was he talking about dogs . . . or kids?

Scripture

"When pride comes, then comes disgrace, but with humility comes wisdom."—Proverbs 11:2 (NIV)

Grace

Dear God Who Sees Us,* please bless this food, our family, our friends, and those in need. We have so much to be thankful for. Show us that having humility means that we think about others rather than trying to get others to think about us. Teach us that it's humility, not pride, that gets us noticed! That's a puzzle, Lord. Your Word teaches us wisdom and an attitude of gratitude. Awesome Lord, awesome words. Amen

El Roi in Hebrew; another name for God.

Grace notes

It's okay to have a healthy self-respect; that's a form of good pride. The kind of pride that God doesn't like is the kind that makes you feel more important than others. To think *I'm better than you* is a sure way to set yourself up for a fall. "It was pride that changed angels into devils," pointed out a great early Christian thinker, Saint Augustine. Then he said, "It is humility that makes men as angels."

Scripture

"We may throw the dice, but the Lord determines how they fall."—Proverbs 16:33 (NLT)

Grace

Heavenly Father, we thank you for this food that feeds us physically and for your Word that feeds us spiritually. Give us reverence for your wisdom and for your mighty ways. Teach us that even though we have the ability to make choices for our lives, you know everything that will happen before it happens. How's that again, Lord? Teach us something of this great mystery we'll come to understand fully in heaven. Lord, we trust in your wisdom; this is called faith. Amen.

Grace notes

You can make all the plans you want. In fact, God wants us to plan and honors good plans, but he has the final say. And sometimes what you think has happened by chance is not chance at all; it's God, working out his plan. God is in complete control, and he'll have his way—you can be sure of that. Someone once said, "Write your plans in pencil but give God the eraser." Good advice. The writer and pastor Max Lucado said, "Jesus gives us hope because He keeps us company, has a vision, and knows the way we should go."

Scripture

"Trust God from the bottom of your heart; don't try to figure out everything on your own. Listen for God's voice in everything you do, everywhere you go; he's the one who will keep you on track. Don't assume that you know it all."—Proverbs 3:5–7 (MSG)

Grace

Dear God, thank you for this food and for the many blessings you give us. Thank you for Mom, Dad, and other good adults in our lives; we trust them a lot. Help us to remember that you are always with us. Teach us that, especially when we lean on you for support, you step in to help us. Give us grateful, trusting hearts, Lord. Amen.

Grace notes

Life is filled with loose ends, but remember that God is always there for you. Jesus, the one who is at the same time both God and man, knows what it's like to be frustrated, confused, lost, or scared. Imagine life being sometimes like an enormous room filled with puzzles. At your feet is one leftover piece. You could spend a lifetime looking for where it belongs, or you could just hand it to God, the great puzzle Master. He'll help you solve whatever "puzzle" is facing you. "Every morning I wake up and thank God," says the Rhythm and Blues singer Aaron Neville. Now there's a wise man!

bay

Scripture

"Wealth you get by dishonesty will do you no good, but honesty can save your life."—Proverbs 10:2 (GNT)

Grace

Dear Father, we're glad to be with you and to share this food and our time together. You number our days with mercy and grace and teach us to be honest and truthful. Remind us that honesty is a true wealth that never loses value. Help us remember that the dishonest actions—which usually start with little things—can multiply and grow until our spiritual lives are in danger. Each dishonest act adds up and the pile gets bigger, until it subtracts from a good name. Thanks, Father, for these good words from Proverbs. We'll add this to our list of right ways to get rich honestly. And thank you for this food, Lord. We ask your blessing and count on your love. We like this kind of arithmetic! Amen.

Grace notes

To be wealthy and honest likely means that your achievements have earned you a good reputation, and the time to develop good habits that will contribute to a good reputation is NOW. Having a good reputation (a reputation is what people think of you), says that what you value—your wealth—is in the right place. A good reputation is like a magnet for bringing great opportunities into your life, including those things that can make you wealthy. Wealth without a good reputation is empty wealth, and moral shortcuts put you outside of God's protection. Being on time (that means you're respectful), being sincere, being pleasant, listening well, and doing even more than is expected of you—these are some ideas for developing qualities of honesty (which is also called integrity). Living honestly also says that you're true to yourself and true to God. What do you think happens if you have a bad reputation? How does a good reputation bring opportunities into your life? "An honest man's the noblest work of God," said the English poet Alexander Pope.

Scripture

"Before daybreak the next morning, Jesus got up and went out to an isolated place to pray."—Mark 1:35 (NLT)

Grace

Heavenly Father, even your Son, Jesus, prays to you! Now it's our turn to pray, thankful for the opportunity to talk to you together. Remind us of how much Jesus, when he was here on earth, loved morning-time prayers to start the day. Remind us of how much Jesus loves to hear us say "Good Morning," too, and picture him reaching out and taking our hand when we do. Encourage us to talk with you, with Jesus, and with the Holy Spirit every day. Sounds good, Father. Really good. We ask your blessing on this food. Amen.

Grace notes

New to praying? Sometimes forget? God knows your heart. Ask him to help you make prayer a habit and a priority. Start with a minute a day, and before you know it you'll wonder how you ever got along without it. "When I pray," explained William Wilberforce, "coincidences happen; and when I don't pray, they don't happen." Ask yourself this question: Do "coincidences" really just happen by chance? What "chance" event in your life or someone you know just might have had God working behind it? Maybe your mom and dad meeting for the first time . . .? William Wilberforce, by the way, was an English politician who worked alongside John Newton to abolish slavery. Preacher Newton, who had been a cruel slave trader, changed his ways, gave his life to God, and wrote the beautiful words of the song "Amazing Grace." Do you know those words? Could you and your family sing them together, right here at the table?

Scripture

"Don't be misled: No one makes a fool of God. What a person plants, he will harvest. The person who plants selfishness, ignoring the needs of others—ignoring God!—harvests a crop of weeds. All he'll have to show for his life is weeds! But the one who plants in response to God, letting God's Spirit do the growth work in him, harvests a crop of real life, eternal life."—Galatians 6:7–8 (MSG)

Grace

Father Almighty, we ask your blessing on this food and give thanks for our family and friends. Fill us with an appetite to see the goodness in others and to show others goodness, too. Plant in us the desire to let you grow in our hearts. Fill us with a need to let the Holy Spirit produce in us his good "fruit" of love, joy, peace, patience, kindness, goodness, faithfulness, gentleness, and self-control.* Amen

*Galatians 5:22–23

Grace notes

Why do you think Paul, the writer of Galatians, names these traits and calls them out as fruit of the Spirit? Notice that he doesn't use the plural *fruits,* which would call attention to each of these traits separately. That's because they're all connected; you can't really have one without any of the others! The fruit of the Holy Spirit is planted within you when you accept Jesus Christ. It's up to you, though, to work to develop these traits. Start by asking the Holy Spirit to help you by his strength. "The fruit of the Spirit is a gift of God, and only He can produce it," said the Bible scholar and spy Dietrich Bonhoeffer (he spied to help defeat the Nazis in Germany during World War II). He went on to say, "They who bear it know as little about it as the tree knows of its fruit. They know only the power of Him on whom their life depends."

mint

Scripture

"'Here is my command. Love each other, just as I have loved you. No one has greater love than the one who gives his life for his friends. You are my friends if you do what I command. I do not call you servants anymore. Servants do not know their master's business. Instead, I have called you friends. I have told you everything I learned from my Father.'"—John 15:12–15 (NIrV)

Grace

Lord Jesus, we bow our heads and ask for your blessing on this food. We thank you for the many blessings of this day. We wonder how it is that you, who made the universe, could seek out each of us and call us friend! Help us to believe that your love for us will never go away—ever. Fill us with gratefulness that you live in us and that our hearts are just where you want to be. Help us see that you are always there to stand by us. And remind us that we can talk to you about anything. You are ever faithful. Help us to be faithful right back. Yay, God! Amen.

Grace notes

A good friend should feel comfortable letting you know when you've crossed the line. Jesus will let you know because he loves you. (Though he calls you friend, it's probably a good idea to remember he's still the boss of you.) The Irish poet Joseph Scriven wrote a hymn that's been a favorite with Christians for 100 years: "What a friend we have in Jesus, all our sins and griefs to bear. What a privilege to carry everything to God in prayer." The Country music star Alan Jackson sings a modern version. Find it on YouTube. It's great!

thyme

Scripture

"Happy is anyone who becomes wise—who comes to have understanding. There is more profit in it than there is in silver; it is worth more to you than gold. Wisdom is more valuable than jewels; nothing you could want can compare with it. Wisdom offers you long life, as well as wealth and honor. Wisdom can make your life pleasant and lead you safely through it. Those who become wise are happy; wisdom will give them life."—Proverbs 3:13–18 (GNT)

Grace

Wonderful Counselor,* thank you for this food and for all of the blessings you give us. How can we become wise, Lord? Teach us that wisdom comes from growing close to you. Show us that it also comes from curiosity, experiences, and making mistakes and learning from them. Give us your guidance to become wiser as we grow bigger and older. Yay, God! Amen.

*Isaiah 9:6

Grace notes

Part of wisdom, or being wise, has to do with doing what is right even if it makes you uncomfortable. Have you ever had to *own up* or admit to something? It doesn't feel so great at first, does it? But this is the way we grow, and there's no getting around it. Question: Who gets to decide what's right and wrong? Answer: God, of course! (But then, you already knew that.) "People grow through experience if they meet life honestly and courageously," Eleanor Roosevelt, the wife of an American president, wisely said. "That's how character is built."

Scripture

"You lazy fool, look at an ant. Watch it closely; let it teach you a thing or two. Nobody has to tell it what to do. All summer it stores up food; at harvest it stockpiles provisions. So how long are you going to laze around doing nothing? How long before you get out of bed? A nap here, a nap there, a day off here, a day off there, sit back, take it easy—do you know what comes next? Just this: You can look forward to a dirt-poor life, poverty your permanent houseguest!"—Proverbs 6:6–11 (MSG)

Grace

Father God, please bless this food and everyone here, and especially bless the cook. Encourage us to show gratitude for the work it takes to put food on the table. Remind us that this preparation gives us all a big benefit: we get to eat! Teach us that your blessings include way more than food, that life's rewards come when we obey and honor you. Remind us that your plan never was for us to live a dirt-poor life in any sense of the word.* Thank you for your teachings—they're our best blessings! We praise your holy name. Amen.

*See what Ecclesiastes 3:12 says about this.

Grace notes

How many people does it take to put your favorite pizza on the table? Don't forget to count the farmers, ranchers, grocers, truck drivers, advertisers, and those who buy it for you! If you knew who they all were, wouldn't you need a lot of thank-you notes! Why not tell Mom and Dad "Thanks" right now, out loud!? Don't you love A. A. Milne's stories about Winnie the Pooh and his friends? In one story "Piglet noticed that even though he had a Very Small Heart, it could hold a rather large amount of Gratitude." Piglet is very observant, isn't he!

parsley

Scripture

"While Jeremiah was still locked up in jail, a second Message from God was given to him: 'This is God's Message, the God who made earth, made it livable and lasting, known everywhere as God: "Call to me and I will answer you. I'll tell you marvelous and wondrous things that you could never figure out on your own."'"—Jeremiah 33:1–3 (MSG)

Grace

Father Almighty, please bless our food, our family, and our friends. We bow our heads to you, amazed that you, the Creator of the universe—who has heaven as your throne and the earth as a footstool*—have a desire to be with us, to love us, to talk with us, and to advise us. Remind us that all we need to do is take you up on your friendship offers! We love you, God, and glorify your name. Hallelujah, mighty God! Amen.

*Isaiah 66:1

Grace notes

God gave authority to certain people, called prophets, whom he called to serve him by speaking his words for him. Jeremiah was one of those. When he said something, people listened. You connect with lots of people whom you should listen to, don't you? They might offer you advice, teach you things, warn you, or protect you. Can you name people like that in your life? Certainly Mom and Dad, Grandma and Grandpa, and your teachers come to mind. But what about police officers, bus drivers, fire fighters, judges, and even school crossing guards? Don't forget that all of these grown-ups are there to help you—that's what they love to do most. Go to them when you need to. Give thanks to them! How can you show your appreciation and respect? Bryant McGill, a writer and Nobel Peace Prize nominee, shares one way: "One of the most sincere forms of respect is actually listening to what another has to say." Can you think of another way to show appreciation and respect?

Scripture

"His disciples began arguing about which of them was the greatest. But Jesus knew their thoughts, so he brought a little child to his side. Then he said to them, "Anyone who welcomes a little child like this on my behalf welcomes me, and anyone who welcomes me also welcomes my Father who sent me. Whoever is the least among you is the greatest."—Luke 9:46–49 (NLT)

Grace

Dear Jesus, you are such a wonderful Teacher. Show us how to look at each other through your eyes. Help us to remember that the least of us can be the greatest and that all of us are equally valuable to you. It's easy for us to slip up and forget; even your disciples needed you to remind them. Teach us that greatness comes from a humble heart of service to you and to each other. Jesus, we thank you for our food and pray for those who are in our hearts. Amen.

Grace notes

We sometimes think that Jesus's disciples were saint-like, don't we? But here we see them arguing about which of them was the greatest! They got caught up in the trap of self-importance, and that can happen to any of us. They forgot for a moment who was really in charge and where all their power and ability came from in the first place. An Englishman named John Ruskin once called it like he saw it: "A man wrapped up in himself makes a very small parcel." Imagine that for a minute! Do you ever find yourself tempted in this way?

Scripture

[Paul asked,] "Do you think I am trying to make people accept me? No, God is the One I am trying to please. Am I trying to please people? If I still wanted to please people, I would not be a servant of Christ." —Galatians 1:10 (NCV)

Grace

Dear Jesus, we are so thankful you are here with us. Please bless our food and each one of us. Fill us up, Lord, with your Spirit and your love, for you are everything. Encourage us to pray, to read the Bible, to try to please you first, and to want to serve you in whatever way you want us to. Inspire us to have a passion for you as Paul did, to learn why Paul was so hungry for your Word. We're reporting for duty, Lord! Amen.

Grace notes

Wouldn't it be great if everyone tried to please God first? What would a day at school look like if that were the case? (That would mean that everyone would treat everyone else exactly the way they would want to be treated—the way Jesus would treat them.) Wow, what a day that would be! Bil and Jeff Keane, who together created the Family Circus cartoons, once made a cartoon that said, "Grandma says of all the things you wear, your expression is the most important." What do you "wear" on your face? Is it more important than the clothes on your back?

Scripture

"Consider it a sheer gift, friends, when tests and challenges come at you from all sides. You know that under pressure, your faith-life is forced into the open and shows its true colors. So don't try to get out of anything prematurely. Let it do its work so you become mature and well-developed, not deficient in any way. If you don't know what you're doing, pray to the Father. He loves to help. You'll get his help, and won't be condescended to when you ask for it. Ask boldly, believingly, without a second thought."—James 1:2–7 (MSG)

Grace

Father God, please bless our family, friends, and food. Thank you for watching over us. "Believe in me," you tell us, "and I'll be there for you." Encourage us to see life's challenges and troubles for what they are: ways for us to grow stronger and teaching tools that show us that we really were made for great and wonderful things. We hear you, Lord, and we promise to believe in you and to ask boldly for your help. Remind us of the good things you do for us through the work of Mom and Dad, too. We have no second thoughts about you, Father; we just believe in you. That's the best way to grow up. Amen.

Grace notes

Don't you hate it when problems seem to blow in out of nowhere? What if you could reprogram your brain to think of them as training exercises instead? The great inventor Albert Einstein once said "We can't solve problems by using the same kind of thinking we used when we created them." Do you think we create our own problems—at least some of the time? Can you name an example? Do you think Mr. Einstein would want us to pray to God for problem-solving help?

bay

Scripture

"If you, God, kept records on wrongdoings, who would stand a chance?"—Psalm 130:3 (MSG)

"Lord, if you punished people for all their sins, no one would be left alive."—Psalm 130:3 (ERV)

"I will forgive their sins and will no longer remember their wrongs."—Hebrews 8:12 (GNT)

Grace

Almighty God, please bless this food and our time together. We thank you that you are so forgiving that you erase our mistakes—letting us start over fresh. We thank you for the blessings you give us each day, and for covering us with hope, kindness, and understanding. Open our eyes to the healing power that comes from being truly sorry and truly forgiven, and remind us that each time we say we're sorry we get stronger and wiser. Thanks, Lord, for family and friends, for those we love and for those who love us, through thick and thin. Help us never to overlook this blessing. Amen.

Grace notes

Since God knows everything, can he *really* forget when we've done things that hurt him or others? The Bible tells us that once we're forgiven God looks at us as though we had never sinned in the first place. When he gazes into our hearts he sees Jesus Christ's sinless heart instead. It's not that God is absent-minded or too busy to keep track of the sins of all his children. He "forgets" our forgiven sins only in the sense that he doesn't hold them against us. Here's another question to think about: If God has forgiven you, does he want you to keep on blaming yourself for something bad you've done? Forgiving yourself is important, too.

65

Scripture

"Children, do what your parents tell you. This is only right. 'Honor your father and mother' is the first commandment that has a promise attached to it, namely, 'so you will live well and have a long life.' Fathers, don't exasperate your children by coming down hard on them. Take them by the hand and lead them in the way of the Master." —Ephesians 6:1–4 (MSG)

Grace

Dear Jesus, thank you for this meal and for the time together with Mom and Dad; we know they love us, and we love them, too. Show us that when we honor our moms and dads we're also showing honor to you. We think Mom and Dad are the best, but sometimes, Lord, we need you to remind us to act like it. Amen.

Grace notes

God makes many promises, but his fifth command from the Ten Commandments is the only one with a promise attached to it. That makes it pretty special, doesn't it? Paul was the author of the book of Ephesians, and in his day fathers were the main ones who disciplined children and provided guidance. So he had an extra word of caution for them. The actor Tim Allen once said that "kids learn by example. If I [as the Dad] respect Mom, they're going to respect Mom." What difference does all-around respect make in a family's life? In what sense do moms and dads show respect for kids?

sage

Scripture

[Luke begins his Gospel (his story of Jesus' life) as a letter to his friend. He says,] "Dear Theophilus: Many people have done their best to write a report of the things that have taken place among us. They wrote what we have been told by those who saw these things from the beginning and who proclaimed the message. And so, Your Excellency, because I have carefully studied all these matters from their beginning, I thought it would be good to write an orderly account for you. I do this so that you will know the full truth about everything which you have been taught."—Luke 1:1–4 (GNT)

Grace

Heavenly Father, thank you for this food and for all your blessings. We thank you, God, for putting the Holy Spirit into Luke so that he could record the truth about your Son's life and ministry on this earth. Thank you that Luke wrote carefully and truthfully, knowing that he would be our eyes and ears to help us understand the wonders of Jesus. Maybe if Luke were around today he would record this most wonderful true story and upload it to YouTube so that everyone could see and hear. Yay, God! You rock and rule! Amen.

Grace notes

Luke was a doctor. It figures—he writes this letter (his Gospel, or story of the Good News of Jesus) as though he were writing an important article for a medical magazine. Did you know that Luke wrote the book of Acts, too? It's a kind of follow-up letter, once again to Luke's friend Theophilus, giving him Part 2 of Jesus' story. Doctors like to research evidence carefully, as Luke did in writing down the events of Jesus' life. Look for that in his writings. As Bugs Bunny likes to ask, "Eh . . . What's up, doc?"

mint

Scripture

[The apostle Paul writes,] "It happens so regularly that it's predictable. The moment I decide to do good, sin is there to trip me up. I truly delight in God's commands, but it's pretty obvious that not all of me joins in that delight. Parts of me covertly rebel, and just when I least expect it, they take charge."—Romans 7:21–23 (MSG)

Grace

Heavenly Father, thank you for our family. Please bless us and our food. This is a big deal, Lord—this being good thing. The thing about obedience, Father, is that if Paul had such a hard time being good we don't stand a chance! We know we can't fix the sin problem by ourselves. Teach us to come to you before times are tough, when times are tough, and after times are tough. We do want to be good, so when we trip up please get us back on our feet right away! Comfort us with your love and forgiveness. Thank you, Lord. Amen.

Grace notes

One of the hardest things to do is to admit mistakes. Most everyone has a hard time with that. Ask God to help you, to give you the courage to speak up—because admitting weakness is the only way to grow stronger. It's easy to believe in something when you don't have to make changes in your behavior, isn't it? But Jesus calls us, as his children, to be the best we can be. A famous Christian thinker and writer, Søren Kierkegaard, had this to say: "It is so hard to believe because it is so hard to obey." Talk about the connection between trusting and obeying. Why are they both so important?

Scripture

"I urge Euodia and Syntyche to iron out their differences and make up. God doesn't want his children holding grudges. And, oh, yes, Syzygus, since you're right there to help them work things out, do your best with them. . . . Celebrate God all day, every day. I mean, revel in him! Make it as clear as you can to all you meet that you're on their side, working with them and not against them."—Philippians 4:2–4 (MSG)

Grace

Heavenly Father, we come into your peace-loving presence, ask for your blessing, and thank you for this food. When we disagree with people, encourage us to look at the situation the way the other person does, and help our friends to do the same. Teach us, too, that we can ask Mom, Dad, or a teacher for help because you often work through others. Remind us that a friend is someone who knows the song in our hearts and sings it back when we forget. Amen.

Grace notes

People in the Bible had interesting names. You probably don't know a single person with the names in today's reading! Here's how to say them: Euodia: Yoo-OH-dee-uh; Syntyche: SIN-tih-kee; Syzygus: Siz-eh-kus. What do you think the last sentence in this grace means? Could it be something about the way good friends know each other so well that they feel comfortable telling each other the truth? "A true friend," said the radio talk show host Bernard Meltzer, "is someone who thinks that you are a good egg even though he knows that you are slightly cracked."

Scripture

"For it is by God's grace that you have been saved through faith. It is not the result of your own efforts, but God's gift, so that no one can boast about it. God has made us what we are, and in our union with Christ Jesus he has created us for a life of good deeds, which he has already prepared for us to do."—Ephesians 2:8–9 (GNT)

Grace

Dear Jesus, your treasure store is endless. Thank you for this food. May we always remember that you are the only one who can open heaven's gates—that only you have the key. Our good works show you that we love you and are grateful, but they can't save us. Inspire us to want to please you and to live for you with purpose and passion. Amen.

Grace notes

God's love and sacrifice have earned you a place in heaven, but that doesn't mean it's goof-off time for you. When you love anyone—and that includes Jesus—you act in loving ways toward them. And when you put your faith into action, Jesus rewards you. "Think of giving not as a duty, but as a privilege," said a very wealthy man named John D. Rockefeller. Mr. Rockefeller gave away hundreds of millions of dollars, but he didn't wait until he was rich to start helping others. He began giving away money from the time of his first job—as an assistant bookkeeper. He was sixteen years old. Can you name ways to show your love and gratitude to Jesus by helping someone else?

parsley

Scripture

"Don't fret or worry. Instead of worrying, pray. Let petitions and praises shape your worries into prayers, letting God know your concerns. Before you know it, a sense of God's wholeness, everything coming together for good, will come and settle you down. It's wonderful what happens when Christ displaces worry at the center of your life."—Philippians 4:6–7 (MSG)

Grace

Heavenly Father, thank you for all your blessings, including your bringing us together as a family. Please bless this meal. Open our eyes, Lord, to the beauty and simplicity of good, honest prayer. Allow the Holy Spirit to guide us and encourage us in the right direction. Center our strength in you, and lead us to your wisdom. Remind us that prayer is a time when you talk to us, too—when your Spirit speaks to our hearts by guiding our thoughts and attitudes. Most of all, Lord, help us turn our worries into prayers. Amen.

Grace notes

There will always be times when worry seems to overtake your brain. Learning to depend on Jesus is so important. When there's a hole in your life, fill it up with prayer. Someone once said, "Worry is an old man with a bent head, carrying a load of feathers he thinks is lead." Imagine that picture. It's funny, isn't it, but maybe a little sad at the same time. When you give your worries to Jesus, they can become as light as a feather. You can stand up straight and tall in him.

sage

Scripture

"Oh—you're my God! I can't get enough of you! I've worked up such hunger and thirst for God, traveling across dry and weary deserts. So here I am in the place of worship, eyes open, drinking in your strength and glory. In your generous love I am really living at last! My lips brim praises like fountains. I bless you every time I take a breath; My arms wave like banners of praise to you."—Psalm 63:1–4 (MSG)

Grace

Heavenly Father, we gather together in your name, asking your blessing. Dear God, your strong love and loyalty to us are so incredibly amazing. How can you know us so well and yet still love us so much? Teach us to be respectful, Lord. Teach us to be grateful, too, and to drink in your glory. You amaze us with your forgiving and loving grace. Amen.

Grace notes

It's thought that King David wrote Psalm 63 while he was running away from his son Absalom, who wanted to destroy him and seize his throne (how sad). Even under those circumstances David was giving thanks to God. It's important to be thankful even in bad times because that's when we're most likely to invite God to help us. Ups and downs are natural parts of life—something we learn as we grow up through the experiences of living. Henry Ford, the founder of Ford Motor Company and the developer of the factory assembly line, had his shares of ups and downs. "When everything seems to be going against you," he said, "remember that the airplane takes off against the wind, not with it." Flying into the wind causes an increased airflow around the wings, reducing takeoff distance. That means the runways don't have to be so long, either. Moving into and then through troubles in our life can help lift us, too—if we have an attitude of gratitude for God's help!

mint

Scripture

"Your words are so choice, so tasty; I prefer them to the best home cooking."—Psalm 119:103 (MSG)

Grace

Abba—"Daddy" God, we are happy to share our meal today. Please bless us all and bless this food, too. Show us that adding grace to the menu makes Mom's best meal even better—no room for half-baked truths here. Inspire us to follow your Word—your recipe—for life; that's what wins the blue ribbon. God, you are amazing, and your words are like delicious food for our souls. Thank you for *all* our food today! Amen.

Grace notes

Mealtimes were very important in ancient days and were often treated as wonderful celebrations of the special relationship between God and his people. Many of Jesus' actions, including his miracles, involved food or drink. Jesus liked to party! Celebrations at your house usually involve food, too, don't they? "The best meals are those prepared by loving hands," said the author Ken Poirot. (Of course, a little pie never hurts, either!)

thyme

Scripture

"My child, pay attention to what I say. Remember my commands. Listen to wisdom, and do your best to understand. Ask for good judgment. Cry out for understanding. Look for wisdom like silver. Search for it like hidden treasure. If you do this, you will understand what it means to respect the Lord, and you will come to know God."—Proverbs 2:1–5 (ERV)

Grace

Dear Lord, you created us and know us inside and out, backward and forward. So you know that it's sometimes hard for us to figure out the right thing to do. Guide us to focus on your Word so we can learn and remember. Help us appreciate that you have given us ways to get to know you. And teach us too, Lord, that we gain wisdom by trying new things, by listening to those who have something to teach us, and by taking little steps forward—even if we feel scared at first. Teach us that a life of playing it safe, of trying to avoid new experiences because we might be afraid, actually becomes a life of avoiding joy. Bless our food, Lord, our family, and all who need your blessing today. (That would be all of us.) Amen.

Grace notes

The joy of following God's commands grows bigger as you dig deeper into God's Word. He opens your heart and rewards you in ways you couldn't have imagined. Learning to do anything well takes time, right? Learning about God is no different. Be patient. And don't ignore God's truth just because part of it is hard to understand. (You don't have to know how a watch is made before you can tell time, right?) The artist Pablo Picasso was hungry to learn. "I am always doing that which I cannot do," he said, "in order that I may learn how to do it." What do you think of that approach to life? What is one way you could follow his example right away, tonight?

Scripture

"The first to plead his case seems right, until another comes and examines him."—Proverbs 18:17 (NASB)

Grace

Just and merciful Father, the heavens are your playground, yet your advice is so down-to-earth! May we never forget that you are everywhere—all at the same time! Sharpen our wits, Lord, so we can understand and accept your truth. Help us always to trust you first, and keep us from believing anything that goes against what we've already learned from you. And no one can object that it's right to thank you for this food, our family, and our friends. That's something we can all agree on. Amen.

Grace notes

How smart you would be to get into the habit of listening to both sides of an argument before jumping to a conclusion. What can seem so obvious at first often makes a lot less sense once you get all the facts. Can you remember a time at school when you took sides quickly and your side turned out to be wrong? "In seeking truth," said the respected news man Walter Cronkite, "you have to get both sides of a story." Why would this be important for someone who publicly writes or talks about stories in the news?

Scripture

"My children, listen to your father's teaching; pay attention so you will understand. What I am telling you is good, so do not forget what I teach you."—Proverbs 4:1-2 (NCV)

Grace

Almighty Father, please bless our food and family and friends. Dear God, open our eyes wide to what is good, and give us big ears to hear what Mom and Dad tell us. Thank you for teaching us how to be obedient kids. We sing your praises, Lord, always remembering how much you love us. Amen.

Grace notes

This proverb is about honoring your parents' words. What are some ways to show them honor? How about respecting and obeying without backtalk or "body language," like glaring, foot stomping, or eye rolling—so not with it! Honoring someone also involves paying attention to their wishes, whether or not they say them out load. Talk about some ways you can show honor to parents, caregivers, teachers, and others in authority over you. Listen to what two famous people have said about their parents. President Abraham Lincoln said "All that I am, or hope to be, I owe to my angel mother." And the Academy Award winning actor Sidney Poitier said "I decided in my life that I would do nothing that did not reflect positively on my father's life." What did Sydney Poitier mean? Will you listen to his advice? Nod your head yes—but only if you mean it!

Scripture

"Enthusiasm without knowledge is not good; impatience will get you into trouble."—Proverbs 19:2 (GNT)

Grace

Lord, please bless our food and family—especially the cook! Help us find things to do that really get us excited, things that create passion in us. Encourage us to chase a dream, but remind us to do a little detective work first. Once we've done some exploring, we might want that thing even more—or maybe less. Teach us that our learning fuels—and guides—our yearning. Yay, God! Amen.

Grace notes

What do you want to be? A pilot, firefighter, musician, or scientist? An actor, builder, parent, pastor, or vet? Maybe you want to help people. Or work outdoors or invent something. How much effort are you willing to put into following your dream? On the other hand, what if you have no idea yet what you want to be? Some ideas: pray about it, explore possibilities, read about jobs that interest you, choose new friends with other interests, or stretch yourself to do something you didn't think you'd be good at. "Neither a wise man nor a brave man lies down on the tracks of history to wait for the train of the future to run over him," said President Dwight D. Eisenhower. That's good advice, even for grown-ups, isn't it?

mint

Scripture

"Do not deceive yourselves by just listening to [God's] word; instead, put it into practice. If you listen to the word, but do not put it into practice you are like people who look in a mirror and see themselves as they are. They take a good look at themselves and then go away and at once forget what they look like."—James 1:22–24 (GNT)

Grace

Heavenly Father, please bless this food, our family, friends, and those in need. Thank you for being part of our lives, and fill us with your Spirit so we can serve you. Show us that good intentions with no follow-up action get us nowhere, and that pretending to be something we're not makes us forget who we really are—your own children. Amen.

Grace notes

What do you think about doing good things? Should your life matter in this way? Most everyone will say yes, but what would that *look* like? President Jefferson understood: "Do you want to know who you are?" he asked. "Don't ask. Act! Action will delineate and define you." Think about some ways to put your faith into action. Offer to do some yard work for an older or disabled person in your neighborhood. Volunteer to help out a person or organization at least once a month. Here are some volunteer activities you might be able to do as a family: Special Olympics, soup kitchens, or beach/neighborhood cleanups. Sponsor a canned food drive, or take part in one. How many ways can you think of to show love and care for others? When you do, be ready for a big surprise at the joy you'll get in return.

Scripture

"Do yourself a favor and learn all you can; then remember what you learn and you will prosper."—Proverbs 19:8 (GNT)

Grace

Awesome Father, please bless our family and this food. Guide us through our days, Lord, and make us eager to learn (Is there an app for that?). Work in us to improve our attitude toward learning. Give us an appetite for your Word and a desire to search for answers there. Remind us that learning is a journey and that it's meant to be fun, with buried treasure to be found along the way. Amen.

Grace notes

It's true—having a happy face and wide-open eyes makes learning and remembering easier. Why do you think that is? Isn't it interesting that you can remember the words to songs you like, no matter how long ago you learned them? Benjamin Franklin knew what it took to learn and remember: "Tell me and I forget," he said. "Teach me and I remember. Involve me and I learn." How might telling be different from teaching? Why do you think being involved—we sometimes call this "hands on"—makes a difference in learning?

Scripture

"We call Abraham 'father' not because he got God's attention by living like a saint, but because God made something out of Abraham when he was a nobody. Isn't that what we've always read in Scripture, God saying to Abraham, 'I set you up as father of many peoples'? Abraham was first named 'father' and then became a father because he dared to trust God to do what only God could do: raise the dead to life, with a word make something out of nothing. When everything was hopeless, Abraham believed anyway, deciding to live not on the basis of what he saw he couldn't do but on what God said he would do. And so he was made father of a multitude of peoples. God himself said to him, 'You're going to have a big family, Abraham!'"—Romans 4:17–18 (MSG)

Grace

Almighty Father, we thank you for our dinner, our family, and all our loved ones. May your blessing and your greatness remind us that though you are the mighty one who creates something from nothing and makes order out of chaos, you still reach out in love to each of us. May we always remember that you reward us not because of what we do or who we are but because of who *you* are. We want to receive your blessing, Lord. Thanks for including us in your big family. Amen.

Grace notes

If you think your life might be too ordinary, take heart! Abraham's story, told in Genesis 12–25, is so inspiring. Here he was, an ordinary shepherd—a nobody, really. And he was a big mistake-maker, to boot. But he came to believe and trust in God, and God rewarded him with a full life, richer than he could ever have imagined. Even though he and his wife were old and childless for a long, long time, God made him the father of millions—including what we call the "spiritual Father" of all of us believers. Abraham's name will forever be known. God can work amazing things in your life, too. "Without the assistance of that Divine Being I cannot succeed," admitted another Abraham, Abraham Lincoln. "With that assistance, I cannot fail." Wow! That goes for you, too!

Scripture

"When Jesus looked up and saw a great crowd coming toward him, he said to Philip, 'Where shall we buy bread for these people to eat?' He asked this only to test him, for he already had in mind what he was going to do. Philip answered him, 'Eight months' wages would not buy enough bread for each one to have a bite!'

"Another of his disciples, Andrew, Simon Peter's brother, spoke up, 'Here is a boy with five small barley loaves and two small fish, but how far will they go among so many?'

"Jesus said, 'Have the people sit down.' There was plenty of grass in that place, and the men sat down, about five thousand of them. Jesus then took the loaves, gave thanks, and distributed to those who were seated as much as they wanted. He did the same with the fish.'"—John 6:5–11 (NIV)

Grace

Dear Jesus, thank you for this food that feeds us, your Spirit that nourishes our souls, and your blessings that fill and lift us up. Test and stretch our faith, Lord. You are the Bread of Life; teach us to believe your promise of a great banquet in heaven for all of us—the party to beat all earthly parties. Show us that with you our life can be joyful and that you are big enough to meet any needs. Jesus, you are our great Provider. Amen.

Grace notes

If Jesus can feed thousands from a few mouthfuls, think of the miracles he can do for you. Miracles are sacred moments—glimpses of himself our Creator gives us to let us know he is there. Keep your eyes open. God's miracles are everywhere if we're only willing to look for them. The scientist and inventor Albert Einstein thought of it this way: "There are only two ways to live your life. One is as though nothing is a miracle. The other is as though everything is a miracle." What miracles have you seen? Not all "miracles" defy the ordinary laws of nature. What about a "coincidence" when something seemed to happen for you at just the time you needed it?

sage

81

Scripture

"If you want people to like you, forgive them when they wrong you. Remembering wrongs can break up a friendship."—Proverbs 17:9 (GNT)

Grace

Dear Jesus, thank you for your blessings. Thank you for this food and for being our friend. Encourage us to appreciate our earthly friends, to treat them right, to forgive them when they hurt us, and to keep them close. Help us see that friendship can be like the beautiful rose attached to a thorny stem; when we get down close to admire the rose we sometimes get a little prick. Encourage us to understand that most of the time it's best to forgive and forget. Lord, you know best—so put us to the test. Amen.

Grace notes

Satan wants you to hold grudges because they lead to ugly thoughts and actions. When someone hurts you, Satan will want you to revisit the wrong—to keep bringing it up or tell others about it. Are you going to let him get the best of you? Don't listen to him! Here's an idea that can help in many situations: say a favorite Bible verse, even if only in your mind. Make a fun project out of decorating cards with some verses you like. Keep them in the car and make a game of memorizing them while you're on the way to school. Have a contest, maybe with your brother or sister! Memorizing is easier than you think, and there are lots of tricks to do it. Joshua Choonmin Kang is an author and pastor of a Korean church in Los Angeles. Listen to his good advice: "When we meditate on the words of Scripture, we begin to bear fruit, directed by the Spirit. The more we commit the Word to memory, the richer our being becomes." *Bearing fruit* means making good things happen! Can you remember that!

mint

Scripture

"My dear friends, don't let public opinion influence how you live out our glorious, Christ-originated faith. If a man enters your church wearing an expensive suit, and a street person wearing rags comes in right after him, and you say to the man in the suit, 'Sit here, sir; this is the best seat in the house!' and either ignore the street person or say, 'Better sit here in the back row,' haven't you segregated God's children and proved that you are judges who can't be trusted?"—James 2:1–4 (MSG)

Grace

Lord Jesus, we are really hungry and really grateful for this food. We are grateful for our friends and family, too, and we pray for them to be happy and to know how much you love them. Help us to see the importance of not jumping to conclusions about others. Help us remember that you love each of us every bit as much as the next person. Teach us to be kind to everyone. Amen.

Grace notes

James isn't advising you as a Christian never to dress your best. Sometimes you need to dress a certain way—like for a special program, a wedding, or a night out for a family celebration. He is warning you instead to guard against making snap judgments about people based on their appearance or using someone else's wardrobe (could be their fancy car, too) as a measurement of their importance or fame. For example, do you automatically think of homeless people as lazy, untrustworthy, or "good for nothing?" "Beware, so long as you live, of judging men by their outward appearance," said the storyteller Jean de La Fontaine about 500 years ago. That advise holds just as true today.

Scripture

"Dear friends, here is one thing you must not forget. With the Lord a day is like a thousand years. And a thousand years are like a day." —2 Peter 3:8 (NIrV)

Grace

Eternal Father, thank you for this food and for our special time together. Help us to remember how much different your ways are than ours. Even time itself is part of your creation. Fill us with patience and with trust that you will keep all your promises; only you know the time and place when they will come true. Teach us that there are some mysteries we won't understand until we're with you in heaven. Teach us that, for now, just knowing that you are bigger and greater than anything we can imagine is enough for us. Thank you for the gift of time, and help us to use it to become better people for service in your kingdom here on earth. Amen.

Grace notes

God isn't bound by the physical world we live in. God invented time for us—because our limited minds couldn't understand reality without taking it in chunks; we think in terms of todays and tomorrows, of past, present, and future. Time doesn't matter to God. To him a minute, a year, or a billion years are all the same! If that's a mystery to you, don't worry—it's a mystery to everyone. Here's another mystery: he has planned out your life to the very second, and yet he can be persuaded to change his mind—and he knows that will happen, too. Don't even try to figure out how these opposites work together. God knows how it all works, and for him it's a piece of cake. A famous early Christian named Saint Augustine put it this way: "How can the past and future be, when the past no longer is, and the future is not yet? As for the present, if it were always present and never moved on to become the past, it would not be time, but eternity." *Come again!* If words like that boggle your brain, don't feel alone. Perhaps Saint Augustine was thinking of this Bible verse: "Everything that now exists has already been. And what is coming has existed before."* In any case, you can be sure that eternity is not a concept easily understood—except by God. As for you, you'll just have to wait and see what it's all about!

*Ecclesiastes 3:15 (NIrV)

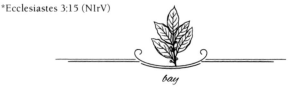

bay

Scripture

"The moment we get tired in the waiting, God's Spirit is right alongside helping us along. If we don't know how or what to pray, it doesn't matter. He does our praying in and for us, making prayer out of our wordless sighs, our aching groans. He knows us far better than we know ourselves, knows our . . . condition, and keeps us present before God. That's why we can be so sure that every detail in our lives of love for God is worked into something good."—Romans 8:26–28 (MSG)

Grace

Dear God Almighty, please bless us. Thank you for our food, so plentiful and delicious. So many times we want to say the right words, but they just won't come—it's so annoying! And yet here you are, Lord, telling us that it's all right—that you already know just what we're struggling to get out. You say "be still, for I am with you."* Remind us to pray and to trust you always, no matter what is going on in our lives. You know how to turn even the bad times into something good and worthy. Blessed be your name, Lord. Amen.

*Psalm 46:10

Grace notes

You feel lost and don't know what to do. Or you feel happy and want to say so. Whatever you feel, share it with the Holy Spirit, who lives in you. He knows what your heart wants to say even if you can't put it into words. Ask him to be your inspiration, and then take a moment and listen for his voice (it won't be out loud, but he'll "talk" to you just the same, through your thoughts and feelings). Listening for him is the best habit ever. Fanny Crosby, in describing her hymn-writing process, said this: "It may seem a little old-fashioned, always to begin one's work with prayer, but I never undertook a hymn without first asking the good Lord to be my inspiration." Fanny knew what she was talking about. She was completely blind but still accomplished amazing things. With the Spirit's help she wrote 8,000 hymns *and memorized the entire Bible—from Genesis to Revelation!* Talk about a *Wow!*

Scripture

"He who guards you never sleeps."—Psalm 121:3(b) (NCV)

Grace

Dear Father, thank you for blessing us and for providing the good food on this table. Lord, your plans are perfect! Imagine if we had to figure out your bedtime so we wouldn't wake you! Encourage us to call you when we need your strength. Let us never forget you are as close to us as our breath. Remind us to whisper your name at any hour, at any time. Just saying your name, even if only in our minds and with no other words attached, can be a prayer to you, Lord, because you read our thoughts, desires, intentions, and feelings. Thanks for who you are. Amen.

Grace notes

How comforting it is to know that God is always present and available, ready and waiting to hear from you. He never sleeps, and his attention is always on you. Ask him in your bedtime prayer tonight to keep his promise to watch over you. He will anyway, but he loves it when you ask because it shows him your love and appreciation. And touching base with God will help you enjoy the best sleep ever. "No pillow so soft as God's promise," someone once said. Here's another thought, written over 400 years ago by playwright Thomas Dekker: "Golden slumbers kiss your eyes, smiles awake you when you rise." Isn't that a pretty picture?

sage

Scripture

"Do the best you can to live in peace with everyone."—Romans 12:18 (ERV)

Grace

Heavenly Father, it's mealtime again; please bless our food, our family, our friends, the hungry, the sick, and those in any kind of trouble. Show us that getting along with others involves more than just a loving feeling. Remind us that if we are going to make a difference it has to be all about doing. Inspire us with energy and eagerness to serve you by serving others. Help us to help others in the same way you help us. We love you, Lord. Amen.

Grace notes

God doesn't ask you to be close buddies with everyone, but he does want you to get along with others as best as you can. And he doesn't want you to give that effort lip service either. Pretending to care about someone is something only actors on a stage should do. If your heart isn't it, the truth will show through, and—if you do it enough—soon you won't like yourself either. If you're finding it hard to like someone genuinely, here are a few things you can do: ask God to help you understand why you don't like someone. Have you ever had a friend you didn't like at first because you thought they were stuck-up, only to find out they were terribly shy around new people? Or maybe they talk mean because they've had a friend walk out on them and don't want to be hurt again. Perhaps you've heard *stories* and made a judgement call. Once you've figured that out it'll be easier to look for the good qualities. Give them a chance. Ask questions to show interest. Be patient. Be forgiving. Seek to understand them. Remember, Jesus loves them, too. "Be able to cite three good qualities of every relative or acquaintance that you dislike, said Marilyn vos Savant, who has the highest recorded IQ ever recorded (Guinness Book of Records).

Scripture

"Don't walk around with a chip on your shoulder, always spoiling for a fight. Don't try to be like those who shoulder their way through life. Why be a bully? 'Why not?' you say. Because God can't stand twisted souls. It's the straightforward who get his respect."—Proverbs 3:30–32 (MSG)

Grace

Dear Jesus, thank you for this meal, and please bless this food, our family, and our friends. Please give us guidance to do the right thing, to be kind, and to lean on your shoulder. We pray today for bullies—yes, not just to keep bullies away from us but to let them know you love them, too. Remind us that most bullies don't recognize how sad they are inside or realize how much you want to help them. Even though it isn't so easy for us to pray for them, we know you want us to. Amen.

Grace notes

Bullying is not only mean but can also be very hurtful and even dangerous. If you're the bully these verses are talking directly to you! So was the Country music singer Joe Nichols when he said, "My message to kids who bully other kids is: You know it's wrong! What's really going on? Try not to make somebody else's life miserable because you are." On the other hand if you, or someone else you see, is the one getting bullied, your first job is to report the problem so it won't keep happening. Tell Mom or Dad or your teacher—they'll know how to handle the situation. Most of the time, though, even when you do get bullied, *you* are not the reason for the bullying. The bully is! Something bad or sad has happened in the bully's life to make him or her react this way. Even though it might not work to make friends with the bully (though sometimes it does!), you can forgive in your heart and pray about the problem. Pray not just for protection from the bully but for God to solve the person's problem and soften his or her hard heart.

Scripture

"So here's what I want you to do, God helping you: Take your everyday, ordinary life—your sleeping, eating, going-to-work, and walking-around life—and place it before God as an offering. Embracing what God does for you is the best thing you can do for him. Don't become so well-adjusted to your culture that you fit into it without even thinking. Instead, fix your attention on God. You'll be changed from the inside out. Readily recognize what he wants from you, and quickly respond to it. Unlike the culture around you, always dragging you down to its level of immaturity, God brings the best out of you, develops well-formed maturity in you."—Romans 12:1–2 (MSG)

Grace

Gracious and loving God, we ask your blessing on this food. Inspire us to live for you—because our lives, and our usefulness in your kingdom, depend on it! Encourage us to practice thankfulness, and remind us that paying attention to you blesses us and others. Make us excited about the wonderful, unexpected things that happen when we allow you to be where you want to be—up front and center in our lives. Thank you for the gift of prayer and for your ear that's always open to us—who else will let us run our mouths all day and gladly listen? Amen.

Grace notes

Why does God want praise from us? He doesn't really need it—he's God, after all! Do you think God's creating us might have something to do with his desire to spend time with us? Or that the times when we're focused on him are the best times for him to work in our lives? "Prayer is simply a two-way conversation between you and God," said Billy Graham. Prayer can seem totally one-sided, can't it? You will have a much easier time hearing God if you first believe God is speaking to you and start listening. Try it, give it some time, and you'll see.

bay

89

Scripture

"Do not neglect to show hospitality to strangers, for by this some have entertained angels without knowing it."—Hebrews 13:2 (NASB)

Grace

Father, please bless our family and this food before us. This verse makes our eyes get big, Lord. Wow! Is it really true that someone could be an angel in disguise? This verse is really about the Golden Rule, isn't it? Encourage us to think about how we want others to treat us, and then do the same for them! If only those angels would reveal themselves—wouldn't that be cool? Show us some wings, Lord! Amen!

Grace notes

Has your family ever thought about inviting a neighbor, a college student from out-of-town, a soldier stationed in your area, a poor person or family living in a shelter, or some person you don't know very well to dinner? Or buying a fast-food meal and giving it to that homeless person standing on the street corner with a sign? If you ask your mom and dad to help you with this and then earn the money first, you'll feel like a million bucks! "I shall pass through this world but once," said a peace-loving leader from India named Mahatma Gandhi. "Any good therefore that I can do or any kindness that I can show to any human being, let me do it now." There's no time like the present (that means now). The other present goes to the person you help!

parsley

Scripture

“Some people ruin themselves by their own stupid actions and then blame the Lord.”—Proverbs 19:3 (GNT)

Grace

Heavenly Father, thank you for the food and for the reminder in this verse. Help us to remember that your gift of free will—our ability to choose for ourselves how we live and what actions we take—is both a great blessing and a big responsibility. And remind us that you’re right there to help pick up the pieces when we blow it. Most of all, keep us from *ever* blaming you for troubles we bring on ourselves. Thank you for that or we’d really be in a pickle. None of us is perfect, except you, Father. Lord, you are perfect in all your ways. Amen.

Grace notes

Free will is the ability to make your own life choices. God gave you that gift. But you also have a responsibility to choose wisely. As long as you’re a kid, your will is limited by your parents or others. You can still choose to disobey—even though you may have to face the music. Free will: it’s a gift that stays with you your whole life long. “You are free to choose, but you are not free to alter the consequences of your decisions,” said Ezra Taft Benson, who served as Secretary of Agriculture under President Eisenhower. Are you glad God gave you free will? Why or why not? What would your life be like if you couldn’t make choices—if God had planned out everything for you, including your reactions and responses?

Scripture

"Your strength will come from settling down in complete dependence on me."

"He's waiting around to be gracious to you. He's gathering strength to show mercy to you. God takes the time to do everything right—everything. Those who wait around for him are the lucky ones." —Isaiah 30:15, 18 (MSG)

Grace

Heavenly Father, please bless our food, family, and friends. Teach us, Lord, that having the trust and patience to rely on you makes us strong. Remind us that just as a mighty ship is no match for a mightier storm, our strength and wisdom can never come close to yours. Help us see that it is only when we let go, realizing that we aren't in control, that we get strong—because we're borrowing your strength. Remind us that you will wait for us—maybe for our whole lifetime—while we figure it out, because you love us that much. Amen.

Grace notes

Does it seem strange to you that depending on God makes you strong? It's just the opposite with people, isn't it? You certainly don't become strong by letting someone else do things for you that you would be perfectly capable of doing yourself. (That's called being lazy.) How do you grow through your dependence on God? Talk to him, serve him, and read his Word. You'll worry less, and your rewards will be great. As you grow up, of course, you'll become less dependent on adults. But it's different with God: as you grow in your faith you become *more* dependent on him. "Dependence upon God makes heroes of ordinary people like you and me," said the teacher and author Bruce Wilkinson. What do you think he meant?

mint

Scripture

"If someone has a hot temper, let him take the consequences. If you get him out of trouble once, you will have to do it again."—Proverbs 19:19 (GNT)

Grace

Dear Jesus, our food is a blessing from you. Accept our thanks and praise! Lord, teach us to know when we can help someone best by not helping—by letting them learn a good lesson the hard way, through the results of their actions. Give us the wisdom to know the difference between a hothead who doesn't care what trouble he puts others through and an angry person who really just needs a friend. Teach us to pray for your guidance in difficult areas like this. Please remind us too, Lord, that this works in both directions—that we, too, gain experience by facing the results—the consequences—of our angry outbursts. Amen.

Grace notes

Someone who continuously gets in trouble *because* of his hot temper is different from a person who has gotten into trouble because he just wasn't thinking. If you have a friend who flies off the handle quickly and easily due to a lack of self-control, you'll end up bailing him (or her) out again and again if you don't set boundaries. He might also expect you to take the blame. What kinds of boundaries could you set to avoid that problem? The Roman Emperor Marcus Aurelius knew plenty about dealing with hotheads. "How much more grievous are the consequences of anger than the causes of it," he said. Think about a situation when you or someone else had a tantrum over practically nothing and then had to suffer big consequences. Was the anger worth it?

Scripture

"When you look into water, you see a likeness of your face. When you look into your heart, you see what you are really like."—Proverbs 27:19 (NIrV)

Grace

Dear Jesus, thank you for this food, for our friends, and for our family. We love you—and we love your Word. Inspire us to develop the traits you want to see in us—qualities like love, kindness, responsibility, and honesty. Jesus, encourage us to write your name on our hearts. When we follow your example we'll learn to see you in us. We'll learn to see ourselves through your eyes. Amen.

Grace notes

What are some traits Jesus would like to see in you? On the other hand, what traits would you say that God, your parent(s)—and you, for that matter—would *not* want to see in you? Did you know that many character qualities are learned and that you can take action to make—or not make—them habits that become part of you? Want a recipe for more joy and less regret in your life? Make kindness, helpfulness, and truthfulness top priorities. Even Mickey Mouse had a word about that: "Live every moment as not to regret what you are about to do." Such a wise little mouse, don't you think?

bay

Scripture

"'You trust God, don't you? Trust me [Jesus]. There is plenty of room for you in my Father's home. If that weren't so, would I have told you that I'm on my way to get a room ready for you? And if I'm on my way to get your room ready, I'll come back and get you so you can live where I live. And you already know the road I'm taking.'"—John 14:2–4 (MSG)

Grace

God Almighty, thank you for this food and for our family. Thank you for being right here with us as we pray. We are in awe of your greatness and tenderness for us. We are amazed that you can be with us and yet be everywhere else, too, all at the same time. And Lord, we really don't understand how there can be a house big enough—or a heaven big enough—for all of us. Help us see that your ways are much bigger than our ways and that though our human minds cannot yet understand, one day everything will be clear to us. May we always reach for you first, because you are the Alpha and the Omega, the beginning and the end of all things. Amen.

Grace notes

Ever wonder what heaven is like? No one knows for sure, but we do know that it's a physical place in which we'll keep busy with lots of creative, fulfilling activities. What you enjoy on earth will be there for you in heaven. The main thing about heaven is that you'll be in God's presence forever. Also, in heaven there will be no pain, death, or tears. The author C. S. Lewis gave some good advice: "Aim at heaven and you will get earth thrown in. Aim at earth and you get neither." What do you think he meant by that?

parsley

95

Scripture

"When you do ask for something, you don't receive it. Why? Because you ask for the wrong reason. You want to spend your money on your sinful pleasures."—James 4:2–3 (NIrV)

Grace

Father, thank you for our food. Bless us at this table, and bless the hands that made this meal. Help us see, Lord, that our path in life has everything to do with the choices we make. Help us appreciate that you—who can command a billion galaxies—are willing to bend down to hold our hand and guide us through life, if we would just let you. More importantly for us, Father God, you *want* to! Help us see, Lord, that your wisdom, sent straight from heaven to us in your Word, is full of goodness, joy, and rightness and can help us make the right choices. Help us understand that as we grow in wisdom and right living, and as we receive the forgiveness we ask for, your loving Spirit blesses us more and more. Lord, please come close; how we need you! Amen.

Grace notes

Why doesn't God always answer your prayers in the way you ask? Maybe a better question is why would you go after what you already know—or would know if you took the time to think about it—wouldn't fit with God's plans. Why would you want him to give you things that wouldn't be good for you? For example, would you take a scissors away from a little kid and then give it back because he cried for it? "I must often be glad that certain past prayers of my own were not granted," said C. S. Lewis, the author of the Narnia children's series, which you may know. The great lion Aslan would certainly agree.

sage

Scripture

"[God has] already made it plain how to live, what to do, what God is looking for in men and women [and boys and girls]. It's quite simple: Do what is fair and just to your neighbor, be compassionate and loyal in your love, and don't take yourself too seriously—take God seriously."—Micah 6:8 (MSG)

Grace

Dear Jesus, you've told us again and again that you want us to have a life of joy and worth. Remind us of your expectation for us: to act fairly and to treat everyone else the way we would want to be treated. Help us to see our neighbors as your children, too. Give us ears to hear and a heart to listen to you, Lord. Please bless this food, and make us ever mindful of the needs of our friends, family, and neighbors, as well as of the strangers around us. Seriously. Amen.

Grace notes

How many neighbors does your family know? Knowing your neighbors makes everyone along your street or in your building feel more connected and contributes to a happier neighborhood. What are some ways you could get to know more of them? How about something as simple as saying hello when you and your parents see someone, and not being afraid to introduce yourself? Another good idea is to be friendly and practice manners; when you smile at a stranger their smile back makes yours even bigger. You could talk to your mom and dad about having a neighborhood garage sale and giving the money you earn together to someone in need. If a family is new to the neighborhood or you know they're going through a hard time, why not put a greeting card at their door—or a plate of home baked brownies? Who knows: maybe you'll gain a friend for a lifetime. Maybe you'll find someone to help or someone who can help you in a time of need. Mother Teresa, the Catholic nun who devoted her life to helping homeless people in India, said this: "I want you to be concerned about your next door neighbor. Do you know your next door neighbor?" she asked. These days we can't take that for granted.

mint

97

Scripture

"Don't you know? Haven't you heard? The Lord is the everlasting God; he created all the world. He never grows tired or weary. No one understands his thoughts. He strengthens those who are weak and tired. Even those who are young grow weak; young people can fall exhausted. But those who trust in the Lord for help will find their strength renewed. They will rise on wings like eagles; they will run and not get weary; they will walk and not grow weak."—Isaiah 40:28–31 (GNT)

Grace

Dear Father, all powerful and always faithful as you are, please bless our food. And bless our family and friends, wherever they may be right now. Encourage us to seek you and to find our strength in you. Provide us strength, Lord, because it's our batteries—not yours—that need recharging. Remind us to plug in to your unlimited, infinite power. Teach us that you can change our circumstances and reward our work. Inspire us to soar, Lord, using the power of your wings. Amen.

Grace notes

Are you going through some tough times? If you are, know that God is standing by, waiting for your call to come and stand by you. You know by now that life comes with tough times; it's a rollercoaster of ups and downs. Be prepared for those hard situations by strengthening your relationship with the Almighty—before you need him in some unusual or special way. Why wait until the last minute? Ask him for guidance for every step, in the good times and the bad. He'll show you how to get to know him better. (Hint: start with the Bible—maybe a simplified Bible intended for kids.) The first American president, George Washington, understood another great way to protect himself from trouble in its many forms. Daily prayer—on his knees, even—was a regular part of Washington's life. "To be prepared for war is one of the most effective means of preserving peace," he said. That's good advice in any of life's "wars."

Scripture

"Get wisdom; develop good judgment. Don't forget my words or turn away from them. Don't turn your back on wisdom, for she will protect you. Love her, and she will guard you. Getting wisdom is the wisest thing you can do! And whatever else you do, develop good judgment."—Proverbs 4:5–7 (NLT)

Grace

Heavenly Father, we honor the wisdom in all your words as we find them in the Bible. Remind us that the easiest road in life doesn't always challenge us—in fact, it can be BORING! Give us the courage to make mistakes, Lord, and to see that a fear of messing up can be the biggest mistake. Help us to grow in our faith and to gain valuable life experiences through daring to try new and hard things. Please bless our food, our family, the cook, and the cleanup crew! Amen.

Grace notes

Why would the fear of making a mistake be a mistake? Goof-ups help us learn, get smarter, and move forward. (Just don't keep making the same mistake over and over again!) Which do you think is truer: we learn more from success, or we learn more from failure? "I have not failed," said Thomas Edison as he worked to invent the light bulb. "I've just found 10,000 ways that won't work." Think of an area in life in which you gained wisdom by messing up.

Scripture

"My thoughts, says the Lord, are not like yours, and my ways are different from yours. As high as the heavens are above the earth, so high are my ways and thoughts above yours."—Isaiah 55:8–9 (GNT)

Grace

Dear heavenly Father, thank you for this food and for our family. Remind us that there's no way we could ever see what you see—even if we had X-ray vision! We know that you see everything, everywhere—past, present, and future—and that your eyes never miss a thing. We just don't know how! All we really need is trust that you will be our eyes and ears if we will just let you. We do trust your ways, Lord, and we want you—only you—at the controls. You are the most colossal, the most awesome, and that makes you COLOSOME! Amen.

Grace notes

Let the almighty, all-knowing, and everywhere present God be your most super superhero. He alone has the qualifications. He never gives up or surrenders, and he understands everything. Yet he will never hold that over you. He knows everything and is willing to fill you with as much wisdom as you can soak up. He's the strongest and the mightiest. You can't go wrong being his sidekick, for with him nothing is impossible. "God is fighting your battle, arranging things in your favor, and making a way even when you don't see a way," pointed out an anonymous author (that means an author whose name we don't know).

Scripture

“Seek your happiness in the Lord, and he will give you your heart’s desire.”—Psalm 37:4 (GNT)

“Delight thyself also in the Lord: and he shall give thee the desires of thine heart.”—Psalm 37:4 (KJV)

Grace

Heavenly Father, may your glory shine brightly in our lives. Encourage us to fill up with your happiness, to carry around within us a heart for you, Lord. Inspire us to always keep in mind the beauty and richness of your work—whatever we do, wherever we look, and wherever we go. Teach us to expect wonderful, amazing, stupendous things from you. Hallelujah! We are happy and grateful for your blessings upon this food and on our family. Amen.

Grace notes

What does it mean to seek your happiness in the Lord? Many people delight only in material, earthly things, like possessions, power, good looks, wealth, or status. But such people will never find the spiritual wealth that can come your way only through a deeper relationship with God. The sad thing is that they probably don’t even realize this. When you find peace and fulfillment in the Lord you become “wealthy” (blessed) in all parts of life. This is a secret discovered only by those who are willing to let him into their hearts. Sad, isn’t it, when people miss out on this recipe for true happiness? “Even though you may not understand how God works,” said Christian writer Max Lucado, “you know he does.” How great does it make you feel to know that God is at work in your heart and life?

Scripture

"God hates cheating in the marketplace; he loves it when business is aboveboard."—Proverbs 11:1 (MSG)

Grace

Dear Jesus, thank you for this food and for our family; we love the way you give us wise words to help us understand the way things should be. Remind us that cheating at any age is low and sneaky. Guide us instead to be truthful and honest. Remind us that every act is a steppingstone that builds our character, in one direction or the other. Please bless each of us and all those in need. Amen.

Grace notes

"Honest Abe" Lincoln had high standards for dealing fairly in his business dealings with others, and they served him well (they certainly did—he became president of the United States). And his ideals didn't apply just to big things. Once he accidently overcharged a customer a few pennies. What did he do? He closed up shop early and walked three miles to return them. "Be sure you put your feet in the right place, then stand firm." he said. What do you think this wise man meant?

Scripture

"Sensible people accept good advice. People who talk foolishly will come to ruin."—Proverbs 10:8 (GNT)

"Stupid people always think they are right. Wise people listen to advice."—Proverbs 12:15 (GNT)

Grace

Dear Jesus, you who are wise and good, please bless this food, our family, and our friends. Please bless also our country's leaders. Remind us that we all need good counsel—even smart people like presidents and Nobel Prize winners seek advice. Teach us that part of being smart means accepting good advice when it's offered. Help us to be your everyday, eager-to-learn people. Amen.

Grace notes

Did you know that there are good and bad ways to accept advice? This advice business can be a funny thing; most people don't give or receive it well. Keep that in mind, and hopefully your first reaction to good advice won't be defensive. (That means mentally putting up your fists to "defend" yourself against something you don't want to hear.) If someone offers you advice, hear them out without interrupting. Keep an open mind; you just might learn something. Repeat back to them what you think they said to make sure you heard correctly. If you're really good about this, you might ask for examples of the kind of changed behavior they have in mind. (If you respond like that when the advice giver is a grown-up, you might have to pick them up off the floor; they won't have expected such wisdom!) Steven Brust, an author of fantasy and science fiction books, made a good point: "Always speak politely to an enraged dragon." Not everyone who gives you advice will be angry, of course, but this is sound advice with all dragon dealings, wouldn't you say?

Scripture

"I, I am the One who erases all your sins, for my sake; I will not remember your sins."—Isaiah 43:25 (NCV)

Grace

Dearest God, we thank you for this food that brings us together. Please bless our family and friends. Remind us, Lord, that your unbelievably gracious love forgives and "forgets" our sins—erases them. Teach us that we can forgive ourselves, too—that our willingness to change direction and set off walking with you on your path is all you need to work miracles in our life. May we always be blessed by your glory and goodness. Amen.

Grace notes

Have you ever had a guilty feeling that wouldn't go away, no matter how sorry you felt about something? Sometimes that guilt will pop back into your head when you least expect it, making you blush inside and feel horrible all over again. Some guilt has value because it causes you to stop and think about what you've done so you can ask for forgiveness and work to make things right. The past can't be changed, but you can learn from it. When it comes to guilt, though, keep in mind that once God forgives you he also frees you from the pain of guilt. "He has removed our sins as far from us as the east is from the west," Psalm 103:12 reminds us. Now it's your turn to free yourself. You can set down that heavy guilt rock by accepting God's forgiveness, thanking him for it, and acting with a grateful spirit to do better. The martial artist, actor, and filmmaker Bruce Lee said it this way: "Mistakes are always forgivable, if one has the courage to admit them."

Scripture

"Don't hit back; discover beauty in everyone. If you've got it in you, get along with everybody. Don't insist on getting even; that's not for you to do. 'I'll do the judging,' says God. 'I'll take care of it.'"—Romans 12:17–19 (MSG)

Grace

Father, thank you for this food. Please bless our family and all those in need—those we know and those we've never even met. We're grateful for your encouragement to get along with others and to look at our differences as a way to widen our vision. Inspire us to look at each other as all of us really are: your creations, beautiful in your sight. Remind us not to try to fill your shoes by judging others. How thankful we are that *you* are the fair and righteous judge. Teach us to be more easy-going, keeping an attitude of gratitude. Amen.

Grace notes

Does this mean that you're not to judge other people? Yes, but it's not the only issue here. Paul's words are also about loving others enough to overlook their weaknesses, realizing that we each have enough of our own. This is about seeking peace, not about cheering when the bad guy—or the guy you don't like—loses out. "I look only to the good qualities of men [and women], said the wise Indian leader Mahatma Gandhi. "Not being faultless myself, I won't presume to probe into the faults of others, he said.

Scripture

"The disciples came to Jesus in private. They asked, 'Why couldn't we drive out the demon?' He replied, 'Because your faith is much too small. What I'm about to tell you is true. If you have faith as small as a mustard seed, it is enough. You can say to this mountain, "Move from here to there." And it will move. Nothing will be impossible for you.'"—Matthew 17:19–21 (NIrV)

Grace

Dear Jesus, we thank you for our food and for Mom and Dad and all those who take such great care of us; please bless them. Show us that faith is big only when it's focused on you, our big and faithful God. Teach us that faith is about having enough confidence in you to let you take charge. Help us understand, Lord, that trusting you means believing in and serving you for who you are, not for what we stand to get out of it. Amen.

Grace notes

When the Gospel writer Matthew talked about moving mountains he was using a literary form of writing called hyperbole (exaggerated ways to make a point about something else). The seed of a mustard tree is very tiny (smaller than the head of a pin), but once planted it can grow into a huge bush, nearly fifteen feet tall! Your faith, little as it may seem, can grow big, too. All you need is the tiniest bit of faith to get that faith-tree started. Nurture it and watch it grow, towering and strong. "Faith," wrote the evangelist Oswald Chambers, "is deliberate confidence in the character of God whose ways you may not understand at the time." Isn't it great that you don't *have* to understand, or see the whole picture, to get the benefit.

sage

Scripture

"In the beginning God created the heavens and the earth. The earth was formless and empty, and darkness covered the deep waters. And the Spirit of God was hovering over the surface of the waters. Then God said, 'Let there be light,' and there was light. And God saw that the light was good. Then he separated the light from the darkness. God called the light 'day' and the darkness 'night.' And evening passed and morning came, marking the first day." Genesis 1:1–5 (NLT)

Grace

Dear God, so *this* is how the world was created—we think first of your almighty hand, but Genesis tells us that all it took was your commanding voice. However long it took, however long that first day—or any day—is to you, focus our eyes not on the part we don't understand but on the beauty and wonder of what we see all around us. Lord, how do you take care of the entire universe and still have time for each of us? Amazing! (We have a hard time keeping up with our homework.) God, you are splendid, colossal, awesome, and loving. Thank you for the food we eat and the family we love. Amen.

Grace notes

America's first president, George Washington, said, "It is impossible to account for the creation of the universe without the agency of a Supreme Being." There is so much debate about the beginnings of the universe, but know this: most languages include words that have different meanings, depending on how you use them; *duck*, *rose*, *bark*, and *bat* are a few examples. (Can you think of others?) The Hebrew word for day can mean: daytime, or 12 hours, or 24 hours, or 1,000 years. The Bible isn't a science book, it's a love story made in heaven. "The Bible," says Galileo Galilei, "shows the way to go to heaven, not the way the heavens go."

mint

Scripture

"It is the Lord who gives wisdom; from him come knowledge and understanding. He provides help and protection for those who are righteous and honest. He protects those who treat others fairly, and guards those who are devoted to him."—Proverbs 2:6–8 (GNT)

Grace

Heavenly Father, the more we learn the more we love you. Thank you for watching over us. May we remember that your power, though invisible, shields us like a great, indestructible cloak. Great are your qualites of faithfulness and fairness; you are our all-powerful God. Let us be faithful in return. Inspire us to accept your Word, Lord. Thank you for our food, our family, and our friends. Please bless those in any need. Amen.

Grace notes

"The mystery of God," said Sister Hildegard of Bingen, "hugs you in its all-encompassing arms." Do you get it that God is close—as close as your breath—all the time? When you're praying, for instance, even though it's okay to ask God to be with you—or with the person you are praying for—be sure to keep in mind that he is already hovering over you! It might be better, instead, to ask for an awareness of his presence. Let him know how much his protection means to you. Close your eyes and feel your hand in his. If he is powerful enough to create the universe, he is certainly powerful enough to help you. Period.

Scripture

"My God, I want to do what you want. Your teachings are in my heart."—Psalm 40:8 (NCV)

Grace

Most gracious God, we thank you for this food, our family, and our friends. Thank you, too, for loving us! Encourage us to think about you with delight, with excitement, and with eager expectation for "what's next!" Inspire in us the kind of faith that causes a tingling sensation up and down our spines. Remind us that the more we seek a relationship with you the more you give us, returning our devotion one-hundred times over with an abundance of joy and meaning in our lives. Our God, we *do* want to do what you want. Your teachings *are* in our hearts. Amen.

Grace notes

Have you ever asked God to reveal your future? Would you really want to know? Corrie ten Boom was a deeply faithful Dutch Christian woman who was captured and sent to a death camp in Berlin, Germany, during World War II for her part in hiding Jews from the Nazis. She survived and ended up having—by her own admission—an amazing life. She saw God's work everywhere. "Every experience God gives us," she said, "every person he brings into our lives, is the perfect preparation for the future that only he can see." God prepared Corrie for what lay ahead, both good and bad. There will be a time in your life when you'll look back and be glad you didn't know what was coming. Treat the gift of today with appreciation, knowing that God is at work preparing you for tomorrow. Oh, what a relief that is!

Scripture

"If you correct conceited people, you will only be insulted. If you reprimand evil people, you will only get hurt. Never correct conceited people; they will hate you for it. But if you correct the wise, they will respect you. Anything you say to the wise will make them wiser. Whatever you tell the righteous will add to their knowledge."—Proverbs 9:7–9 (GNT)

Grace

Dear Father, thank you for this food and for the many blessings of this day and every day. Please help us to know when we should speak up and when we are better off to keep quiet. Remind us that it's your job—not ours—to fix others' lives. This is a great time, though, to speak up about Mom's yummy dinner. Keep our hearts thankful, we pray! Amen.

Grace notes

Giving advice is a learned skill. If someone asks you for advice, it's perfectly okay to say "Let me think about it first." You can also answer a question with a question, like this: "Well, what do *you* think?" Also, if you find yourself giving the advice to make yourself look good (instead of to be helpful), that's not the right place to be, either. The important question is to ask how well you would take advice if the shoe were on the other foot. Take this advice from the writer Logan Pearsall Smith: "It takes a great man to give sound advice tactfully [delicately], but a greater one to accept it graciously."

parsley

Scripture

"Anyone who hides hatred is a liar. Anyone who spreads gossip is a fool."—Proverbs 10:18 (GNT)

"A useless person causes trouble, and a gossip ruins friendships." —Proverbs 16:28 (NCV)

"No one who gossips can be trusted with a secret, but you can put confidence in someone who is trustworthy."—Proverbs 11:13 (GNT)

Grace

Dear Jesus, we thank you for this food and for our friends and family. Help us to be kind and loving toward each other, just as you were here on earth. Help us see that gossiping says more about the gossiper than about the person being talked about—and who of us would want to see an ugly thought about ourselves freeze-framed for all to see? Teach us to put our thoughts to the test before releasing them as words: Is what we are about to say kind? Is it true? Good advice, Jesus, and that is surely the truth. Amen.

Grace notes

Have you ever found out that someone has said something mean or untrue about you behind your back? (That's why gossipers are sometimes called backstabbers.) How did that make you feel? Do you think those people who like to gossip get gossiped about? And why do you think people gossip in the first place? For one thing, telling secrets about others might make themselves seem like an *insider*. They might also do it to feel important or because they're jealous. There's never a good reason to gossip, though, is there? It's important to ask yourself these *Why?* questions about your motives when you find yourself tempted to speak negatively about other people. You know that God loves you, and the other person, too, right? The cowboy and humorist Will Rogers had it right when he said, "Live in such a way that you would not be ashamed to sell your parrot to the town gossip."

sage

Scripture

"If you are lazy, you will never get what you are after, but if you work hard, you will get a fortune."—Proverbs 12:27 (GNT)

Grace

Father in heaven, please bless our food, our family, our friends, and all those in need, whether or not we know them or their troubles. Motivate us always to do our best for you and others, teach us good judgment, and remind us to use wisely the smarts you've put into our heads. Help us see that clear thinking and willing attitudes will move us forward—no walking backward here! Help us understand how the past affects the present and the present affects the future. Amen.

Grace notes

Ever feel lazy? That's okay now and then, but do you often find yourself trying to avoid or delay those dreaded *have-tos*, hoping they'll magically disappear? Sometimes there could be other issues going on: the fear of failure, health problems, lack of sleep, or too much junk food. But mostly being lazy is just—being lazy. You'll never make a fortune, never win any titles by laziness—except perhaps those of "couch potato," "airhead," or "slacker." "It is necessary to relax your muscles when you can," said the Formula One race car driver Sir Stirling Moss, "but relaxing your brain is fatal." That's a good point. Laziness is mostly a mind game—one you should aim to lose.

mint

Scripture

"If you eat or drink, or if you do anything, do it all for the glory of God."—1 Corinthians 10:31 (NCV)

Grace

Heavenly Father, to think of you in whatever we do—what a great way to live our lives. Teach us that to give you glory—honor, praise, and worship—is soothing to our souls. It also reminds us that you're in charge, that you're always with us, and that you always provide. Lord God, you are the source of life, and we glorify you when we behave with love and in agreement with your ways. Teach us to love you and ourselves enough to honor our bodies with a healthy lifestyle. What a wonderful partner we have in you, almighty Father. Thank you for feeding our minds; our hearts; and, right now, our tummies. Amen.

Grace notes

When you think about someone you love, what qualities about that person come to mind? The author and theologian A. W. Tozer said this: "What comes into our minds when we think about God is the most important thing about us." *Hmmm!* What pops into your mind first when you think of God? Here's a fun idea: Make an alphabetical list of God's qualities. For instance: A—Amazing. B—BIG! . . . T—Teacher. How far can you get? Q and Z are always hard, aren't they? And, oh dear, what to do for X? How about X-citing!?

Scripture

"My friends, fill your minds with those things that are good and that deserve praise: things that are true, noble, right, pure, lovely, and honorable. Put into practice what you learned and received from me, both from my words and from my actions. And the God who gives us peace will be with you."—Philippians 4:8–9 (GNT)

Grace

Creator God, we ask your blessing on this food, on our family, and on our loved ones. We are told that practice makes perfect. Encourage us to be careful about what we practice and about what we think—because, sure enough, that's what we'll get good at. Father, we'd like to be saints in the making—all it takes is practice. Amen.

Grace notes

Change your thinking, change your life. You'll probably hear a lot of that growing up. Easier said than done, though, isn't it? Try this. Write down what occupies your thoughts. Use positive words to describe those thoughts, as Paul did in today's reading. If you find that difficult, chances are you need to reboot. Concentrate on good things. Read and watch things that are true, right, and honorable. Ask God for help. (After all, he can do anything.) Over time little steps will cover long distances, and goodness will shine brightly from you. "How far that little candle throws his beams! So shines a good deed in a weary world," said Portia, the heroine of William Shakespeare's play "The Merchant of Venice." Good thoughts to practice!

Scripture

"The first thing I want you to do is pray. Pray every way you know how, for everyone you know. Pray especially for rulers and their governments to rule well so we can be quietly about our business of living simply, in humble contemplation. This is the way our Savior God wants us to live."—1 Timothy 2:1 (NCV)

Grace

Thank you, Jesus, for the food we eat and for the family in our lives. Help us to make prayer a part—an important part!—of every day. We pray now for our school, our church, our country, and the world and its leaders, asking you to help all of them do what's right. Give all those who are in positions of authority—whether or not they follow you—your guidance and wisdom, because leadership can be a hard and lonely job. We pray that you keep them strong. Help us to understand that praying for others—including people everywhere we've never even met—is an important way to help them. We ask you to help us live the way you want us to. We pray with hearts of gratitude for all the blessings you give us. Amen.

Grace notes

When is a good time to pray? Silly question—always! Here are some examples of short but meaningful prayers. In the morning: "Thank you, Jesus, for today. What would you like me to do?" Last thing at night: "Just checking in, Lord; I know you think about me all day." And what should you pray for? How about wisdom, guidance, safety for you and others, strength to overcome temptation, and help in becoming stronger spiritually? Not all prayer, of course, is *for* something. It's important to praise and thank God for what you have and to ask for forgiveness. Pray to be a better person, too. But what about those times when you don't know *what* to pray? That's okay, too; you can ask for help with that! John Wesley, one of the founders of the Methodist church back in the 1700s, understood the power of prayer. "Prayer is where the action is," he said. Sounds like a pretty cool guy, even if he is over 300 years old!

Scripture

The apostle Paul said, "I have been a constant example of how you can help those in need by working hard. You should remember the words of the Lord Jesus: 'It is more blessed to give than to receive.'"—Acts 20:35 (NLT)

Grace

Lord Jesus, thank you for this food; we are so grateful. We ask your blessing upon us all, including our family, our friends, and those in need. Inspire us to share what we have because you love it when we do. Remind us, too, in case we've forgotten, how wonderful sharing can make us feel—especially when it's our own idea. Teach us that whatever we do for others we do for you. Hallelujah! So the *giving* turns out to be the *getting*. That's cool, really cool. Amen.

Grace notes

There are lots of reasons why giving can feel as good as getting. Jesus tells you to give to others, of course, but did you know that even scientists and doctors say you're happier when you give than when you don't? There is always something to give, too, like love, your time, a warm smile, a willing hand, encouragement, and—of course—money. Jesus has more to say about giving, too. He says that the *more* you give the *more* you'll receive.* Sounds like a formula for happiness, doesn't it? "We make a living by what we get. We make a life by what we give," someone once said. And *that* you can take to the bank!

*Luke 6:38

sage

Scripture

"Remember what happened long ago. Remember that I am God, and there is no other God. I am God, and there is no one like me. From the beginning I told you what would happen in the end. A long time ago I told you things that have not yet happened. When I plan something, it happens. What I want to do, I will do."—Isaiah 46:9–10 (NCV)

Grace

Almighty God, we thank you for loving us so much. We thank you for this food and for being with us every moment. Help us see that your plan for each of us contains wondrous things not yet dreamed of. Remind us that our true meaning and purpose in life come from you. Inspire us to give our lives wholeheartedly to you, for they were always yours to begin with. Amen.

Grace notes

How reliable is the Bible? Short answer: very. Or, better even: totally. A longer answer would make a good research project, but for now know that the Bible is studied under the same strict criteria used to examine all historical works, and it gets the highest marks possible. The Bible has passed every standard—religious or nonreligious—for trustworthiness, too. What's more, no facts presented in the Bible have ever been proven false. (Keep in mind, though, that the Bible was never intended to be a science book. Its writers didn't know, for example, that the world is round.) Here's what Robert Dick Wilson, who had mastered *fifty* languages (yes, fifty!), said: "[T]he result of my 45 years of study of the Bible has led me all the time to a firmer faith that in the Old Testament, we have a true historical account of the history of the Israelite people." And about the New Testament, here's a headline from a *Time Magazine*, December 18, 1995, cover story: "Is the Bible Fact or Fiction? Answer: "Reputable scholars now believe that the New Testament account is reliable history." Sounds pretty conclusive, doesn't it?

mint

Scripture

"I love the Lord because he hears my voice and my prayer for mercy. Because he bends down to listen, I will pray as long as I have breath!" —Psalm 116:1–2 (NLT)

"Pray without ceasing." —1 Thessalonians 5:17 (KJV)

Grace

Father God, you know our voice and tilt your head to hear us, bending down to listen. Thank you for your goodness, your greatness, and for knowing our names. Thank you for caring for each of us so much that you keep our tears in a bottle.* How can we best honor you, Lord? Give us guidance and wisdom, for we surely want to follow you—that's part of being your children. May we think of the love you have for us as we share our thanks for this food and ask for your blessing. Remind us that you long to hear us in prayer. Lord, we hear you, too. Amen.

*Psalm 56:8

Grace notes

Isn't it amazing that God hears all your prayers? Can you picture him bending down to look directly into your eyes? Sometimes, though, when your prayer doesn't seem to get answered, you might think that God can't hear you or, worse, isn't listening. But your relationship with God isn't an "I'll give you this prayer, and you give me what I want" game. Every once in a while, just let God know that a connection with him is enough for you. That will make his whole face light upon you! Sometimes, too, it's hard to concentrate on God's replies to your prayers, but know that God doesn't mumble. Listen closely and you'll hear him. Maybe not in word, but he will speak to your heart. "We must be open to the possibility of God's addressing us in whatever way he chooses, or else we may walk right past a burning bush instead of saying, as Moses did, 'I must turn aside and look at this great sight, and see why the bush is not burned up,'" said the great thinker Dallas Willard.

Scripture

"Remember: A stingy planter gets a stingy crop; a lavish planter gets a lavish crop. I want each of you to take plenty of time to think it over, and make up your own mind what you will give. That will protect you against sob stories and arm-twisting. God loves it when the giver delights in the giving."—2 Corinthians 9:6–7 (MSG)

Grace

Dear Jesus, you see how big our smile gets when we see the happiness on someone else's face because of something we did for them. Encourage us to give before we're even asked because that shows those around us that you live in our heart. Thank you for this food, Lord, and for Mom and Dad. Help us always to remember how generous they are in their love for us. Amen.

Grace notes

Grumpy generosity is really no gift at all. What's in your heart is where the gift starts. Did you know that generosity is more than just giving things away? It starts with giving away something of yourself and moves on from there. "Money is not the only commodity that is fun to give," pointed out the author Steve Goodier (isn't that a great last name!?). "We can give time, we can give our expertise, we can give our love or simply give a smile. What does that cost? The point is, none of us can ever run out of something worthwhile to give," he said. Why not go around the dinner table right now and have everybody name one good gift that won't require any money and can be offered at any time—like maybe right now!? (Show some teeth—in the grinning way; no snarls here!)

bay

Scripture

"Rain and snow fall from the sky and don't return without watering the ground. They cause the plants to sprout and grow, making seeds for the farmer and bread for the people. The same thing is true of the words I speak. They will not return to me empty. They make the things happen that I want to happen, and they succeed in doing what I send them to do."—Isaiah 55:10–11 (NCV)

Grace

Creator God, we are happy for our time together. Thanks for helping us understand things we need to learn. We love your Word, Lord; it helps us think about how things work together, just as a seed needs rain to turn it into grain to make bread. Help us see that we can't grow in the right way without your Word, either. Guide us, Lord, to *stand in your rain,* receiving your words, so we can grow into exactly the *whos* you mean for us to be. Your Word reminds us to let you know how grateful we are for this food, to tell you that we love our family, and to ask for your blessing. Amen.

Grace notes

There will be times when you re-read something in the Bible and find a whole new meaning. It's exciting when that happens. The clue as to why it does is found in these words of Isaiah. God reveals things to you when he knows you're ready for them (taking in everything at once would be like trying to drink from a fire hose). Your understanding will deepen and grow as God prepares you each step of the way. The founder of Paramount Studios and the father of the Hollywood film industry, Cecil B. DeMille, would have agreed: "After more than sixty years of almost daily reading of the BIBLE, I never fail to find it always new and marvelously in tune with the changing needs of everyday," he said. Maybe he should have made a movie out of the Bible! Oh, wait—he did—more than one! One of them, a 1956 blockbuster called *The Ten Commandments*, made Moses a movie star. You can bet Moses never saw *that* coming!

parsley

Scripture

"You are proud and you brag. All of this bragging is wrong."—James 4:16 (NCV)

Grace

Jesus, we thank you for our food, family, and friends. Fill us with knowing that your love for us knows no bounds and that you already know everything, and you're the one who counts. Remind us, Lord, that you really see us. *You see us.* Help us keep you always in mind, because without you we would have—or be—nothing. Let's never forget that you are the one who creates conditions that allow us to shine, and that you love to see us build each other up. May we always remember that if you are with us, what does it matter who is against us?* Amen.

*Romans 8:31–32

Grace notes

"The biggest challenge after success is shutting up about it," said the poet Criss Jami. Often people who brag don't really feel good about themselves on the inside, even though it sounds like they do. They think that bragging about themselves is the only way to get your approval. Do you know anyone like that? (Is it just possible that some of their bragging would stop if they were complimented every once in a while?) People who boast might not even realize they are hurting other people's feelings, putting others down to make themselves look better. God loves them; don't they know that? Don't they know they only need the applause of one? Him? Maybe you could tell them. Here's a good reminder from the American humorist Evan Esar: "Only one man has the right to boast, and that's the man who never does." Who do you know who never brags? Why is it, do you think, that you've noticed that?

sage

Scripture

"When you are praying, if you are angry with someone, forgive him so that your Father in heaven will also forgive your sins."—Mark 11:25 (NCV)

Grace

Dear Jesus, please bless this food and accept our thanks for all your gifts. Give us a heart that is calm and kind, as well as eyes that see the best in everyone. Help us see the wrong in asking for your forgiveness if we haven't forgiven others. Teach us too, Lord, that *pretending* to forgive is not the same thing as forgiving—that holding grudges, even after we've said the right words, hurts all of us. Amen.

Grace notes

It certainly makes sense, doesn't it? If you expect Jesus to forgive you your wrongs, shouldn't he be able to make the same request of you? Is it anger, sorrow, or resentment that keeps you from forgiving others? "Forgiving someone for deeply hurting us isn't easy," recognize the pastors Ken and Pam Ingold, "but perhaps it is the way in which we approach it. . . . [T]hink of forgiveness as a gift." To hold a grudge means that your attention is focused on the "wrong that was done you." That means that the person who has "wronged you" holds great power over your thoughts and actions; this is destructive, like acid eating away at your attitude, and it will change you into someone you don't like if you allow it to. Is that what you really want? Diffuse that negative power with forgiveness. Give yourself a gift—the freedom of no longer being held captive. You may have to seek the advice of someone to help you, but don't forget who to ask first for help: Jesus. After all, you can do all things through Christ, who strengthens you.* Buddha (also known as Siddhartha Gautama) gave wise counsel about the power of anger: "Holding on to anger," he said, "is like grasping a hot coal with the intent of throwing it at someone else; you are the one who gets burned." That's a word picture that's really hot! How cool!

*Philippians 4:13

mint

Scripture

"I know what it is to be in need and what it is to have more than enough. I have learned this secret, so that anywhere, at any time, I am content, whether I am full or hungry, whether I have too much or too little. I have the strength to face all conditions by the power that Christ gives me."—Philippians 4:12–13 (GNT)

Grace

Jesus, thank you for this food and for our family. May we have peace around our table with you. Show us that true joy and contentment come when we trust you and put you first. When we do that things have a way of amazingly falling into place, and everything we have becomes more than enough for us. Help us see that it matters so much how we live. Teach us that you didn't come to earth to give us a religion but to connect with us. Our trust is in you. Lord, you are awesome! Amen.

Grace notes

Paul (the apostle who wrote Philippians) knew that Jesus would give him the resources he needed to weather any hardships—and he suffered a lot of them! When were you last beaten, shipwrecked, or imprisoned (hopefully never!)? Paul was referring mostly to spiritual needs, but he understood that his physical needs were important to Christ, too, and that things would either get better or he would learn to adjust. In the end Paul only needed to know that if God was with him it didn't make any real difference who might have been against him. Remind yourself when you face those bad times that God is in complete control and that even if you don't know the whys of life, he does. "Complain and remain. Praise and be raised," said the evangelist Joyce Meyer. That just could be the difference between standing still, in our troubles, or rising above them with God's help.

123

Scripture

"The Lord said to Job [his name rhymes with 'robe'], 'Do you still want to argue with the Almighty? You are God's critic, but do you have the answers?' . . . Then Job replied to the Lord, 'I am nothing—how could I ever find the answers? I will cover my mouth with my hand. I have said too much already. I have nothing more to say.'"—Job 40:1–5 (NLT)

Grace

Mighty God, this feels like too much—Job arguing with you. Remind us that we, too, have been there and acted like that. Teach us that just when we think we know it all, trouble can loom. Assure us that you don't mind when we're honest enough to wrestle with you—that you welcome our complaints and hard questions, too, accepting them all because you love us so much. Give us grateful hearts for this food, our family, and our life; we ask you now to bless us all. Amen.

Grace notes

Do you know Job's story? It's a tough one, but Job stayed true to God, and in the end God blessed him with riches and rewards greater than he could ever have dreamed of before the hard times. It turns out that Job understood much more about God than his know-it-all friends—or Satan—did. Job loved God even when his whole world dropped out from under him. Somehow he understood that what really mattered was his relationship with and dependence upon God—through thick and thin. You'll be amazed at how God came through (check out the rest of the story in Job 42:7–16). "God can do nothing for me until I recognize the limits of what is humanly possible, allowing Him to do the impossible," said the famous evangelist, teacher, and author Oswald Chambers.

bay

Scripture

"God is our shelter and strength, always ready to help in times of trouble. So we will not be afraid, even if the earth is shaken and mountains fall into the ocean depths; even if the seas roar and rage, and the hills are shaken by the violence."—Psalm 46:1–3 (GNT)

Grace

Almighty God, our eyes get big when we think about the earth shaking under our feet. Help us to see in our mind's eye what you mean: that you are a tremble-proof fortress in times of trouble. Help us to realize that life with you is less scary, especially if we picture you holding tightly to our hand. Let our eyes get big right now with delight at the food before us. Fill us up, Lord, physically, spiritually, and in every other way; you are our Provider and Protector. Amen.

Grace notes

Our fears—those giants in front of our mind's eyes—change throughout our lives. Can you think of something that was once s-o-o-o-o-o scary but doesn't even faze you anymore? How about bad dreams, thunder, or your first solo bike ride? Or maybe it was a big test or, if you're older, that first job interview. Scary? You bet. Courage has been described as the ability to act in spite of your fear. God's got you covered on that one, and don't forget when you're scared that he offers his own strength for you to borrow. Think about this as the writer Max Lucado does: "Focus on giants—you stumble. Focus on God—Giants tumble." Obviously, Goliath had no clue, did he?

125

Scripture

"Without faith no one can please God. Anyone who comes to God must believe that he is real and that he rewards those who truly want to find him."—Hebrews 11:6 (NCV)

Grace

Wonderful Jesus, we want to shout out to the world that you are Lord and Savior! Just as we know there's a sun by feeling its warmth, and just as we know there is thunder by hearing it rumble, so we know that you are there without our having to see you; our faith carries us through to the rewards we receive. Thank you for our food, family, and friends. We ask you to bless us, in the faith that you always do and will and that your grace is your very best gift to us. Amen.

Grace notes

Crazy, wouldn't it be, to go to God in prayer without believing in . . . God! (But do you think we sometimes act that way?) If you do truly trust in God, your actions can't help but show it. And when you make the effort to get to know him better (he isn't hiding, after all), you will become more and more confident that he rewards faith. "Take the first step in faith," said Dr. Martin Luther King Jr. "You don't have to see the whole staircase," he said. "Just take the first step." Reverend King was right. Having faith—trust—in God always leads to action. You get on the plane because you trust the pilot. You get on the school bus because you trust the driver. You trust the bank, so you put money there. What other ways do you show trust? In the same way, how does your faith—trust—in God affect your actions?

Scripture

"God has made us what we are. In Christ Jesus, God made us new people so that we would spend our lives doing the good things he had already planned for us to do."—Ephesians 2:10 (ERV)

Grace

Gracious Father, thank you for this food and for our family. Please bless us and encourage us to live big, big lives for you! Remind us that in you we are new creations and that we can do wondrous things. Remind us that, in your strength, no dream is too big. At the same time, though, help us remember that no worry or fear is too small to hand over to you. Please Lord, cast us in your play and be our director. We invite your Spirit—the Holy Spirit—to help us with our lines! Amen.

Grace notes

Jesus is the greatest teller of true stories, and he can help you bring *your* story—the great one God has planned for you—to life! That story doesn't have to be one the world falls in love with, either; just knowing that God loves your story—and you—should be enough. And when he sees how faithful you are, look out! It's only going to get better. The Christian writer Max Lucado knows this too: "God cast you in His play, wrote you into His story," he said, going on: "He has a definite direction for your life. Fulfill it and enjoy fulfillment. Play the part God prepared for you and get ready for some great days." Oh, just imagine the reviews!

Scripture

"In view of all this, what can we say? If God is for us, who can be against us? Certainly not God, who did not even keep back his own Son, but offered him for us all! He gave us his Son—will he not also freely give us all things?"—Romans 8:31–32 (GNT)

Grace

Lord, we come to you with grateful hearts because you bring us life in all its fullness.* Father, we know you are with us, but there are days when everything seems to go wrong, when problems seem to line up at the door. Remind us to come to you in prayer in those times. Teach us that you are forever and that everything else—including whatever troubles want to get us—is temporary. Jesus, you ask us to come to you not only with our joys but also with our sadness and disappointments. Thank you for all you so freely give us, Lord, and please now bless our food. Amen.

*John 10:10

Grace notes

How confident are you of God's work within you and for you? No one, not even the devil, is a match for him—you can be sure of that. Your purpose, your faith, and your love are more important to him than anything else. Let that truth sink in and become a part of you; let it transform you so you can conquer the world! The author A. W. Tozer put it this way: "An infinite God can give all of Himself to each of His children. He does not distribute Himself that each may have a part, but to each one He gives all of Himself as fully as if there were no others." Picture our great God giving *his all* for you—and then doing the same thing for everyone else around your table and in the world. You only have one *all*, but his love and ability have no end. No, you can't begin to understand that, . . . but don't let that stop you from believing!

Scripture

“In the same way, younger people should be willing to be under older people. And all of you should be very humble with each other. ‘God is against the proud, but he gives grace to the humble’”*—1 Peter 5:5 (NCV)

*Proverbs 3:34

Grace

Gracious Father, we thank you for this food, our family, and our health. Inspire us with a *sir-and-ma'am* respect in our vocabulary. Teach us, young and old, to show that we value each other's abilities and are open to learning something, for everyone has a story to tell. Remind us how much you appreciate humility and how you long to flood our lives with your great grace. Amen.

Grace notes

You see it more and more these days: technology is moving so fast that it's easier for younger people than for older ones to get it. Kids deserve respect for catching on so quickly. What you may not recognize, though, is that older people have their own skills and insights to offer the younger generation: like experience, knowledge of consequences, discipline, critical thinking ability, and practical life skills. They, too, have earned respect. Treat each other as though all of you were teachers with skills to pass along. The genius inventor Albert Einstein had many reasons to be stuck up, but he wasn't. (It isn't every physicist, after all, who is offered the presidency of Israel!) Imagine what the world would be like if all of us treated each other the way Albert Einstein did: “I speak to everyone in the same way,” he said, “whether he is the garbage man or the president of the university.” Humility is the mark—and the strength—of a great person.

bay

Scripture

"God says, 'Be still and know that I am God.'"—Psalm 46:10 (NCV)

"I pray to the Lord, and he will answer me from his holy mountain. *Selah*."—Psalm 3:4 (NCV)

Grace

Incredible, almighty God, we bow our heads as we join in offering up this grace. Help us to be still for a moment—quiet in unspoken reverence. *Selah*. [Take a moment of silence.] . . . We give you thanks now for our family, friends, health, and food. Give us the desire to sit quietly so we can hear you. *Selah*. Jesus, show us that quiet time is a time to praise your name, to listen for your words spoken in quiet heart whispers; what amazing ideas you put into our heads. *Selah*. And Amen.

Grace notes

Selah is a Hebrew word used 74 times in the books of Psalms and Habakkuk. (It isn't in Psalm 46:10, but it could be!) The word means to pause, to think, to "listen up." In the psalms it may also have meant a place to stop in a worship service and play some music. *Selah* is also thought to have been a word used to emphasize the truth of what had just been said. Here are some statements that could easily be followed by *Selah* (you can use "Amen" in the same way): God is your biggest fan! *Selah!* God always tells the truth. *Selah!* We love Thanksgiving! *Selah!* The chemist Louis Pasteur said this: "The more I study nature, the more I stand amazed at the work of the Creator." We could add a *Selah!* Why not go around the table and have each of you think of a *Selah* sentence?

parsley

Scripture

"Long before he laid down earth's foundations, God had us in mind, had settled on us as the focus of his love, to be made whole and holy by his love. Long, long ago he decided to adopt us into his family through Jesus Christ. (What pleasure he took in planning this!) He wanted us to enter into the celebration of his lavish gift-giving by the hand of his beloved Son."—Ephesians 1:4–6 (MSG)

Grace

Almighty God, thank you for being here with us and for blessing us. We give thanks for this food. How amazing to discover that you had each of us in mind before you created the universe. Wow! You created us so you could love us—so we could be your children who would give glory to you and love you right back. Wow again! Your grace is amazing. We praise and thank you for always being here, for never giving up on us. Lord, you reign! Amen.

Grace notes

God's heart and mind are immeasurably bigger than ours, and we aren't able to understand how much he loves us—only that it's more than our human minds can possibly imagine. Think about what Max Lucado said about God's love: "If God had a refrigerator, your picture would be on it. If He had a wallet, your photo would be in it. He sends you flowers every spring and a sunrise every morning. Face it, friend. He is crazy about you!" That paints a great picture, don't you think? Give it a try—how can you describe God's love? Maybe something like "God loves me so much, he . . ." Why not give it a try—each one of you can take a turn!

Scripture

"Love one another deeply. Honor others more than yourselves. Stay excited about your faith as you serve the Lord. When you hope, be joyful. When you suffer, be patient. When you pray, be faithful."—Romans 12:10–12 (NIrV)

Grace

Dear Jesus, great are your blessings and your teachings. Show us, Lord, how caring for others can produce joy and hope in our hearts. Show us, too, how patience produces strength and how faithfulness leads to answered prayer. Teach us that praying for someone who is hurting touches your heart and moves you to action. Remind us to pray for someone who is unhappy or sick because we know you will hear us. We thank you for this food and family; please bless both. Amen.

Grace notes

Jesus tells us to love one another. Love in action (not just a loving feeling) is what today's reading is about. When you love others you show it. When you hope, you look forward to a joyful outcome. Your patience tells God and others that you know God is blessing you, even through your pain. When you pray for faithfulness, God hears and strengthens you. The author and Bible teacher Joyce Meyer reminds us of the depth of God's faithfulness and love coming in our direction: "Our prayers are heard by God not according to what we try to be when we pray, but who we are when we are not praying." Think about her statement for a moment. That's the action part, isn't it?

mint

Scripture

"Oh, what joy for those whose disobedience is forgiven, whose sins are put out of sight. Yes, what joy for those whose record the Lord has cleared of sin."—Romans 4:7–8 (NLT)

Grace

Dear Jesus, you are so patient with us. Your glory shines brighter than anything in creation. We thank you for loving us so much. Sometimes we get stuck in past sins, and our face gets red thinking about those times. Help us understand that your amazing love propels us forward, forgives our sins, and clears our name. Jesus, you are our Lord of Second Chances, the one who sees and loves us, just the way we are. Thank you for the food—and for your blessing. Amen.

Grace notes

Guilt. It's what makes you feel bad when you've done something wrong or when you don't do something you should have done. Is guilt good or bad? Guilt is good if it alerts you to a wrong and causes you regret and sorrow, . . . and then moves you to do what you can to fix the problem. God gives you grace, and in the process you become a better person. Guilt is a terrible thing, though, if you don't learn from it, if you let it take over your life or don't believe that God is willing to forgive you. If God says you get another chance—which he does—and you refuse to believe him, you'd better think again. "When grace moves in . . . guilt moves out," said the Christian author Max Lucado.

Scripture

"Continue praying, keeping alert, and always thanking God." —Colossians 4:2 (NCV)

Grace

Dear Jesus, we thank you for our food and for your blessings. Help us understand that prayers are like conversations; some are short and to the point and some are longer. Inspire us to see life as you do, filled with so many reasons to love and to be thankful and happy. Remind us that when we talk to you, you talk right back to us in our hearts; you never send us into voice mail. Amen.

Grace notes

"I know that when I pray, something wonderful happens," said the author Maya Angelou. "Not just to the person or persons for whom I'm praying, but also something wonderful happens to me. I'm grateful that I'm heard," she said. God wants you to share your thoughts with him all day long. Here are some short examples (short means just as much to him as long!): "Awesome sunset!"—"Jesus, help me to focus on my homework!"—"Please keep Mom and Dad safe driving to work."—"Lord, what do you want me to do today?"—"Wow, did you see that?"—"Goodnight, Jesus." What thoughts would you like to share with Jesus right now?

Scripture

"Remember that I have commanded you to be determined and confident! Do not be afraid or discouraged, for I, the LORD your God, am with you wherever you go."—Joshua 1:9 (GNT)

Grace

Everlasting Father, help us remember that because of your protection we can be brave, bold, and lionhearted. Safeguard us, Lord, with the mighty armor of faith. Help us see that goodness needs the courage to stand up to wrongdoing; may we pray often for that. Please bless this day, this food, our family, and especially those timid ones who have never experienced the courage that comes from knowing you. Amen.

Grace notes

After Moses died God appointed Joshua to take his place as the leader of the Israelites. How Joshua must have trembled—having to follow in the footsteps of Moses! After all, he was taking over for *Moses*—as in the Moses-who-talked-with God Moses! It was so important for Joshua to understand that God's strength and protection would go with him as he led God's people into the promised land, where they would have to fight. "We forget," said the author Max Lucado, "that IMPOSSIBLE is one of God's favorite words." Why do you think that is? Could it be because that's when he goes to work to make the impossible possible? Oh, how he loves to do that!

Scripture

"Don't be quick to fly off the handle. Anger boomerangs. You can spot a fool by the lumps on his head."—Ecclesiastes 7:9 (MSG)

Grace

Gracious Father, we're glad to be together, happy it's mealtime, and grateful for all your blessings. Thanks too, Lord, for the heads up about anger. Teach us to ask for guidance and patience in dealing with others; we don't want to be a bunch of hotheads. We know you're awesome, wise, and perfectly fair. Thank you now for the food we're about to eat, the friends we enjoy, and the family we love. Amen.

Grace notes

You might be surprised by how much a deep breath, count-backwards-from-ten approach helps people get along. That's because while you're counting you're also *thinking* (you're a good multi-tasker, right?). How often, after all, does trouble happen because we speak before we think? The trick is to count *before* you get angry—or at least before the anger you're starting to feel moves from your head to your mouth. Make a little game of it by practicing a countdown in ordinary conversations (like right now at your table). Baltasar Gracián, a seventeenth-century philosopher, had this to say: "It is better to sleep on things beforehand than lie awake about them afterwards." Four hundred years later that's still good advice, wouldn't you say?

Scripture

"We can rejoice, too, when we run into problems and trials, for we know that they help us develop endurance. And endurance develops strength of character, and character strengthens our confident hope of salvation. And this hope will not lead to disappointment. For we know how dearly God loves us because he has given us the Holy Spirit to fill our hearts with his love."—Romans 5:3–5 (NLT)

Grace

Lord Jesus, please bless our food and those at our table. Fill our hearts with love and our minds with an understanding of the Holy Spirit's presence in our hearts. Help us see that strength comes through tests and challenges and that you'll use even our setbacks as setups for good things. Teach us also that the way we react in the tough times makes all the difference in developing good character and great habits. Set us up, Lord! With you on our side we can only get stronger. Now *that's* something to rejoice about! Amen.

Grace notes

"Character cannot be developed in ease and quiet," said Helen Keller. "Only through experience of trial and suffering can the soul be strengthened, ambition inspired, and success achieved." Helen Keller was blind and deaf, which made it hard for her to speak well, yet she graduated from college and went on to do great things. (And you think your classes are rough!) There's a great movie about her called *The Miracle Worker*, starring Patty Duke and Anne Bancroft. Try this at dinner: discuss someone you know or have read about who faced terrible odds and yet came out triumphant on the other side. Look for God's glory in their story.

Scripture

"A spiritual gift is given to each of us so we can help each other. To one person the Spirit gives the ability to give wise advice; to another, the same Spirit gives a message of special knowledge. The same Spirit gives great faith to another, and to someone else the one Spirit gives the gift of healing."—1 Corinthians 12:7–9 (GNT)

Grace

Father God, we're amazed that you pay such close attention to each of us and bless us with our own special abilities. May we use our gifts well to help us love others; that's how we share in the joy of your riches. Teach us to look for, appreciate, and develop the gifts we have, not to be sad about the ones we don't or jealous of those who got the gifts we wanted. Bless this food—and aren't we happy about the talents of the cook! Amen.

Grace notes

To be happy about someone else's abilities or accomplishments without feeling a twinge of envy gets easier the more you practice. After all, why count others' blessings when you have so many of your own? Why not go around the table right now and take turns saying how grateful you are for the gift you've been given (if someone doesn't recognize their talents, the rest of you can help them out). No matter what your gifts, with God's help they're enough for you to do the great things he has in mind for you. "We never become truly spiritual by sitting down and wishing to become so," said the preacher and author Phillips Brooks. "You must undertake something so great that you cannot accomplish it unaided."

Scripture

"Come, let's sing for joy to the LORD. Let's shout praises to the Rock who saves us. Let's come to him with thanksgiving. Let's sing songs to him, because the LORD is the great God, the great King over all gods. The deepest places on earth are his, and the highest mountains belong to him. The sea is his because he made it, and he created the land with his own hands."—Psalm 95:1–5 (NCV)

Grace

Heavenly Father, we're in awe over the wonders of your creation, and especially over the wonder of life. Thank you for this food and for the blessings we could never begin to count. Teach us to read the psalms as though we are singing them, for many of them were written that way. Encourage us to make up our own lyrics, maybe something like this: "God, you are so loving and patient. All the beauty in the world, we know, existed first in your heart. All the great ideas in the world are first yours. You give them to us to share with each other. You give them to us to help each other. Mighty Lord, there is no other like you. Your majesty and goodness are over the top; we see them in every mountain, flower, bird, butterfly, . . . and human being. You love us for all time. You love us for all time." Amen.

Grace notes

Many of the psalms are prayers written as poetry (poems don't have to rhyme). Read Psalm 95:1–5 out loud prayerfully one more time with this thought in mind. See if they speak to a place deep within you. (If they don't, they will in time. That's why it's important to read God's Word again and again.) These poems and songs cover the entire range of human emotion. The psalms are praises to God that are timeless in their beauty (beautiful to people of all ages and times). The Mexican poet and diplomat Octavio Paz charms us with these words: "To read a poem is to hear it with our eyes. To hear it is to see it with our ears."

Scripture

Jesus said, "To you who are ready for the truth, I say this: love your enemies. Let them bring out the best in you, not the worst. When someone gives you a hard time, respond with the energies of prayer for that person. If someone slaps you in the face, stand there and take it. If someone grabs your shirt, gift wrap your best coat and make a present of it. If someone takes unfair advantage of you, use the occasion to practice the servant life. No more tit-for-tat stuff. Live generously."—Luke 6:27–31 (MSG)

Grace

Dear Jesus, we thank you for this food, and we try to count our many blessings. We pray for a good understanding of your Word. Fill us, Lord, with compassion for others because we are all your children. Remind us that though it's easy to be nice to the nice guy and girl, it takes strength to be nice to the not-so-nice guy. Give us that strength, Jesus, for it's because you gave that we also can give—because you forgave that we too can forgive. Amen.

Grace notes

Words are often used to paint a picture in our minds. What do you think "a slap in the face" could mean? Maybe not an actual slap, but what about an insult—a rude remark? What about someone who "grabs your shirt" in today's Scripture? Could Jesus be talking about someone who would love to have your clothes because he is too poor to have anything decent? Jesus is calling upon you to recognize that people who are poor in their heart or in their pocket need help. Be the kind of person who "would give the shirt off your back" to help someone in need. "Love is the only force," said Dr. Martin Luther King Jr., "capable of transforming an enemy into a friend."

Scripture

Jesus said, "If you walk around with your nose in the air, you're going to end up flat on your face, but if you're content to be simply yourself, you will become more than yourself."—Luke 18:14(b) (MSG)

Grace

Jesus, thank you for this food and for our family. May we always be grateful for your blessings. Teach us to think thoughts that are genuine, honest, and caring and then to act in the same way. Remind us to listen to you—not to the values of this material world. Teach us that humility is a way of encouraging others by putting them first. Remind us that those who understand humility don't have to boast about it—they display it. Amen.

Grace notes

To be humble means that you are always teachable; no one is going to call you a know-it-all, and that's a good thing. To be humble also means accepting the idea that you're not always going to be right. C. S. Lewis had another way of saying it: "Humility is not thinking less of yourself, it's thinking of yourself less." Can you think of some real-life situations where humility plays a part? Here's some ideas to get you started: an athlete giving credit to his teammates; a person who lets someone in a big hurry cut in line; or the star athlete who offers to clean up the locker room after the game. Get the idea?

Scripture

Jesus said, "I am the good shepherd. As the Father knows me and I know the Father, in the same way I know my sheep and they know me. And I am willing to die for them."—John 10:14–15 (GNT)

Grace

Dear Jesus, good shepherd, please bless our food. We're so grateful for your love and protection. May we never forget that you watch over us day and night—that you protect us, find us when we get lost, and rejoice when we are found. This is a BIG deal, Jesus. How we praise you for your love, faithfulness, protection, compassion, and guidance. You'll never pull the wool over our eyes. Teach us to know your voice—always. Lord, you are awesome! Amen.

Grace notes

Are you one of those people who is puzzled over the notion that Jesus has compared us to sheep? After all, sheep aren't very smart. But that's not the point. Jesus, as the shepherd, said he would take care of us, so it's all about the relationship. And besides, we do have enough things in common with sheep to get you to think twice about that comparison. For instance, sheep are known to wander aimlessly. Do you ever feel lost? Sheep kick and struggle when they're being sheared. They hate it, yet they will literally die if they don't get shorn regularly. We sometimes don't take care of our bodies very well, do we? Overeating? Drugs, anyone? Sheep have no thoughts of defending themselves or staying out of harm's way. Temptation anyone? Still think it odd to be compared to sheep? Jesus knows you need a shepherd—and he, the creator of the universe, is willing to assume that role because he loves you that much. We sometimes forget that. "Too many leaders," said the business advisor Ken Blanchard, "act as if the sheep [their people] are there for the benefit of the shepherd, not that the shepherd has responsibility for the sheep." With Jesus, our leader, it's the right way: he came to serve us and gave his life to save us (Luke 10:45). Did that solve the puzzle?

mint

Scripture

"'I tell you,' [Jesus] replied, 'that to those who have something, even more will be given; but those who have nothing, even the little that they have will be taken away from them.'"—Luke 19:26 (GNT)

Grace

Precious Jesus, thank you for our dinner and for our family. May we be filled to overflowing with your blessings. Teach us that when we're faithful to you we'll be rewarded with your grace—with your undeserved favor and kindness. And that trusting you makes our faith grow, bringing more of your grace, which in turn strengthens our trust in you. This is the circle of life—the circle of grace and faith—for which we praise your holy name. Amen.

Grace notes

This is a call to faithfulness. Not only does God want you to believe in him, but he expects you to act out that trust. When you do he will reward you. He also expects you to depend on him and wants you to receive his grace; when you do he will bless you many times over, adding to your life what you cannot do for yourself. Jesus loves you and wants so much to be part of your life—a BIG part. There's another side to this as well: the responsibility to obey Jesus. "For those to whom much is given, much is required," declared President John F. Kennedy (he was quoting from Luke 12:48).

Scripture

"In those days Israel had no king; everyone did as they saw fit." —Judges 21:25 (NIV)

Grace

Gracious Father, please bless our family and our food. Thank you for all the blessings of this day. Help us to see what a topsy-turvy world it would be if each one of us made up our own rules as we went along. Just as Mom seems to have eyes in the back of her head, may we always remember that you know and see everything. Amen.

Grace notes

The book of Judges is about the faithlessness (or unfaithfulness, depending on which part we're talking) of the Israelites and their punishments when they deliberately disobeyed God. Especially at the end when each Israelite made up his own rules and then changed them to suit whatever situation he found himself in at the moment. Talk about a mess! You *can* make up your own rules, of course, since God gave you a free will. Nothing bad may happen—for a while—and you might even be tempted to forget about God. But you *will* get into trouble sooner or later. Then what? God will forgive you if you ask him to, but what have you lost? What will be the consequences? How long will it take you to recover the ground you lost—to get back to square one? The Spanish novelist Carlos Ruiz Zafon took a more modern approach: "You don't win a game by hitting the ball out of the court."

Scripture

"Much is required from the person to whom much is given; much more is required from the person to whom much more is given."—Luke 12:48(b) (GNT)

Grace

Gracious Jesus, we thank you for our food and family and pray for all those in need, including both friends and strangers. Lord, teach us this truth: the more you've given us the more you expect us to give, and the more we give the more you will give again to us. Lord, this is an amazing upward spiral; it just keeps getting bigger and wider! Inspire us and guide us so that our hearts remain giving, that we may become more like you and that you will find us ever faithful. Amen.

Grace notes

Just what is it that we should give? Is it our time? Our money? Our talent? Yes to all three! And don't forget those things that aren't even there until you give them away. *What?* Well, how about kindness, thoughtfulness, hugs, and smiles—to name a few? You get the picture. The best part about a truly giving spirit was summed up by Princess Elizabeth Bibesco: "Blessed are those who can give without remembering, and take without forgetting."

Scripture

Jesus said, "Whoever can be trusted with a little can also be trusted with a lot, and whoever is dishonest with a little is dishonest with a lot. If you cannot be trusted with worldly riches, then who will trust you with true riches? And if you cannot be trusted with things that belong to someone else, who will give you things of your own?"—Luke 16:10–12 (NCV)

Grace

Heavenly Father, please bless our food, our family, and everyone—especially those who haven't yet come to know you. Inspire us to write Jesus' words on our hearts: to tell the truth in all things. Show us that telling the truth is how we ourselves become trusted—a treasure no one can take away. Inspire us to go after the kinds of riches that please you, and reward our faithfulness with more responsibility in your kingdom. Amen.

Grace notes

When you trust someone you believe that person will keep their word. And when that someone can be trusted you will probably be comfortable around them, too. How do you feel when someone breaks that trust? It hurts, doesn't it? God always keeps his promises. (It might seem sometimes as though he doesn't, but that's because you can't see the big picture and because he isn't finished with you yet!) Benjamin Franklin, a very wise man, said this: "Watch the little things; a small leak will sink a great ship."

sage

Scripture

"Nothing in all the world can be hidden from God. Everything is clear and lies open before him, and to him we must explain the way we have lived."—Hebrews 4:13 (NCV)

Grace

Almighty God, may you always remind us that you see the best and the worst of what we do; there is no hiding from your gaze. Lord, your joy in us, your patience with us, and your faithfulness to us know no bounds. Teach us that you are slow to anger and filled with unfailing love, forgiving every kind of sin and rebellion.* Encourage us to check in with you, even if just with a "How we doin', Lord." Please bless and strengthen us with this good food. Amen.

*Numbers 14:18

Grace notes

Here's a puzzle: (1) God sees everything. (2) People get to choose what they want to do and how they want to act (free will). (3) God knows everything that's going to happen. *What?* Don't try to piece this one together because you never will. God's ways are much too high and wise for our human brains to understand. Can a bug understand how an airplane flies? Does a bird understand windows? It's not that you're small and simple; it's just that you don't have God's brain. So what's it going to be? Will you approach this puzzle with frustration and denial or with love, trust, and acceptance? James Weldon Johnson, a songwriter, lawyer, and civil rights activist, had a unique way of looking at this: "Young man—Young man—Your arm's too short to box with God." Hugs work a whole lot better!

Scripture

"It is by faith we understand that the whole world was made by God's command so what we see was made by something that cannot be seen."—Hebrews 11:3 (NCV)

Grace

Dear Jesus, thank you for this food, and please use it to nourish and strengthen us all for your service. Remind us that a bold faith connects us to you, the Creator.* May we lift our praise and prayers to you, who created everything that exists out of nothing, and may that truth remind us that you will keep all your promises to us. We ask you into our hearts and invite your Spirit to dwell within us, too—always loving us, always our strength. We trust you and your plan for us. Amen.

*John 1:3; Colossians 1:15–17

Grace notes

Do you think that having belief and faith in God means that you are committed to everything he stands for, both the seen and the unseen? One thing you can be sure of: growing a strong faith isn't the easiest thing to do, but it is the most rewarding. It takes time, too—this repeated process of learning, growing, falling down, and getting back up again. The Spirit works within you, of course, although your degree of cooperation with him is your choice. "Nothing shapes your life," pointed out Pastor Rick Warren, "more than the commitments you choose to make." What commitments are shaping your life?

thyme

Scripture

Jesus said, "Pay attention to how you hear. To those who listen to my teaching, more understanding will be given. But for those who are not listening, even what they think they understand will be taken away from them."—Luke 8:18 (NLT)

Grace

Lord Jesus, thank you for dinner; we ask now for your blessing and protection. We are especially grateful for our family and friends. We like to spend time with them and want to hear all the news of their days. We listen to their advice, too, because we know they want what's best for us. It's the same way between us, Lord—between us and *you*, that is. Help us to listen attentively to your Word, and increase our understanding more and more as we come to know you better and better. Make us eager learners. Yay, God! Inspire us to get close to you, Jesus! We're listening! Amen.

Grace notes

It's one thing to hear but quite another to listen. Listening requires concentration and brainpower, doesn't it? (Did you know that your brain uses 25% of your oxygen intake?) Ever had a parent ask "Did you hear me?" (or maybe "Weren't you listening to what I *just said*?"). Jesus wants your full attention, too. He has such good things in mind for you; make sure they don't go in one ear and out the other (where have you heard that before?). Jesus sent the Holy Spirit to fill you with his power. Did you know that you can ask the Spirit to help you listen and understand? Pastor Mark Batterson explained it this way: "In my experience, take the Holy Spirit out of the equation of your life and it spells boring. Add it into the equation of your life and you never know where you are going to go, what you are going to do, or who you are going to meet." Wow, did you *hear* that!

bay

Scripture

“Be cheerful no matter what; pray all the time; thank God no matter what happens. This is the way God wants you who belong to Christ Jesus to live.”—1 Thessalonians 5:16–18 (MSG)

Grace

Dear Lord, thank you for dinner and for our family. May your deep, endless love guide us and give us strength. May we be encouraged and gratefully express our thanks, not *for* all things but *in* all things, rejoicing that your hand is in our lives. May we never let Jesus think that we want to be his friend only when everything is going our way. Amen.

Grace notes

This is a hard lesson: to give thanks *in* all circumstances—both the good and the not so good. Jesus has the last word in everything, and he loves you more than you can imagine. Remember that he alone sees the big picture and knows how everything will turn out in the long run. Don’t put so much stock in what you see, but trust him based on what he sees. And don’t forget to count your blessings, even in the hardest times. Trust him, not because you have to but because he has promised to work at all times and in all circumstances for the good of those who love him. Do you want God working for you? “I have lived to thank God,” said the English poet Jean Ingelow, “that all my prayers have not been answered.”

parsley

Scripture

"Do you, my friend, pass judgment on others? You have no excuse at all, whoever you are. For when you judge others and then do the same things which they do, you condemn yourself. We know that God is right when he judges the people who do such things as these."—Romans 2:1–2 (GNT)

Grace

Gracious Jesus, we thank you for such wise words and for this food, our family, and our friends. Encourage us to imitate your ways, Lord, and to remember that you will judge all people fairly, without any coaching from us. Help us see that feelings of superiority have no place in your kingdom. Remind us that your message of love extends to everyone, for we are all sons and daughters of God, your Father, through faith in you and acceptance of your sacrifice for our salvation.* When we slip up, Jesus, we know you will be patient with us. How grateful we are for that. Amen.

*Galatians 3:26–29

Grace notes

Judging other people can be a tricky thing. And criticizing others for the same kinds of things you also have done or said—or might be tempted to do or say—is wrong. Jesus doesn't like it when people judge others harshly just because they're different. Can you think of situations where that might happen—like making value judgments based on someone's skin color, their clothes, their hairstyle, their body type, or the way they talk? What if everyone were to respond instead to everyone else with interest and gratitude that we all have something different to add to the world? "Be not angry that you cannot make others as you wish them to be," cautioned the fifteenth-century author Thomas à Kempis, "since you cannot make yourself as you wish to be."

Scripture

"And the Holy Spirit helps us in our weakness. For example, we don't know what God wants us to pray for. But the Holy Spirit prays for us with groanings that cannot be expressed in words."—Romans 8:26 (NLT)

Grace

Wonderful Holy Spirit, please watch over us and all those in need, and work in our hearts, guiding us to do the Father's will. Thank you for assuring us that even though we may not know what to ask for in our prayers or how to ask for it, you know what we can't put into words and can say it for us. We lift our hearts in thanksgiving and ask the Father's blessing on this food. Amen.

Grace notes

The Holy Spirit is God—a divine person with a mind, emotions, and a will. He is the third person of the Trinity, sent by the Father to comfort us. Do you ever wish you'd been around when Jesus was—what it would've been like to talk to him? Here's something to think about: Jesus is sometimes called Immanuel, which means "God with us," but the Holy Spirit is even closer. Think of the Holy Spirit as "God *within* us." Think of the Holy Spirit as God within *you*! Jesus himself—in his human form—could be in only one place at a time, but today every one of us carries the Holy Spirit along with us wherever we go. When it comes to prayer, God doesn't expect you to use fancy words; the Spirit knows exactly what's in your heart, even if you can't put it into words. Call on the Spirit to help you, trusting that he will. The television preacher Rod Parsley said the same thing in a different way: "The baptism of the Spirit will do for you what a phone booth did for Clark Kent, it will change you into a different being." Super!

mint

Scripture

"I love you, Lord; you are my strength. The Lord is my rock, my fortress, and my savior; my God is my rock, in whom I find protection. He is my shield, the power that saves me, and my place of safety."—Psalm 18:1–2 (NLT)

Grace

Father God, thank you for our food and for our family. We are so grateful that you are with us always. May your unending love remind us how happy and creative we can be, knowing that you are our safety net, surrounding us with strength and protection. Help us never to waste our energy on fear or worry. Amen.

Grace notes

God promises to protect you, not just from bad people but from sin itself; that's why he sent Jesus to pave the way for you to enjoy eternity with him. Even so, you are bound to have troubles in your life—that just goes with the territory of being human. Sometimes God *allows* trouble in our lives, but he *never causes* it; that's an important difference. He promises also to strengthen you and improve the quality of your life after the crisis time. Just as a shield can't be of any use unless you pick it up and use it, God can't protect you if you turn away from him, rejecting his plan and purpose for your life. Be faithful to God, and he will be faithful to you—every day. "It's incredible to realize that what we do each day has meaning in the big picture of God's plan," pointed out the author and pastor Bill Hybels.

Scripture

"God can give you more blessings than you need. Then you will always have plenty of everything—enough to give to every good work." —2 Corinthians 9:8 (NCV)

Grace

Heavenly Father, please bless our food, our family, and all those in need. Instill in us a desire to do what is good, to find the excitement and fun in every good work. Help us understand what it means to be blessed, Lord. Teach us to trust you to provide all our needs, and work in our hearts to make us generous to others, knowing that you will bless us, giving us that much more to give back in your service, as well as paying us back with the enjoyment of your glory and riches. Amen.

Grace notes

God is the source of all good things. He creates the universe and everything in it; surely he can turn his face to you, bless you, and make your life meaningful and rich in all that matters. Sometimes you might hear people talk not just about praising God but about *blessing* him. How does that work? We can't offer him anything he doesn't already have. "Blessing" God is really a way of recognizing that he is the source of our blessings; it's a way of expressing our thankfulness. There are three things we *can* give him, though, and he delights in all three: glory, praise, and love. In a way we're giving him something else, then, too: joyfulness! The Country and Western singer Willie Nelson knew the importance of blessings. "When I started counting my blessings, my whole life turned around," he said.

Scripture

"Some people like to do things their own way, and they get upset when people give them advice. Fools don't want to learn from others. They only want to tell their own ideas."—Proverbs 18:1–3 (ERV)

Grace

Father God, we ask your blessing on this meal and thank you for loving and watching over us. Help us to understand and grow in your Word. And help us to notice how we talk to others. Show us that our talk reveals our heart and our character and that this is what you see and notice about us. Give us open hearts, Lord, willing to listen and learn from the ideas of others. Amen.

Grace notes

It's boring to listen to someone who talks just to show off. Have you ever felt as though someone like that is talking *at* you, not *to* you, and that they don't really want your opinion or response? Let's face it, most people love positive attention and congratulations. Most people don't mind talking about themselves, either; it's just best not to overdo it. If you really want to shine, you'll choose instead to be a good listener. Be sincerely interested in others; do that and you will be liked by everyone. As long as you're genuinely attentive you don't have to be smart, charming, witty, or talented. "Encouragement is awesome," said the radio preacher Chuck Swindoll. "It can actually change the course of another person's day, week, or life." Do you know you have that power?

Scripture

"When you do things, do not let selfishness or pride be your guide. Instead, be humble and give more honor to others than to yourselves. Do not be interested only in your own life, but be interested in the lives of others."—Philippians 2:3–4 (NCV)

Grace

Dear Jesus, we are so grateful for your many blessings. Your abundance is all around us; help us to honor you and appreciate your wonderful creation. We pray for guidance in our relationships with friends; motivate us to show real interest in what they say and do, even when we'd rather talk about what interests us. Remind us to follow the golden rule: to treat others in the same way we want to be treated—it works every time! We turn our thoughts to you, Lord, thanking you for this food and asking your blessing on us all. Amen.

Grace notes

You will be amazed at the interesting things you can learn when you show interest in others. Be curious, ask questions, and let them see that what they have to say matters to you. No matter what your age or situation, being polite (even though it might be hard sometimes) will teach you genuine respect—a trait in people that is too rare and always admired. "People who inspire others are those who see invisible bridges at the end of dead-end streets," said the wise preacher Chuck Swindoll. What do you think he meant? To inspire others it helps to first listen to their dreams, right?

sage

Scripture

"It's better to have a partner than go it alone. Share the work, share the wealth. And if one falls down, the other helps, but if there's no one to help, tough!"—Ecclesiastes 4:9 (MSG)

Grace

Gracious Father, thank you for this food, and please bless us today. Your advice is music to our ears, and friendship is the golden instrument for getting along in life. Help us see how much more we can accomplish when we're willing to help each other. Show us that helpfulness is a great way to make friends. Lord, *you* are our best partner in life. Thank you that we never have to go it alone. Amen.

Grace notes

Ralph Waldo Emerson was a poet and a great thinker. "There is no limit," he said, "to what can be accomplished if it doesn't matter who gets the credit." Keep that in mind and you have a great formula for working as a valued teammate. Have you ever found it easier to solve a problem when two or more of you put your minds to it? Not only are things easier, but it feels great to share in the accomplishment, doesn't it? No one has to feel one-upped or left out, and you can celebrate together.

Scripture

"My children, we should love people not only with words and talk, but by our actions and true caring."—1 John 3:18 (NCV)

"Let us think about each other and help each other to show love and do good deeds."—Hebrews 10:24 (NCV)

Grace

Dear Jesus, thank you for reminding us how important our actions are. Encourage us to make our love visible through everything we do. Teach us to think of love and generosity at the same time. Nurture our spirits to encourage others with good thoughts, good words, and good deeds. Thanks for our food, Lord, and for the many other blessings you give us—way more than we can begin to count. May we be, and *act*, grateful. Amen.

Grace notes

How could you make your love *visible* after dinner? Help with the dishes? Wow! Do your homework right away? Super! Pick out your clothes for tomorrow to avoid last-minute frustration? Smooth. Climb into bed at the right time? Marvelous! "Home is the comfiest place to be," said Winnie the Pooh. He'd probably like your home, too!

Scripture

"The Lord is kind and shows mercy. He does not become angry quickly but is full of love."—Psalm 145:8 (NCV)

Grace

Heavenly Father, thank you for this food; we eat with happy feelings about being together. Thank you for these expressions of your love and goodness; they're like sweet-smelling desserts to our soul. We lift up our praise to you, God, knowing that our mistakes can never be bigger than your willingness to love and forgive. Lord, you get us. Amen.

Grace notes

Does God ever get angry? You bet. But God's anger—and his judgment—never result from his being bad-tempered, irritated, or out of control. And God extends his great mercy—his forgiveness—to you all the time. Jesus willingly gave his life and took on your sin so you could enter heaven—that's as powerful as love gets, isn't it? And just so we're clear, God's love isn't impersonal. Even if you were the only human being on this planet Jesus would have made the same sacrifice just for you. Now, don't you feel special—you should! "Our prayer and God's mercy are like two buckets in a well; while the one ascends the other descends," said Mark Hopkins, the president of Williams College in Massachusetts. God is never too busy to hear you and to respond in grace and love.

bay

Scripture

Jesus said, "If you work the words into your life, you are like a smart carpenter who dug deep and laid the foundation of his house on bedrock. When the river burst its banks and crashed against the house, nothing could shake it; it was built to last. But if you just use my words in Bible studies and don't work them into your life, you are like a dumb carpenter who built a house but skipped the foundation. When the swollen river came crashing in, it collapsed like a house of cards. It was a total loss."—Luke 6:47–48 (MSG)

Grace

Dear Jesus, we thank you for this meal and for loving us always. Help us keep your Word in our minds and hearts throughout our day, to make it a part of who we are, of what we think and feel, and of what we do. Don't let us forget that this is about walking *your* talk and talking *your* walk—which are always right and perfect. Inspire us to build a foundation with you NOW so that in times of trial and trouble we'll know just what to do. Encourage us to have such an appetite for your Word that we want to spread it like homemade jam over everything we do and everything we are. May we accept your invitation to enter your house of grace—which is always open, with your welcome sign beckoning us in. Amen.

Grace notes

Would you expect to become a doctor without going to medical school? Would passengers be comfortable if they knew their pilot had only flown a two-seater? Would God know that you loved him if you didn't spend much time with him? Getting to know God is an effort worth making. "How often we expect big things from God without preparing for big things from him," said the Bible teacher Beth Moore. God will surprise you, all right—over and over again. Just don't be surprised that he has surprised you!

Scripture

"My friends, if someone is caught in any kind of wrongdoing, those of you who are spiritual should set him right; but you must do it in a gentle way. And keep an eye on yourselves, so that you will not be tempted, too."—Galatians 6:1 (GNT)

"And be ye kind one to another, tenderhearted, forgiving one another, even as God for Christ's sake hath forgiven you."—Ephesians 4:32 (KJV)

Grace

Father, thanks for this food and for our family, and please bless us all. Inspire us to hold up one another in support and encouragement. May we remember to be kind, to never feel high-and-mighty in our helping, especially since we're far from perfect ourselves. We praise you, Lord, for your wise and wonderful ways. Amen.

Grace notes

There's a fine walk between being judgmental and holding someone else accountable. Being judgmental is condemning someone, and if you're doing it behind their back you'll be gossiping at the same time. Holding someone accountable means helping the person look at their problem behavior so they can recognize the issue and do what they can to make things right. Before you can do that well you'll have to have a good relationship with that person. Do you trust each other? Do you know what other things are going on in their life? It's important to also think about why you're holding their feet to the fire, so to speak. Is it really your desire to help them, or might you secretly enjoy putting them down, even if you're doing it in the "nicest" way? Pray before you talk; that really helps. Make sure your approach is gentle, too. "Only the weak are cruel," said the teacher and motivational speaker Leo Buscaglia. "Gentleness can only be expected from the strong." Why might weak and insecure people act cruelly? Why can strong and confident people risk being gentle? (Mom and Dad can be a big help with these questions.)

Scripture

"One day Jesus told his disciples a story to show that they should always pray and never give up. 'There was a judge in a certain city,' he said, 'who neither feared God nor cared about people. A widow of that city came to him repeatedly, saying, "Give me justice in this dispute with my enemy." The judge ignored her for a while, but finally he said to himself, "I don't fear God or care about people, but this woman is driving me crazy. I'm going to see that she gets justice, because she is wearing me out with her constant requests!" Then the Lord said, 'Learn a lesson from this unjust judge. Even he rendered a just decision in the end. So don't you think God will surely give justice to his chosen people who cry out to him day and night? Will he keep putting them off? I tell you, he will grant justice to them quickly!'"—Luke 18:1–8(a) (NLT)

Grace

Dear Jesus, we love dinnertime and thank you that we can gather together around this table. Please bless our meal. Inspire us to pray always. Teach us that even though you know everything that happens long before it happens, you still listen to and answer our prayers. Assure us that we don't need to understand your mysterious ways. Instead, Lord, continue to remind us that our prayers make all the difference with you. Inspire us to pray, to be persistent, to be patient, to be bold, and to be faithful. Amen.

Grace notes

Jesus told a story about a judge who didn't care about a widow but still granted her request just so she wouldn't keep interrupting his afternoon nap. How much more, Jesus asks, will God, who loves you more than you can begin to imagine, answer you when your request is right and good? "God is able to do more than man can understand," said the fifteenth-century author Thomas à Kempis. That's what we call an understatement—an awesomely true statement made in a quiet, matter-of-fact way. If it wouldn't sound disrespectful, we might be tempted to say "You *think?*"

mint

Scripture

"I look up to the mountains; does my strength come from mountains? No, my strength comes from God, who made heaven, and earth, and mountains."—Psalm 121:1–2 (MSG)

Grace

Dear Father, we thank you for today and ask your blessing upon this food and upon our family. We are so grateful for your guidance, strength, and shelter. Remind us of the delicious peace that comes our way when we trust in you. We are amazed by your promises of protection night and day, no matter the time, no matter the situation. Teach us that our strength is stronger when we seek you. That's because you inject us with an extra dose of *your* strength to top it off. We praise you for your perfect ways. Amen.

Grace notes

There is no greater joy than knowing that God loves you—really loves you. As you learn more about Jesus you'll be amazed how those simple words seem to increase in meaning and how their truth changes your heart. Think of joy as being the state or condition in which nothing can come between Jesus and you. Spell out the word joy like this: **J**esus—**O**—**Y**ou. This is another way to look at it: Jesus + Nothing = Everything. Any way you look at it, the joy of the Lord is yours for the asking. "Don't measure the size of the mountain; talk to the One who can move it," said Max Lucado. No mountain—or anything else—is ever an obstacle to God.

Scripture

"It's in Christ that we find out who we are and what we are living for. Long before we first heard of Christ and got our hopes up, he had his eye on us, had designs on us for glorious living, part of the overall purpose he is working out in everything and everyone."—Ephesians 1:11–12 (MSG)

Grace

Mighty God, we thank you so much for our food and for our family. Please bless those in any need, friend or stranger. Help us see that you created everything in the universe according to your great plan. Remind us that each one of us, too, was created *on* purpose, *for* a purpose, and that our life matters very much to you. We love you, Lord, and thank you for telling us again, in so many ways, just how greatly you have loved us first. Inspire us to give you our heart so you can fulfill your wonderful plan in us. Amen.

Grace notes

You have a power in you that is unequaled in all the universe! It's the Holy Spirit (sometimes called the spirit of Christ)*—God himself. When you allow him to fill you up, you give him free rein to teach you, lead you, and guide you. Let him do his work and you will have an unimaginably fulfilling life. Be his, and he'll be yours. "Do not pray for tasks equal to your powers, pray for powers equal to your task," urged the preacher and author Phillips Brooks. That Spirit power is yours, just for the asking.

*Romans 8:9

bay

Scripture

"No one can see God, but Jesus Christ is exactly like him. He ranks higher than everything that has been made. Through his power all things were made—things in heaven and on earth, things seen and unseen, all powers, authorities, lords, and rulers. All things were made through Christ and for Christ. He was there before anything was made, and all things continue because of him."—Colossians 1:15–17 (NCV)

Grace

Jesus Christ, we glorify you for your creation of all things, big and small, strong and delicate. We honor you for making yourself one of us through your willingness to take on our human form. Inspire us to put you first in our lives and to use you as an example of how to live. Jesus, you are our rock. Thank you for making us who we are. May we grow to appreciate our own special gifts, talents, and abilities, knowing that no one else is quite like us, that you gave us these abilities for a purpose, and that you also give us the desire and strength to serve you well. Oh, and thanks for producing our food; please bless our bodies through its nourishment. Amen.

Grace notes

God wants to have a relationship with you—to share his life with you. You could say that God made the entire universe for us (for *you*), choosing and preparing this magnificent planet, Earth, to be our just-right home. The grandeur all around you is his, and his alone, but he joyously shares it with you. Jesus Christ—let's just say God, because Christ *is* God—is the center of creation; without him there would be absolutely nothing. He planned all that exists far in advance; the universe is no accident, no fluke coincidence of nature. If God made Jesus for us, and Jesus came to Earth for us, you can know for certain that he considers you, along with all Earth's inhabitants, to be of unlimited importance. That truly is God's way—so different from ours! Remember Jesus in your prayers and ask him, the one who created the world, to be the center of *your* world. Your asking is the first step. In the words of Max Lucado (speaking for God, not himself): "Remember, you are special because I made you. And I don't make mistakes."

Scripture

Jesus said, "You did not choose me; I chose you. And I gave you this work: to go and produce fruit, fruit that will last. Then the Father will give you anything you ask for in my name."—John 15:16 (NCV)

Grace

Heavenly Father, you amaze us. Thank you for the way you love us. What if your Son, Jesus, had loved us so much that he was willing to come to this Earth to show us how to live and then to sacrifice his own life so we could have a life with you, for all eternity? Oh—that's right!—that's just what he did. Help us to remember that our talents are a gift from you, Lord; make us truly grateful. Remind us that staying connected to you produces in us a fruit-bearing life, full of your blessings. Father, we are thankful for this food and for our loved ones, and we ask your continued blessing on all of us. Amen.

Grace notes

Do you want to change things? Make your home or your school a better place? Or perhaps your sights are set on something even bigger. Here's the first step on whatever road you take, be it short or long: put your hands together and pray. That's the very first—and best—starting point. The power of prayer ignites your fire and keeps it burning victoriously, like the Olympic torch, all the way to the finish line! "It is impossible to worship God and remain unchanged," pointed out the pastor Henry Blackaby. How do *you* know that's true?

sage

Scripture

"Give yourselves completely to God. Stand against the devil, and the devil will run from you. Come near to God, and God will come near to you."—James 4:7–8 (NCV)

Grace

Jesus, our Savior, please bless our food and our family. Bless those in any trouble; give them eyes to see you and a desire to accept you into their lives. Remind us that Satan is no match for you and that he'll run away as fast as he can if he sees you standing there beside us. Lord, we want you to be near us always. Thank you for loving us and for promising to never let us go. Amen.

Grace notes

Sometimes the truth is so simple. Humanity has a problem. God sent Jesus to solve that problem. You meet his terms and are rewarded with a wonderful life in heaven. All you have to do is obey him, and you obey because you want to. Simple. The professional baseball player turned preacher Billy Sunday made an unusual point: "Hell is the highest reward that the devil can offer you for being a servant of his." Remember, it's God alone who offers heaven. Satan takes the dregs.

Scripture

"Love your neighbor as you love yourself. If you love others, you will never do them wrong."—Romans 13:9(b)–10(a) (GNT)

Grace

Heavenly Father, thank you for your presence at this table, for this food, and for your Word. May our souls magnify you, Lord, and our actions magnify (enlarge) our soul. Let our actions be as good as our word, and may all our words and actions be driven by love. Help us to remember that our friends and neighbors—everyone everywhere—are people you cherish. Amen.

Grace notes

What if you were to treat all those with whom you come into contact as friends? (We're not talking here about stranger danger situations; God wants you to be safe). Would you smile when you see them? Would you say hello? Would you help them if they had their arms full? Would you root for them at their game? "Of course!" you may say. But if you've ever felt like laughing at someone's mistake, or calling someone a name, or pretending you didn't know someone, resist that temptation! God wants you to honor others, honor yourself, and especially him with kind and loving actions—to consider love as a debt you owe, and one that can never be repaid in full. "Friends show their love in times of trouble, not in happiness," said the fifth-century Greek playwright Euripides. It's easy to show love in the good times; let Christ's love motivate you to love others in their bad times, too.

168

Scripture

"Take control of what I say, O Lord, and guard my lips."—Psalm 141:3 (NLT)

Grace

Father, thank you for this food. Please bless our family and friends. Bless also those who say mean things because they need love in their hearts. Would you call us wise, Lord, if we decided to memorize this verse; to say it to ourselves whenever we're tempted to say something else we might later regret? We think we know the answer. While we're on the subject, thank you for the gift of your Word—all of it. Amen.

Grace notes

This verse is not just about saying angry things. To use another example, do you sometimes find yourself saying "I promise"—letting it roll smoothly off your lips—and then not following through? Do you know how disappointing that can be to others? Not something you want to get in the habit of doing, is it? "Promises," said the author Norman Vincent Peale, "are like crying babies in a theater, they should be carried out at once."

Scripture

"You made all the delicate, inner parts of my body and knit me together in my mother's womb. Thank you for making me so wonderfully complex! Your workmanship is marvelous—how well I know it. You watched me as I was being formed in utter seclusion, as I was woven together in the dark of the womb. You saw me before I was born. Every day of my life was recorded in your book. Every moment was laid out before a single day had passed."—Psalm 139:13–16 (NLT)

Grace

Thank you, Lord, for this food and for this time together. Almighty God of creation, we marvel that you know each of us so well; we are grateful that you provide our food. Please bless us all. To learn that you have been watching over us before our time began—You, God, were the first to count our stubby little fingers and toes—Wow! Thanks for showing us that *you* don't step into *our* story—we step into yours. May we use our gifts wisely in your service. Glory be to you, dear Father. Amen.

Grace notes

What kind of relationship do you want with God? Figure out what part you want to play and what part you want God to play. Yes, you do get to choose. Think about the game of soccer, for instance. There are rules, yet what you do within those rules makes all the difference. How you prepare, how you play, how you react—it all counts. God does let you call the shots in your life, but you're wise to keep in mind that there are consequences—good and bad—in the choices you make. "Without God, we cannot," said the great early Christian St. Augustine. "Without us, God will not."

Scripture

"When you look up into the sky and see the sun, moon, and stars—all the forces of heaven—don't be seduced into worshiping them. The LORD your God gave them to all the peoples of the earth."—Deuteronomy 4:19 (NLT)

Grace

Heavenly Father, thank you for our food, our family, and all the blessings you have given us today. Thank you for reminding us that the stars don't guide us—you do. Help us to always keep in mind that it's you, Father, who alone knows our future and promises to guide us through to eternity. We agree with Moses: don't trust the stars; trust the one who made them and gave them brilliance. That's you, God. How we trust you! Amen.

Grace notes

Moses wrote the book of Deuteronomy; its name means a second reading of the Ten Commandments, first recorded for us in Exodus 20. This book adds an important detail: God himself inscribed (wrote) the commandments on the two stone tablets. That very act tells you that in all the universe—in all of creation—we people are the most important masterpiece in God's eyes. Just imagine how much he must love us: look at all the details he worked out so we could have a relationship with himself. Hundreds of years ago the Italian astronomer Galileo Galilei looked up and saw God's works. "The Sun," he said, "with all the planets revolving around it, and depending on it, can still ripen a bunch of grapes as though it had nothing else in the Universe to do." Oh yah, God does that. All of that.

Scripture

"The Fear-of-God is a spring of living water so you won't go off drinking from poisoned wells."—Proverbs 14:27 (MSG)

"O give thanks unto the Lord; for he is good: for his mercy endureth for ever."—Psalm 136:1 (KJV)

Grace

Father, we thank you for our food and for our family. Please bless the food that nourishes our bodies, and may your Word nourish our souls. May our actions always show respect, awe, and loyalty to you. Keep us a little fearful of you, Lord, because that will remind us of your great power. Keep our eyes open wide for danger, too, so that big, big trouble doesn't sneak up on us. Teach us to remember that you are always good and that your way is always the best. May we always remember too, Lord, that your mercy and love never quit. We drink your living water. How it quenches our thirst! Amen.

Grace notes

To whom do you look up? Do you see how you can really like someone and still be fearful—respectful—of their authority? Who in your life best fits that description? Your parents, teachers, coaches? The respectful attitude you have toward them makes you teachable: because you look up to them you're going to pay attention to what they say. And they can help you to be a better person by the way they use their authority. "Happiness," said the writer Shannon Alder, "is always on the other side of being teachable." Think of something that made you very happy once you had learned it.

Scripture

"A gentle answer quiets anger, but a harsh one stirs it up."—Proverbs 15:1 (GNT)

"With patience you can convince a ruler, and a gentle word can get through to the hard-headed."—Proverbs 25:15 (NCV)

Grace

Dear God, it's dinnertime, and we thank you for the food and for our family. May grace and peace live in our home, settling in and filling up every corner. Inspire us to listen to your advice about gentleness. Remind us that patience is always the quiet, wise choice. Teach us that strength lies in refusing to allow anger to control our voice, our words, our decisions, or our relationships. Amen.

Grace notes

Everything seems to be going along just fine, and then something happens. All of a sudden things go haywire, and home suddenly feels like a zoo—with everyone screaming and shrieking like riled up monkeys. Only these little monkeys aren't so cute, are they? Did you know that there are ways to disagree peaceably, without all the yelling? Agree on the ground rules ahead of time, when no one's mad. Write down a list of what will and will not be allowed, and up it goes—on the refrigerator. Then when there's a difference of opinion and someone forgets a rule—just as in a football game—someone can call foul and everybody will have to stop behaving badly. "You don't always have to chop with the sword of truth. You can point with it, too," pointed out the writer Anne Lamott. Good point, Ms. Lamott!

Scripture

"Is there anyone around who can explain God? Anyone smart enough to tell him what to do? Anyone who has done him such a huge favor that God has to ask his advice? Everything comes from him; Everything happens through him; Everything ends up in him. Always glory! Always praise! Yes. Yes. Yes."—Romans 11:34–36 (MSG)

Grace

Almighty God, even as we ask your blessing upon us and our meal we are humbled by your greatness. We know you are wiser and more powerful than all seven billion of us on this planet put together. Never let us forget, though, that you know us, love us, and pay attention to each of us—as though we were your only child. Remind us that although we may at times question you, we do know that you want only what's best for us. It's good to know that you have all the answers, Lord. That's not something we question. We praise your name. Yes. Yes. Yes. Amen.

Grace notes

Just when you think you've got things all figured out, something happens that you didn't see coming. Sometimes what you thought you knew you didn't, or what you didn't know you do, or what you thought you saw wasn't there! Got that? It's a confusing world, for sure. You can be sure of one thing, though: God's in charge and he's got your back. "This is God's universe and he does things his way," said the pastor and radio minister J. Vernon McGee. He went on to say, "Now, you may have a better way of doing things, but you don't have a universe."

bay

Scripture

"God's Message, the God who created the cosmos, stretched out the skies, laid out the earth and all that grows from it, who breathes life into earth's people, makes them alive with his own life: 'I am God. I have called you to live right and well.'"—Isaiah 42:5–6(a) (MSG)

Grace

Great God, we give you all the praise and all the glory. Thank you for this food and for your many blessings; may your Word, our greatest treasure, nourish our souls. Thank you for sending your Son, Jesus, who paid for our sins so that we could become right with you. Show us how best to honor you for your greatness, faithfulness, mercy, and love. Please bless those who don't know your Word and bring people into their lives who do know you, so that through them their eyes may be opened. Glory be to you, Father God, and to our Lord and Savior Jesus Christ, the one you sent to show us the way to live rightly and well. Amen.

Grace notes

God is asking us to be good, Isaiah says. But how can you do that when God is perfect and you aren't? How great it is that God has it all worked out. He sent Jesus to pay for your sins, and that's just what Isaiah was talking about. (Through God's Spirit Isaiah knew about Jesus 700 years before Jesus was even born.) Invite Jesus into your heart, and you'll be amazed as he helps you start to live right and well, just as God has called you to do. "Jesus became what we are that he might make us what he is," said Saint Athanasius, the fourth-century church Father. Now *there's* a tradeoff for all time!

parsley

Scripture

"We are God's masterpiece. He has created us anew in Christ Jesus, so we can do the good things he planned for us long ago."—Ephesians 2:10 (NLT)

Grace

How great you are, Lord; you offer us the way for right living through Jesus Christ, our way, our truth, and our life.* We thank you for this food. Help us see why you call us your masterpiece—because of the good things we can do through your grace and mercy. Remind us what a wonderful life awaits us if we will only trust you and obey. Thank you, Lord, for your many blessings, your grace, for Mom and Dad, and for this food. Amen.

*John 14:6

Grace notes

"Strength will rise as we wait upon the Lord."* What a great line from a song that tells us of God's plan and purpose for us. When you pray, ask God to help you know him better. Don't demand that he do this or that; instead, let him know that you trust him and his ways. You'll be amazed at how clear your vision will become. You'll be amazed at how strong your values will become.

*"Everlasting God," lyrics by Brown and Riley

Scripture

Jesus said, "Live in me. Make your home in me just as I do in you. In the same way that a branch can't bear grapes by itself but only by being joined to the vine, you can't bear fruit unless you are joined with me."—John 15:4 (MSG)

Grace

Dear Jesus, thank you for all your gifts, for this food, for our family, and for this earth you give us to protect and enjoy. We love it that you make your truth so easy to understand: you're the vine, we're the branches, and staying connected to you produces the wonderful fruit of the Holy Spirit—love, joy, peace, patience, kindness, goodness, faithfulness, gentleness, and self-control.* Inspire us to keep you in our hearts so we can bear beautiful fruit in tribute to you. Amen.

*Galatians 5:22–23—good verses to memorize

Grace notes

It can be life changing when you get it—really get it—that you're connected to Jesus. Here's the part, though, that gets a little complicated: he lives in you at the same time you live in him! Just like the branch that thrives as long as it stays connected to the vine (or to a tree or plant), you stay strong, growing and full of live when you remain in Jesus. (What happens if you cut yourself off? You wither, just like a branch separated from the vine.) With Jesus you are never alone; the gift of peace of mind and heart is yours for the taking. Here's what Max Lucado had to say about that: "We are Jesus Christ's; we belong to him. But even more, we are increasingly him. He moves in and commandeers our hands and feet, requisitions our minds and tongues. We sense his rearranging: debris into the divine, pig's ear into silk purse. He repurposes bad decisions and squalid choices. Little by little, a new image emerges." What a great picture of Jesus living in you and doing what he does best through you!

Scripture

"You've all been to the stadium and seen the athlete's race. Everyone runs; one wins. Run to win. All good athletes train hard. They do it for a gold medal that tarnishes and fades. You're after one that's gold eternally."—1 Corinthians 9:24–25 (MSG)

Grace

Gracious Father, thank you for the many blessings you give us, for our food, and for the privilege of gathering around this dinner table as a family. Thanks for reminding us that your prize is the really big one that will last forever! Inspire us to train with you so we can be part of your winner's circle. Let us never forget who wrote the training manual, that you know what it takes to win, and that you're the greatest coach ever! Encourage us to keep training, and help us live our lives in ways that bring you glory and honor. Encourage us to run the race of the Christian life with your finish line in our sights. Glory be to you, God, forever and ever. Amen.

Grace notes

You know how important it is to take the time to train in your chosen activity, whether it be sports, music, dance, other arts, or anything else. Your performance has everything to do with the time and effort you put into it. Making a commitment to Jesus is like that, too. If you want a relationship with him, you have to make him your focus. Eric Liddell was a good example. He was devoted to running, but God came first. Eric faced an unexpected decision when, in the 1924 Olympics, the 100-meter heats (the preliminary races) were held on Sunday. Because the Lord was his number one priority, he refused to run on God's day and gave up the chance to compete, even though he was favored to win. Eric ran on another day, and even though this 400-meter wasn't his best event, he won and took home the gold medal, setting a record that would stand for 12 years. (If you're interested in Eric's story, see the movie *Chariots of Fire*). "I give all the glory to God. It's kind of a win-win situation," said another Olympic gold medalist, Gabby Douglas. "The glory goes up to Him and the blessings fall down on me." Wow! That's a Gold Medal statement!

Scripture

"Grow in the grace of our Lord and Savior Jesus Christ. Get to know him better. Give him glory both now and forever. Amen."—2 Peter 3:18 (NIrV)

Grace

Almighty Father, you tell us that the Holy Spirit gives us wisdom to understand you better, and that the more we are willing to listen the closer we get to you. How awesome, Lord, that the Holy Spirit stays with us to guide us and make us stronger and wiser as we grow in our faith. Inspire us to read your Word, to help others, to listen to Mom and Dad, and to pray. Great is our heart for you, Lord; great unto the day of eternity. We give you thanks (especially for the food). Jesus, take control. Amen.

Grace notes

Do you have your very own Bible? There's something special about having one all to yourself, especially if it's one with special features that are just right for your age. You can write in it, color in it, and talk to God with it. You can get to know God the Father and Jesus the Son better, because reading God's Word is like reading their diaries (with their permission, of course!). If you can't afford a Bible there are lots of ways to get a free one (you can, for example, Google free Bibles for kids). "The book to read is not the one which thinks for you, but the one which makes you think. No book in the world equals the Bible for that," said the Princeton University professor James McCosh. Does that make you think?

bay

Scripture

"When you sit down to eat with someone important, keep in mind who he is. If you have a big appetite, restrain yourself. Don't be greedy for the fine food he serves; he may be trying to trick you."—Proverbs 23:1–3 (GNT)

Grace

Father in Heaven, this advice sounds like it's coming straight from Mom and Dad. Remind us now, while we're kids, to avoid being greedy and to mind our manners, no matter who we're with. Remind us, too, to be more impressed by a person's character than by how important they supposedly are. Let us also learn to say grace with respect and reverence, before we even pick up a fork. Thank you for our food—our hearts are full of your love. Amen.

Grace notes

Be careful of someone who is trying to impress you with their greatness or importance—they may want to catch you off guard, trick you into doing something you know isn't right, or distract you from more important things. This is also a warning about your appetite. Are you ruled by it? If so, other qualities, like self-discipline, might be at risk. The publisher William Feather said this about that: "If we do not discipline ourselves the world will do it for us." Ouch! That can't be a good thing.

Scripture

"I will praise the Lord. Deep down inside me, I will praise him. I will praise him, because his name is holy. I will praise the Lord. I won't forget anything he does for me. He forgives all my sins. He heals all my sicknesses."—Psalm 103:1–3 (NIrV)

Grace

Lord, there is power in your holy name. All praise belongs to you. We wish to keep you in our hearts and minds—please help us with that. Help us see that our praises reach you in our prayers but also in our actions. Thank you for forgiving our sins. We pray for peace and healing for those who especially need it tonight. Thank you for taking care of us, for our food, and for our family. Halleluiah! Amen.

Grace notes

Some think that King David wrote this psalm when he was old. He had been through so much with the Lord and was very close to him. David spent a lot of time praying and trying to live an obedient life, but like all human beings he had his failings. God forgave David for some big-time sins because his heart was true. "Let this be your chief object in prayer, to realize the presence of your heavenly Father. Let your watchword be: Alone with God," said the South African preacher Andrew Murray. Mighty King David would surely have agreed.

Scripture

"LORD, you have seen what is in my heart. You know all about me. You know when I sit down and when I get up. You know what I'm thinking even though you are far away. You know when I go out to work and when I come back home. You know exactly how I live. LORD, even before I speak a word, you know all about it. You are all around me. You are behind me and in front of me. You hold me in your power. I'm amazed at how well you know me. It's more than I can understand."—Psalm 139:1–6 (NIrV)

Grace

Father God, the fact that you are everywhere and see everything at once is something we can't begin to imagine, but how great is that!? You're the superhero of superheroes. We say out loud how awesome it is that you know what's in our hearts, and being good is what we aim for. Give us confidence to know that you will help us to be what you want us to be. Thank you for everything—for our food, our parents, our grandparents—for all our family. Thank you for loving them, too. Amen.

Grace notes

Imagine being the coach of a sports team. You have to be able to see what everyone's doing at the same time—helping all the players be the best they can be, both individually and together, as a team. Life is like that, as the Washington Redskins Football Hall of Fame Coach Joe Gibbs has described it: "You and I are players, God's our coach, and we're playing the biggest game of all. We have a loving God that made us. We need to get on His team. It says in His word, there's only one way to Him and that's through Jesus Christ." Coach Gibbs is a very wise man.

mint

Scripture

Jesus said, "Don't worry. Don't say, 'What will we eat?' Or, 'What will we drink?' Or, 'What will we wear?' People who are ungodly run after all of those things. Your Father who is in heaven knows that you need them. But put God's kingdom first. Do what he wants you to do. Then all of those things will also be given to you. Do not be like [babbling pagans], for your Father knows what you need before you ask him." —Matthew 6:31–33 (NIrV)

Grace

Dear Jesus, thank you for dinner, and please bless us all. Inspire us to plan for the future and to work hard to do what we can to make our dreams come true. Remind us, though, of how important it is to put you first in our priorities, plans, and preparations. Remind us that worry is really substituting fear for faith in you. Great is your love for us; we praise you for it. Amen.

Grace notes

It's okay to be uncertain about what God may do next in your life—or what he may want you to do next; just don't ever be uncertain about God. This verse doesn't tell you not to prepare for your future—that would be a cop-out. God is inviting you to trust in him, to walk with him, and to be ready to do whatever needs to be done; he'll let you know when the time is right. Don't forget that he knows you and your needs and abilities a whole lot better than you do. The Nazi death camp survivor Corrie ten Boom said it this way: "Never be afraid to trust an unknown future to a known God."

Scripture

"As it is written: 'What no eye has seen, what no ear has heard, and what no human mind has conceived'—the things God has prepared for those who love him—these are the things God has revealed to us by his Spirit."—1 Corinthians 2:9–10 (NIV)

Grace

Lord, we thank you for this food and ask that it nourish our bodies. We thank you for your Word, too, knowing that it is more than enough to nourish our minds, hearts, and souls. Fill us up, Father, with truth from your Word and Spirit. Inspire us to learn excitedly and passionately, preparing for the incredible life you have promised. Please bless our friends and family. Father, you are our amazing God! Amen.

Grace notes

Jonathan Swift, the author of *Gulliver's Travels*, said, "Vision is the art of seeing things invisible." Even an extraordinary vision or imagination, though, won't get you a good description of heaven ("What no eye has seen . . ."). No, we don't know exactly what heaven will be like, but we do have some facts. In heaven you'll never be bored because you'll always love what you do. There will be no pain or suffering, and there will be plenty of room for everyone. (You won't turn into an angel, by the way, nor will you want to.) Most important of all, you'll be face-to-face with your Lord and Savior—the *most* overwhelming, indescribable joy. You won't know whether to grin or to tear up with pure joy! Pastor Rick Warren summed it up this way: "You will not be in heaven two seconds before you cry out, why did I place so much importance on things that were so temporary?"

Scripture

"My dear brothers and sisters, take note of this: Everyone should be quick to listen, slow to speak and slow to become angry, because human anger does not produce the righteousness that God desires."—James 1:19–20 (NIV)

Grace

Dear Jesus, please join us for dinner and give us your blessing. James, your very own earthly brother, knew that it's never smart to speak first and think second. Lord, help us to remember that, because it's hard to put into practice. Remind us, too, that half-listening is really not the same as listening. Teach us to think about the power words have—and to choose them carefully; the direction of our lives may just depend on it. We hear you, Lord. Amen.

Grace notes

"You're not listening!" Ever hear that one before? Or ever hear of a "non-versation"? Okay, that's not quite a word—yet, but it means having a meaningless talk with someone. That happens when someone only half listens—a sure recipe for communication disaster. Can you think of times when half-listening got you into trouble—especially if it involved a parent or other authority figure? God wants you to honor your mother and father. You can do that by looking at them when they're talking and even repeating back to them what you think they said to check your understanding. You'll be amazed at how much easier life gets for you when you make a point of really listening to others. "The first duty of love is to listen," said the philosopher Paul Tillich. Hey, did you just hear that?

Scripture

"It is better to have wise people reprimand you than to have stupid people sing your praises."—Ecclesiastes 7:5 (GNT)

Grace

"Heavenly Father, thank you for dinner and for your blessings on this day. Thank you for those wonderful words of wisdom, from you and from other people, that teach us about growing up. Encourage us to listen and learn from those—like Mom and Dad—who know stuff and are willing to share it. Give us the wisdom to know when someone is saying nice things only to get their way—help us not to do that, either, because it doesn't really help anybody. Thank you for being our friend and teacher, Lord. We sing your praises—and that's being smart—very smart. Amen.

Grace notes

Having to listen to lectures from parents and teachers is part of growing up, isn't it? Even if you don't always appreciate it, learn to really listen to those experienced people. Be on the lookout for false praise from others, knowing that it can give you the wrong idea about yourself. Honest praise is sincere and encouraging and given with no hidden motive. There's a word, though, for false praise: *flattery*. It's saying something nice with the expectation of getting a favor in return. In this case both sides lose. How's that now? Discuss it with your family if that would be helpful. "Flattery is like chewing gum. Enjoy it but don't swallow it," said Hank Ketcham, the creator of the Dennis the Menace cartoons.

Scripture

"Don't eavesdrop on the conversation of others. What if the gossip's about you and you'd rather not hear it? You've done that a few times, haven't you—said things behind someone's back you wouldn't say to his face?"—Ecclesiastes 7:21–22 (MSG)

Grace

Father, thank you for this day and for our food. Thank you for your wisdom; may we hear you and remember. Lord, are you telling us not to get so riled up over what others say, as though we've never said something not-so-nice ourselves? Forgive us, Lord, when we're careless with the treasure you've given us of words and language. Teach us that Solomon's words stand the test of time*; he got his wisdom straight from you, and his words in Proverbs and Ecclesiastes are in the Bible to pass that wisdom along. Sharpen our wits, Lord. Some things never change, like your love for us and our praise for you. Amen.

*Solomon wrote Ecclesiastes 3,900 years ago, and his wisdom still helps us. A wise guy indeed!

Grace notes

There's a word for secretly listening in on a conversation: *eavesdropping*. The way eavesdropping works is that we don't often get the chance, even when we want to, to hear the *whole* conversation. The pieces of the whole we do catch are "out of context" (that's like looking at one little piece of a puzzle and trying to guess the whole picture). Do you see how easy it would be to reach a wrong conclusion? And would you want someone to listen in on your private conversation? "I have long since come to believe that people never mean half of what they say," said the social activist Dorothy Day, "and that it is best to disregard their talk and judge only their actions." If you accidently overhear something unflattering about yourself or someone else, would you rather get worked up over it or shrug it off—like a dog that's just come in out of the rain?

Scripture

"The Lord has given us eyes to see with and ears to listen with."
—Proverbs 20:12 (GNT)

Grace

Gracious Father, we praise you and ask your blessing on this food. Show us that more than looking and more than hearing, our eyes and ears help us to *know* you. Teach us that when Mom or Dad tell us to "focus," it's time to pay close attention with our minds and hearts. Thank you, Lord, for your grace. Amen.

Grace notes

If you have eyes and ears—and they're in good working order—the Lord wants you to use them wisely. They aren't just for hearing and seeing but also for listening and understanding. They help you pay attention, which is key in the process of becoming wise and good. "Right is right, even if everyone is against it; and wrong is wrong, even if everyone is for it," said William Penn, the founder of the American colony (later the state) of Pennsylvania. You can be sure he used his eyes and ears wisely.

Scripture

"Nehemiah said, 'Go and enjoy good food and sweet drinks. Send some to people who have none, because today is a holy day to the Lord. Don't be sad, because the joy of the Lord will make you strong.'" —Nehemiah 8:10 (NCV)

Grace

Heavenly Father, we're grateful for the food you've set before us today—ours is a table of plenty! Teach us to love our time together because, like good food and drinks, it's all part of a joyful, fulfilled, and happy life. May we show others through our generous actions how much we love you; may they become strong in you, too, so we can all rejoice together. Make us grateful not just for our dinner but for all that you do for us. Amen.

Grace notes

The Scripture right before today's verse describes God's people weeping because they had just realized how sinful they had been. The wise leaders wanted to show them God's love and grace, so they set aside that day as a holiday—holy and joyful to the Lord. God wants to forgive the sins of all his children, and he takes delight in our joy over his forgiveness. Nehemiah wanted to reassure the people that God is a loving God, just and full of mercy. He wanted them to know that restoration—becoming right with God again—was possible when they responded to him in prayer. Had Saint Augustine been around to talk to them, they might have been comforted by his words: "Do not seek to understand in order that you may believe, but believe so that you may understand."

Scripture

Jesus said, "Pay close attention to what you hear. The closer you listen, the more understanding you will be given—and you will receive even more. To those who listen to my teaching, more understanding will be given. But for those who are not listening, even what little understanding they have will be taken away from them."—Mark 4:24–27 (NLT)

Grace

Lord, we thank you for this food and for your many blessings. Encourage us to make you a priority in our lives—to experience the meaning of "the hungrier we get, the more we are fed." Make us truly hungry for your Word! Remind us that when we're learning something it might not make sense at first, but later . . . it does! Help us to think of it like learning to read music; at first we see just scribbles on a page, but soon we're following those markings and making music! Keep us listening, Lord, and help us understand. Amen.

Grace notes

Sometimes the words and ideas in the Bible are hard to understand, aren't they? Do you have a study Bible? They're available for people of all ages, and they include notes, often at the bottom of each page, to explain stuff! George Müller, the director of the Ashley Down Orphanage in England, cared for 10,024 orphans during his lifetime. He was very busy but always made time to read his Bible. "The less we read the Word of God," he said, "the less we desire to read it, and the less we pray, the less we desire to pray." Remember that. It's a good reminder to keep you on track.

parsley

Scripture

"Jesus went on: 'Does anyone bring a lamp home and put it under a washtub or beneath the bed? Don't you put it up on a table or on the mantel? We're not keeping secrets, we're telling them; we're not hiding things, we're bringing them out into the open. Are you listening to this? Really listening?'"—Mark 4:21–23 (MSG)

Grace

Heavenly Father, thank you for the food we eat; thank you, too, for our family and friends. Please bless us. Please bring people who love you into the lives of others who don't. (They need to know how much you love them, too.) Encourage us to see the wonders of life hidden in plain sight—all we have to do is open our eyes to your truth and our ears to your words in your Word. May we be filled with the Holy Spirit and come to see your light and glory. Amen.

Grace notes

When you turn on a flashlight you expect it to light up and show you the way, don't you? And when you no longer need it, you turn it off. Jesus is calling on you to never turn off the light of your faith. Keep that flashlight turned on and Jesus will draw ever closer to you and your life will become better. How can you shine your light as he asks you to do? Interact with others, be a good example, nurture friendships with kindness. Keep in mind, too, that this light is not an attention-getting device. If it were you would only be serving yourself—not others and definitely not Jesus. William Law was an eighteenth-century priest who gave up his position at Emmanuel College in Cambridge, England, rather than taking the required oath of allegiance to the king. Did that end his career? No, he taught privately and had a great life, and his writings cast a light that still shines today. "If you have not chosen the Kingdom of God first," he said, "it will in the end make no difference what you have chosen instead."

Scripture

"What God the Father considers to be pure and genuine religion is this: to take care of orphans and widows in their suffering and to keep oneself from being corrupted by the world."—James 1:27 (GNT)

"Learn to do right; seek justice. Defend the oppressed. Take up the cause of the fatherless; plead the case of the widow."—Isaiah 1:17 (NIV)

Grace

Jesus, we thank you for this meal and for giving us a family to love. Give us kind feelings toward those with no earthly family, and remind us to pray for their safety and well-being. Teach us that doing so honors you, dear Jesus. We are saved by faith to do good, and that goes full circle: our good works help others, you help us, and we all become better people. May your love shine through us. Amen.

Grace notes

We are called by God to "stand up for those beaten down, to be fair to those wronged, and to give food to the hungry."* God seeks to defend orphans and widows and asks for our participation. "Seek justice and encourage the oppressed," Moses told the Israelites in Deuteronomy 10:18. And Jesus said, "Truly I tell you, whatever you did for one of the least of these brothers and sisters of mine, you did for me."** Wow! Next time you help someone, think of that. It's a wonderful feeling. The famous English novelist Charles Dickens wrote often about the poor and oppressed. "No one is useless in this world," he said, "who lightens the burdens of another."

*Proverbs 14:31 and Psalm 146:7; **Matthew 25:40

mint

Scripture

"Moses said to the Lord, 'Please, Lord, I have never been a skilled speaker. Even now, after talking to you, I cannot speak well. I speak slowly and can't find the best words.' Then the Lord said to him, 'Who made a person's mouth? And who makes someone deaf or not able to speak? Or who gives a person sight or blindness? It is I, the Lord. Now go! I will help you speak, and I will teach you what to say.'"—Exodus 4:10–12 (NCV)

Grace

Gracious Father, we thank you for bringing us together to talk about your goodness and strength and guidance. Thank you for our food. May we not forget, Lord, that you can take a weakness and turn it into a strength for your kingdom cause. Remind us that when we listen to your voice great things are in store for us. May we never forget your power and glory. Amen.

Grace notes

Moses was in a whiny mood here. "Oh no, not me, Lord," he might have said. "You've got the wrong guy." Really? Didn't Moses realize who he was arguing with? So God can create the universe but can't correct a slow tongue? *Hmmm!* If God calls you to it, he will see you through it. If you think he's calling on you to do something, ask for his instructions. "Expect great things from God; attempt great things for God," said William Carey, known today as the father of modern missions. And don't worry: God will back you up.

Scripture

"This is my prayer for you: that your love will grow more and more; that you will have knowledge and understanding with your love; that you will see the difference between good and bad and will choose the good; that you will be pure and without wrong for the coming of Christ; that you will be filled with the good things produced in your life by Christ to bring glory and praise to God."—Philippians 1:9–11 (NCV)

Grace

Loving Jesus, soon our tummies will be full; please fill our hearts and souls with your goodness and blessing, too. We pray for new understanding of what it means to love each other—to feel how much more is involved than just saying "I love you." We ask for guidance in putting our love into practice and pray for good things in our life through knowing you. We belong to you, Lord, and we praise your name. Amen.

Grace notes

Sometimes good thoughts get stuck in the planning phase. Instead of thinking about ways to show love, just get out and do it. Just start, and the momentum will carry you through. Each action builds upon the last, and it gets easier every time. C. S. Lewis made the same point in a slightly different way: "Do not waste time bothering whether you 'love' your neighbor; act as if you did."

Scripture

"Being respected is more important than having great riches. To be well thought of is better than silver or gold."—Proverbs 22:1 (NCV)

Grace

Gracious Father, thank you for the richness of this meal and for those who prepared it. Please bless us all. Teach us that although having money is not a bad thing, the value we place on it and the ways we use it matter. Help us to remember that being honorable—ensuring a good reputation—is the real prize. Help us to be better people, Lord. We praise you for your splendor. Amen.

Grace notes

Do you know what it means to be respected? It's being admired for your qualities. Can you list some of the characteristics that will cause others to think well of you? How about these for a short list? Do more than you say you will. Be a good teammate. Focus on solutions instead of blame. Share what you know (but not in a know-it-all-way). Show interest in others. None of that's so difficult, is it? The professional baseball player turned preacher Billy Sunday shared these thoughts: "The fellow that has no money is poor. The fellow that has nothing but money is poorer still." Oh, that thought is rich, indeed!

Scripture

"A healthy tree does not bear bad fruit, nor does a poor tree bear good fruit. . . . A good person brings good out of the treasure of good things in his heart; a bad person brings bad out of his treasure of bad things. For the mouth speaks what the heart is full of."—Luke 6:43, 45 (GNT)

Grace

Heavenly Father, thank you for blessing our food. Fill us now with the goodness it has for us. Thank you for your Word; fill us to overflowing with its goodness, as well. Lord, teach us that our character is evident to all from the fruit we produce—it's right there for everyone to see (including you, Lord). Remind us, too, of the importance of not making snap judgments about other people based on one action; everyone has a bad day now and then. Help us keep in mind that Christians aren't perfect—they're just forgiven. Amen.

Grace notes

One of the first things people notice about you is the light behind your smile. A ready smile says so much about the state of your soul. (Think of someone who says hello without smiling—Ugh.) Your genuine smile not only makes the other person happy but, according to scientists who study faces, makes *you* happier, too. An authentic smile will help you feel better, and that in turn helps you to do better, act better, and *be* better. All that! Who knew! "Wear a smile and have friends; wear a scowl and have wrinkles," said George Eliot, the author of the novel *Silas Marner*.

Scripture

"Telling lies about others is as harmful as hitting them with an ax, wounding them with a sword, or shooting them with a sharp arrow."
—Proverbs 25:18 (NLT)

Grace

Father God, thank you for dinner and for all your other blessings—way too many to shout out or count. Thank you for teaching us wisdom from your Word. Teach us to be very, very careful of our words and make us aware of how an untruth can turn on us like a boomerang, hurting everyone in the picture. Encourage us to be uneasy around friends who tell lies and mock you, Lord; we don't want to start thinking and acting like them. And that's the truth. Amen.

Grace notes

A lie, even a small one, is a serious deal to God. Being untruthful affects others' willingness to trust us, too, and can dilute the quality of a friendship. Even those little white lies—you know, the ones you say to spare someone's feelings, like "No, those pants don't make you look fat!"—may be more about protecting yourself from a fear of not being liked. Know that the farther you stretch the truth, the more stretchable it seems to become, and the more negative your emotions become. That's a real danger. The habit of dishonesty, like any other, may develop a little at a time, but sooner or later you get comfortable with it. As you mature the art of being tactful (telling the truth in a kind, gentle manner) becomes more important ("I think those black pants would look better on you"). It's a good skill to learn, but it takes attention and doesn't come automatically. We aren't born knowing how to be kind. The poet William Blake summed up the truth about truth-telling like this: "The truth that's told with bad intent beats all the lies you can invent." Oh, how true!

mint

Scripture

Jesus said, "If anyone comes to me and does not hate father and mother, wife and children, brothers and sisters—yes, even their own life—such a person cannot be my disciple."—Luke 14:26 (NIV)

Grace

Dear Jesus, thank you for this food. Thank you for our family and for the many blessings of today. We love each other, Jesus, so what are you telling us here? Help us understand that in the ancient Greek language "to hate" also meant "to choose over." Help us see that you're asking us to choose you first and to be ready to give you everything—family, friends, money, work, and play. Remind us that when we do that everything else in our lives will fall into place. We love you, Jesus, and yet we know you love us more. Amen.

Grace notes

Many time Jesus spoke of the importance of spiritual relationships with the Father and fellow believers over other worldly relationships,* and that is what he is doing here. Often, and to emphasize the importance of his words, Jesus would say things in a way that would shock you into listening closely. He wants you to get it—really get it. In today's Scripture his words are an exaggeration, like when you say "I'm so hungry I could eat a horse." Everyone knew you never had any intention of eating a horse, but you wanted others to know you were really hungry. Would anyone take your serious hunger seriously if you just said "I'm hungry?" or "I'm so hungry I could eat a head of lettuce"? Get it? The more you read the Bible the better you'll understand its many different tones, techniques, and ways of saying things, and anything worth accomplishing takes effort. Get a good study Bible geared to your level of understanding, and feel free to write in it when new insights come your way! Set aside some time to focus on God's Word, being sure to get rid of distractions (that means turn off the cell phone, radio, or TV). Be patient and ask Jesus to guide you as you begin reading. "When first things are put first, second things are not suppressed but increased," said C. S. Lewis. Can you come up with some examples together?

*For example, Mark 3:33–35 and Matthew 19:29

Scripture

"When you're given a box of candy, don't gulp it all down; eat too much chocolate and you'll make yourself sick; and when you find a friend, don't outwear your welcome; show up at all hours and he'll soon get fed up."—Proverbs 25:16–17 (MSG)

Grace

Gracious Father, thank you for our family, friends, and neighbors. Please bless us all. Thanks for reminding us that too much of an (earthly) good thing is just as bad as having to do without. Help us develop habits of willpower and good manners. Fill us up with good things—but not too many or too much. Amen.

Grace notes

Eat too much honey and you get a tummy ache. Drink too much caffeinated, sugary soda and weight gain and sleepless nights may be in your future. Moderation (taking it easy) *in all things* is a good rule to live by. (All except for God's love, right?) You realize that's what good habits and willpower are for: denying yourself something now in favor of a payday later. In what other areas of life have you noticed that willpower and good habits pay off? The Australian actor F. M. Alexander also taught other actors, and he was big on developing positive habits. "Men do not decide their future," he said. "They decide their habits and their habits decide their future."

Scripture

"Whoever is your servant is the greatest among you. Whoever makes himself great will be made humble. Whoever makes himself humble will be made great."—Matthew 23:11–12 (NCV)

Grace

Father God, teach us that just as your Son Jesus calls himself the servant of people, so we are called to serve others. Inspire us to serve humbly, in the spirit of God's intent—not out of self-importance, duty, or guilt but because of our love and gratitude for you. Thank you now for our food. Just as you serve us, Lord, may we willingly serve you. Amen.

Grace notes

To become a great leader, you must first be a great follower. Working in the trenches—doing ordinary, everyday work—improves your leadership abilities because you become aware of the needs of others and what it takes to accomplish the various jobs followers do. You learn to notice what needs to be done and how to become a good team member. Here's another way to look at it. The job of a follower is to make the leader look good, and the job of a leader is to make the follower look good. "I pray to be a good servant to God, a father, a husband, a son, a friend, a brother, an uncle, a good neighbor, a good leader to those who look up to me, a good follower to those who are serving God and doing the right thing," said the American actor, producer, and rapper Mark Wahlberg. Name some roles in which *you* can be a good servant. Name some ways you can be a good leader, too.

Scripture

"Praise be to the God and Father of our Lord Jesus Christ. In Christ, God has given us every spiritual blessing in the heavenly world." —Ephesians 1:3 (NCV)

Grace

Eternal Father, we praise you for blessing us; thank you for this food and family. Help us understand that your blessings are ours for the asking if we're only willing to invite Jesus to live in our hearts. Show us that you draw us into your life so you can work in our lives. We praise you, Father, and honor you for your goodness and grace. Lift us up, we pray, to "soar on wings like eagles"* along with you. Amen.

*Isaiah 40:31

Grace notes

The Lord has a plan for your life. It's a short life, relatively speaking, but it prepares you for eternity. So what can you do now to get ready? Start with baby steps. Love Jesus and others, for starters. As you grow in his Word the way will open up for you. Benjamin Disraeli, who twice served as prime minister of Great Britain, understood: "The greatest good you can do for another," he said, "is not just to share your riches but to reveal to him his own." God has gifted each of us with spiritual blessings. To help others see and develop their gifts is a great gift to yourself—and others.

Scripture

"Not all those who say 'You are our Lord' will enter the kingdom of heaven. The only people who will enter the kingdom of heaven are those who do what my Father in heaven wants."—Matthew 7:21 (NCV)

Grace

Heavenly Jesus, we believe in your faithfulness and thank you for blessing us. Remind us that the true measure of who we are is in our hearts, a place that cannot be hidden from you. Show us that doing the right thing is harder—but so much more worthwhile—than trying to lip-sync our praise or fake our obedience. Give us the desire, Jesus, to do what you and your Father want us to do. Teach us that when we do our happiness multiplies. Amen.

Grace notes

God, the maker of the human heart, is impossible to fool; he can easily recognize a *wolf hiding in sheep's clothing.** In other words, a "Look at me, look at me; I'm so good" attitude, when you're really thinking about something quite the opposite of good, or serving God only for appearances sake, just won't cut it with him. Here's the thing: don't worry so much about rules; just get the love in your heart right, and the rules will usually take care of themselves. That's because you'll want to do the right thing. Someone once said "walk your talk, talk your walk." What does this have to do with throwing out the double standard—with *being* the sheep instead of just pretending to be?

*Matthew 7:15

mint

Scripture

"Praise the Lord, my soul! All my being, praise his holy name! Praise the Lord, my soul, and do not forget how kind he is. He forgives all my sins and heals all my diseases. He keeps me from the grave and blesses me with love and mercy. He fills my life with good things, so that I stay young and strong like an eagle."—Psalm 103:1–5 (GNT)

Grace

Dear Lord, for food and family dear,
We ask your blessings always, here.
May grace and love shine on us all.
With thanks and praise to you we call.
We ask for strength and all good things,
Your healing ways upon each day.
In Jesus' name alone we pray. Amen.

Grace notes

God wants to hear your praises. (Not just for his sake, but also for yours, as a reminder of your connection to him.) He also wants you to share your troubles and your wishes with him because he delights in helping you! But don't try to put God in a box by telling him how to help you; leave that to him. Phillips Brooks, the pastor who wrote the Christmas carol "O Little Town of Bethlehem," understood this well. "Pray the largest prayers," he said. "You cannot think a prayer so large that God, in answering it, will not wish you had made it larger. Pray not for crutches but for wings!"

Scripture

"Listen before you answer. If you don't, you are being stupid and insulting."—Proverbs 18:13 (GNT)

Grace

Dear Jesus, please bless our family, friends, and food; we give thanks for all your gifts. This verse is a great tip, Lord. Listening is a sure way to learn tons of stuff—maybe even enough to get on *Jeopardy*! Teach us, Jesus, that the answers to all our questions about life can be found in your Word—the Bible. Remind us, too, that people are drawn like a magnet to a good listener. Thanks, Lord—we hear you. We hear Mom and Dad, too. Help us listen and learn. Amen.

Grace notes

Question: Who wants to be considered stupid and insulting? Answer: No one! The art of listening is highly underrated, and those who listen well are far ahead of the game. Good listening helps you solve problems, opens your mind to new ideas, and is one of the best ways to find and keep friends. (How might not listening well cost you friends?) Here are some ways to develop your listening skills: Talk less than you listen. Listen with your whole self and try to picture what the speaker is saying. Maintain eye contact. When you hear frustration in someone's words, repeat back what you've heard; they may not be saying—or you may not be hearing—what they mean to be saying. Don't talk over someone else who's talking. Wait your turn, without interrupting or thinking of an answer before they're finished. "I like to listen. I have learned a great deal from listening carefully. Most people never listen," said the Nobel prize-winning author Ernest Hemingway. Wow! Do you think good listening is really that rare?

Scripture

"This is my command—be strong and courageous! Do not be afraid or discouraged. For the LORD your God is with you wherever you go." —Joshua 1:9 (NLT)

Grace

Dear Lord, our God, thank you for your blessings. Continue to watch over us, our family, and all those in need tonight. Teach us to be bold and courageous and to live with purpose; to believe that you'll part all of our Red Seas for us, tear down our walls of Jericho, and be with us always. Open our eyes to your presence and your power, Lord. Teach us that the more we sense your nearness the less energy we'll waste in fear or worry. Amen.

Grace notes

Courage means being able to do something even though you're afraid. It means being strong even when you're in pain or sorrow. Courage also means that you might have to be the first one to speak up when something is wrong. And your character grows when you work up the courage to do things you think you can't do. The famous preacher and evangelist Billy Graham shows us another benefit: "Courage is contagious. When a brave man takes a stand, the spines of others are stiffened." How do you think *that* works?

Scripture

"My God will use his glorious riches to give you everything you need. He will do this through Christ Jesus."—Philippians 4:19 (ERV)

Grace

Dear Jesus, we know you love us and shower us with an abundance of good gifts; the most important gift ever given, we know, is your gift of yourself. Look into our hearts and find joy and gratitude there. Help us see that trying to earn our own way into heaven by taking credit for your work makes us stingy and conceited—as though we think we don't need you. Thank you, Lord, for your blessings on this food. Amen.

Grace notes

Did you know that the Father, the Son, and the Holy Spirit, even though they are distinct and individual persons, are all God and never disagree or act separately? And did you realize that they talk to each other *about you*? They know who you are, your name, and everything about you. They know what you need, too, and see what's in your heart. Someone has said "First, give yourself to God. You may be sure he'll look after what is his." That means you!

sage

Scripture

"Jesus went up a hill to pray and spent the whole night there praying to God. When day came, he called his disciples to him and chose twelve of them, whom he named apostles: Simon (whom he named Peter) and his brother Andrew; James and John, Philip and Bartholomew*, Matthew and Thomas, James son of Alphaeus, and Simon (who was called the Patriot), Judas son of James, and Judas Iscariot, who became the traitor."—Luke 6:12–16 (GNT)

*Some think Nathanial, mentioned by John as an apostle, and Bartholomew are one and the same.

Grace

Dear Jesus, thank you for this food to nourish our bodies and for your Word to feed our souls. We think the disciples (later called apostles) had an awesome job: to go out and spread the gospel—the news about *you*, the best news ever! Teach us that you have called us to be disciples, too. Awesome!

Our job, you say: Good News to teach,
As your disciples, we seek and reach.
Like Peter, Andy, Jim, and John,
Philip, Bart, Matt, and Tom.
James, Simon, Thaddeus (called Jude)—
And then there was Judas, who became devil's food.
Lord fill our minds so we can speak,
Filled with your Spirit to shepherd your sheep. Amen.

Grace notes

Jesus called all of us to spread the word about God—to be his disciples. His command is called the Great Commission; you can read it in Matthew 28:18–20. Invite a friend to church; your action might just result, through the working of the Holy Spirit, in their finding a relationship with Jesus! James Brown, known as the Godfather of Soul music, was a big believer in Jesus. "When I'm on stage," he said, "I'm trying to do one thing: bring people joy. Just like church does. People don't go to church to find trouble; they go there to lose it," he said. Now, there's some food for the soul!

mint

Scripture

"Blessed are the poor in spirit, for theirs is the kingdom of heaven." —Matthew 5:3 (NIV)

"You're blessed when you're at the end of your rope. With less of you there is more of God and his rule."—Matthew 5:3 (MSG)

Grace

Lord Jesus, thank you for this food and for your teaching. Teach us that being *poor in spirit* is a good thing because it means saying YES to being close to you and becoming rich in *your* Spirit. Help us to walk in your footsteps, Jesus. We are grateful for all your blessings. Amen.

Grace notes

This verse comes from the Beatitudes—the eight blessings spoken by Jesus as part of his Sermon on the Mount. Being poor in spirit means being spiritually or emotionally poor or needy. Someone who says "I don't need any help" when they obviously do is either too proud or too self-confident. When you recognize that God is your provider and that it's his strength that carries you, you're giving God the space to do his best work in you. Admitting your weakness allows him to be stronger in your life, enriching you in ways you could never have imagined. "The deeper we grow in the Spirit of Jesus Christ, the poorer we become—the more we realize that everything in life is a gift," said the American author Brennan Manning. Those words are worth reading again!

thyme

Scripture

"In the beginning was the Word, and the Word was with God, and the Word was God. He was with God in the beginning. Through him all things were made; without him nothing was made that has been made. In him was life, and that life was the light of all mankind. The light shines in the darkness, and the darkness has not overcome it."—John 1:1–5 (NIV)

Grace

Heavenly Father, we give thanks for this day and ask your blessing on our food. Fill us with the understanding that Jesus Christ is also God. Through him you made everything, including us. You, God, just spoke, and the universe was created. Thank you that Jesus, your Son, was willing to come to this earth in human flesh and blood (Wow!) to take the punishment for the sin of all people. Teach us that you love us a lot—more than we can imagine. May we come to know and appreciate all the treasures you offer us. We love your amazing grace. Amen.

Grace notes

Try this experiment: turn off the lights at nighttime and turn on a single flashlight. You can't help but look toward the light, can you? Now think of James's words about Jesus being a light in the darkness: Come near to God and he will come near to you.* How can you be a light for Jesus in the world? Here are some ideas to explore: be careful what you say, think about how you use social media, and encourage instead of criticizing. A man named John Hagee put it this way: "We are indeed the light of the world . . . but only if our switch is turned on."

*James 4:8

bay

Scripture

"I am the Alpha and the Omega—the beginning and the end," says the Lord God. "I am the one who is, who always was, and who is still to come—the Almighty One."—Revelation 1:8 (NLT)

"Jesus Christ is the same yesterday, today, and forever."—Hebrews 13:8 (NLT)

Grace

Heavenly Father, we bow our heads in gratefulness for this food and for our family. Crazy, topsy-turvy things are going on all around us, yet you are always with us, unchanging and ever faithful. Make us stronger in our faith and hope, and help us understand a little better your awesome words, "Heaven and earth will pass away, but my words will never pass away."* Wow! And Wow again! Amen.

*Luke 21:33

Grace notes

God never, never, ever changes. He's always the same, has no limits, is ever-faithful, is a promise-keeper, is perfectly just and fair, and loves you eternally. So if something happens and you change your mind about God, remember that *he* isn't the one who has changed—*you* have. "If the Lord be with us, we have no cause of fear. His eye is upon us, his arm over us, his ear open to our prayer—his grace sufficient, his promise unchangeable," said John Newton, a slave trader who repented and later wrote the well-loved hymn "Amazing Grace."

parsley

Scripture

"Children, do what your parents tell you. This delights the Master no end. Parents, don't come down too hard on your children or you'll crush their spirits."—Colossians 3:20–21 (MSG)

Grace

Dear Jesus, we thank you for this food, for everything we are and have, and for telling it like it is. May we never forget that our obeying Mom and Dad makes you happy, Lord. Help us see that Mom and Dad care for us like potters who work with soft clay; they have to be gentle, firm, and patient to produce something beautiful and valuable. The real potter, though, is *you!* In your hands each of us becomes a true work of art! Thank heaven for Mom and Dad, and for all those who care for us and use their time, energy, and love to teach and mold us. Amen.

Grace notes

Robert Fulghum, who wrote the book *All I Really Need to Know I Learned in Kindergarten*, had this to say to grown-ups: "Don't worry that children never listen to you. Worry that they are always watching you." Think about this question: Are you more likely to copy what your parents say or what they do? If you're like most kids, you'll copy the way Mom and Dad act more quickly than you'll do what they say. Sometimes moms and dads come down hard on their kids because, as kids once themselves, they've been there, done that same thing—Oops! Being a parent sounds easy, but it's a lot harder than it looks to follow Jesus and be a great example to watching boys and girls. Don't be too critical: someday it may be your turn.

Scripture

"There will be glory and honor and peace from God for all who do good—for the Jew first and also for the Gentile. For God does not show favoritism."—Romans 2:10–11 (NLT)

Grace

Dear Jesus, we thank you for all that is good—that's everything that comes from you. Help us to always want to be good and to try our hardest to follow your example. Remind us that *all* people, from whatever background, who love you, believe in you, and accept your sacrifice to save us from our sins are part of your very own chosen people. Teach us that your love is perfect and that it never goes away. Teach us to pay attention to what you think—not to what others think. Help us to be more like you, Lord. Thank you that you lead us to your table of plenty. We praise your name and thank you for this meal and for our family. Amen.

Grace notes

The gospel (that's the Good News of Jesus) was brought first to the Jewish people (the same people who were called the Israelites in the Old Testament) and then to the Gentiles (all people who are not Jewish.) God chose Israel to represent him to the world, and his plan from the beginning of time was to bless the whole world through Israel. God promised that, from the ancestors of the Jewish king David, he would bring forth Jesus Christ, the Savior of the world. This has nothing to do with the Israelites or Jews being better or more important than other people; we are all special in God's eyes. It's about Israel being given that big responsibility to bless the entire world. "There are only two kinds of people in the end," said the author C. S. Lewis: "those who say to God, 'Thy will be done,' and those to whom God says, 'Thy will be done.'" It doesn't matter in God's eyes whether we are Jews or Gentiles; it only matters whether we're willing to let God take control of our lives.

Scripture

"Give, and you will receive. You will be given much. Pressed down, shaken together, and running over, it will spill into your lap. The way you give to others is the way God will give to you."—Luke 6:38 (NCV)

Grace

Loving Father, thank you for this food and for our family. Thank you for teaching us so many important things in your Word, the Bible. Teach us to be generous in our thoughts, words, and actions. Teach us to be people others can count on, to be truthful, and to be aware that the way we treat others is the way you, God, will treat us. Lord, you are awesome! Please bless us all, in Jesus' name. Amen.

Grace notes

Jesus doesn't want you to forget the kinds of people the world would like to forget: the poor, hungry, sick, disabled, oppressed, victims of crimes, prisoners, widows, or orphans. He wants you to remember that each of them is as important as every other person; he loves everyone equally. You can make a difference in someone else's life, and that will feel wonderful for both of you. There are lots of ways to do this. You might want to consider donating your time or giving your own money to a charity or directly to someone in need. Here's something that could make a big difference today: after dinner go find something of your own—make sure it's in good condition—to give away to someone who needs it. "Giving is a two-week cruise—with pay," said the comedian, actor, dancer, and author Bob Hope. What kind of pay do you receive from giving?

Scripture

"Bridle your anger, trash your wrath, cool your pipes—it only makes things worse. Before long the crooks will be bankrupt; God-investors will soon own the store."—Psalm 37:8–9 (MSG)

Grace

Dear Jesus, thank you for this food, and please bless us all. Thank you for coaching us in cool ways to grow up—and that includes teaching us to keep our cool. Remind us of how uncool it is to use mean words. Remind us, too, that controlling our anger takes practice. Teach us that true strength comes gently. Teach us, Lord, to forgive. Amen.

Grace notes

Do you know what pushes your buttons (what makes you mad)? If you don't, ask others—they'll tell you! Be prepared, though, for your own reaction; listening to their answers might make you angry. If it doesn't take much to rile you up, follow the wise words of Thomas Jefferson: "When angry count to ten before you speak. If very angry, count to one hundred." Hopefully by that time you'll have overlooked what set you off. If someone bugs you, think before you speak—and then speak gently.

Scripture

"If you make the Lord your refuge, if you make the Most High your shelter, no evil will conquer you; no plague will come near your home. For he will order his angels to protect you wherever you go."—Psalm 91:9–11 (NLT)

Grace

Father in heaven, please bless our meal, our family, and all our loved ones. Teach us that your strength and protection are meant for us and that in times of trouble you will always be there to help us get through. Inspire us to make you our number one, God, and richly reward* us with your divine protection. Help us remember that although trouble comes in this sinful world, nothing can ever happen that is out of your control. Praise be to you, Lord. Amen.

*Ruth 2:12

Grace notes

It is far better to face life with God as your coat of armor than to try to go it alone or to depend on other people. Trust God and know that he is in charge. Plant that thought in your head each morning, and be sure to talk to God every day—then stop to listen for his answers. You might not hear the flap of angel's wings, but you *will* feel the quiet strength of God's protecting arms around you. You can believe, though, that God's angels are also there for you. "I could not have made it this far had there not been angels along the way," said the actress and jazz singer Della Reese.

Scripture

"Then [Jesus] said, "Beware! Guard against every kind of greed. Life is not measured by how much you own."—Luke 12:15 (NLT)

Grace

Gracious Lord, thank you for this food and for our friends and family. Encourage us to measure our success not by how much we have but by how little we need. Remind us that everything we do have is from you and that you don't want our possessions to rule our actions. Teach us, Jesus, that when we give we also receive; help us always to give away the important things of life through acts of love, care, encouragement, and forgiveness. Thank you for your wisdom, Lord. Help us to take it to heart. Amen.

Grace notes

How you feel about the importance of money and material things, not whether you have the right amount of stuff, is the lesson here. If you want to feel truly rich, count the things you have that money can't buy. "There is no dignity quite so impressive, and no independence quite so important, as living within your means," said the U.S. president Calvin Coolidge. If you get an allowance, or have some money saved, what does it mean to live within your means? How does this help you set the kinds of priorities Jesus would want you to have? Matthew* tells us to seek first Christ's kingdom, knowing that he will then give us everything else we need.

*Matthew 6:33

sage

Scripture

"You may believe you are doing right, but the Lord judges your reasons."—Proverbs 21:2 (NCV)

Grace

Lord God, how well you know us; how patient and loving you are. We recognize that your way is the best way and ask you to guide us to do what is right. Teach us that making excuses is for small thinkers and in the long run never solves anything. Help us see that on your playing field the best defense is a good offense—that if we want to score for your kingdom we have to make the moves that make you happy. May we always remember that you know our intentions and that we can run but can never hide from your searching, loving eyes. Thank you, Father, for this food and for our family. Amen.

Grace notes

Do you know what self-deception is? The word means misleading yourself about yourself. For instance, you might convince yourself that it's okay to cheat on a test because *everyone* else is doing it. Or, if you're a little older, that it's okay to sneak in after curfew because your friends have dared you to. When you talk yourself into things like this you hurt yourself, you hurt others, and sooner or later you'll have regrets. "You can be sincere, but you can be sincerely wrong. The fact is, it takes more than sincerity to make it in life. It takes truth," said Pastor Rick Warren. And that includes true and right thinking about ourselves and our actions.

mint

Scripture

"Let's hear it from Sky, with Earth joining in, And a huge round of applause from Sea. Let Wilderness turn cartwheels, animals, come dance, put every tree of the forest in the choir—an extravaganza before God as he comes, as he comes to set everything right on earth, set everything right, treat everyone fair."—Psalm 96:11–13 (MSG)

Grace

Heavenly Father, we are grateful for all you have provided and for the beauty you created to declare your existence. Please bless our food, our family, and all those in need, especially those who cannot yet see that creation is yours. May we always remember our purpose: to have a relationship with you and to invite others to have one, too. Amen.

Grace notes

When Jesus Christ comes and reigns over all the nations, the world—the entire universe—will experience a state of joy and will cry out, so to speak, the words of this psalm. And you'll be there to experience it if you have let Jesus come into your heart. "There is one spectacle greater than the sea: that is the sky," said the French poet and writer Victor Hugo. He went on, "There is one spectacle greater than the sky: that is the interior of the soul." What do you think he meant?

Scripture

"This is the day the LORD has made; we will rejoice and be glad in it."—Psalm 118:24 (NIV)

Grace

Almighty Father, please bless our day, our evening, our night, our tomorrow, our family, and this meal. Fill us with joyful hope for the coming days. Teach us to look forward to finding the miracles in each one of them and to depend, day by day, on your strength and love. Watch over us in the days to come. We praise your name. Amen.

Grace notes

"The hardest arithmetic to master is that which enables us to count our blessings," said the American philosopher Eric Hoffer. Can you add up today's blessings? It's easy to see nothing but blessings when the day is fun, or when nothing is going wrong, isn't it? But how about when the day isn't going so well? A gratitude attitude is the answer. Like learning to like new foods, we have to learn thankfulness. Who or what are you thankful for? Going around the table, help each other find reasons to be grateful. Have each of you name three good things that have happened during the day and why you believe they happened. Studies show that when you focus on the positive instead of on the negative you are more enthusiastic, alert, determined, and attentive. Wow, those are some benefits! Every evening before falling asleep, tell Jesus why you're grateful. You'll be amazed. Practice right now, so you'll be ready for bedtime: "I am grateful for . . ."

Scripture

"The gentle are blessed, because they will inherit the earth."—Matthew 5:5 (HCSB)

"You're blessed when you're content with just who you are—no more, no less. That's the moment you find yourselves proud owners of everything that can't be bought."—Matthew 5:5 (MSG)

Grace

Father God, thank you for our family, our friends, and this meal. We give thanks for knowing you because it puts us on solid ground. Teach us that being gentle isn't the same thing as being weak—it means power through controlled strength and not feeling as though we need to prove ourselves to others. Teach us that those who are gentle are blessed with lots of peace and are guided and taught by the Lord, lifted up, and saved.* Lord, this is a great lesson for us to think about. Amen.

*See Psalm 25:9.

Grace notes

Some Bible translations use the words "meek" or "humble" instead of "gentle." Jesus and Moses both described themselves as being meek.* How about that!? A gentle person shows his or her strength by not reacting with anger or frustration. Take time to respond; that way you'll have better control over what you say or do. "Nothing is so strong as gentleness," said Saint Francis de Sales, "nothing so gentle as real strength." What do you think that means? How can strength and gentleness be connected?

*Matthew 11:29; Numbers 12:3

Scripture

"The next day John [the Baptist] saw Jesus coming toward him and said, 'Look! The Lamb of God who takes away the sin of the world! He is the one I was talking about when I said, "A man is coming after me who is far greater than I am, for he existed long before me."'—John 1:29–30 (NLT)

Grace

God Almighty, thank you for being all-important in our lives. Thank you for this food and for all your blessings. Please watch over us so we don't become so full of ourselves that we lose our appetite for you. Help us to realize your truth that says the less important we feel (the more humble we are) the more important—valuable—we can be in your kingdom. Teach us why: when we honor you as being the most important you do great and wonderful things through us. Lord, your greatness knows no end. We praise you. Amen.

Grace notes

John the Baptist called Jesus the Lamb of God not because he knew Jesus to be good, gentle, and rarely angered, but because he knew ahead of time that Jesus, like a lamb about to be put on the altar,* would offer himself as the final sacrifice for our sins. John the Baptist knew well the Old Testament Scriptures, and everyone understood that lambs were an important part of Israel's religious traditions: a sinner's acceptable substitute payment for sins. John knew, though, that this kind of sacrifice was only temporary and that it would take an act as extreme and conclusive (final) as the crucifixion of God's only Son to give us eternal life with him. Just as Jesus did not come to our world to be served but to serve others (like us!), we are to serve others as well. "Only a life lived for others is a life worthwhile," said the great physicist Albert Einstein.

*Isaiah 53:7

Scripture

"God is strong and can help you not to fall. He can bring you before his glory without any wrong in you and can give you great joy. He is the only God, the One who saves us. To him be glory, greatness, power, and authority through Jesus Christ our Lord for all time past, now, and forever. Amen."—Jude* 1:24–25 (NCV)

*Jude was Jesus' half brother

Grace

Almighty God, we give praise to you for your great glory. Thank you for your many blessings, including this food. Grant that we may belong to you, Lord, and only you, knowing that no one else deserves our love and loyalty. Remind us to show mercy and compassion to those who do not know your Good News. Help us to be more like Jesus so that others may see you in us. Amen.

Grace notes

Glory. Greatness. Power. Authority. Take a little time to talk together about each of these four words. The Bible uses these and other, similar words many times to express the character of God. The last three you can probably understand, but that first one, "glory"—is hard to explain. For now, think of glory as God's awesome presence and magnificence. Want to fill up with God's glory? Picture the brightest, purest light you can imagine, with angels singing heavenly notes in the background—and then open your heart and soul in prayer, inviting in the full majesty of God. How amazing that such a glorious God cares so much about little you! "God has no phone, but I talk to him," an unknown author is quoted as saying. "He has no Facebook, but he is still my friend. He does not have Twitter, but I still follow him." How about you?

Scripture

"Dear friend, do not imitate what is evil but what is good. Anyone who does what is good is from God. Anyone who does what is evil has not seen God."—3 John 11 (NIV)

Grace

Father God, we thank you for this food and for all your blessings. Help us understand that there is a difference between good people who sin* and people who choose to be wicked or who live their lives *for sin*. Those who know you, Lord, will ask for forgiveness; those who don't, won't. Encourage us to avoid those who do evil on purpose, because they want to, especially those who do bad things while pretending to be good. Help us to be smart and careful in associating with people who might harm or be a bad influence on us. Amen.

*All of us have sinned. See Romans 3:23.

Grace notes

In his short letter of 3 John, the apostle John was warning a group of early Christians about a traveling preacher who was creating disagreement among its members by promoting false ideas about Jesus. John put forth a careful plan to deal with this, urging his readers to encourage and support those who were teaching the truth and to not give any audience to the false teachers who had hidden underhanded motives. John knew that while no one *has to* believe in or obey God, people will have to deal with the consequences if they choose against him. "The Devil is not afraid to preach the will of God provided he can preach it his own way," warned the American writer Thomas Merton. Beware! Those who are against God often have a way of twisting his words to make them seem to say something different. Yes, it's still true today: if you play with sin, sin will play with you.

thyme

Scripture

"I am writing to remind you, dear friends, that we should love one another. This is not a new commandment, but one we have had from the beginning. Love means doing what God has commanded us, and he has commanded us to love one another, just as you heard from the beginning."—2 John 1:5–6 (NLT)

Grace

Dear Jesus, we want to be filled with your love and goodness, so full we can't wait to pass it along. Encourage us to think about the ways we want our friends to act toward us—and then act the same way to them (that goes for our non-friends, too)! Remind us that our love for you involves a whole bunch of attitudes and actions—one is gratefulness and another is obedience. Help our love for you spill over in our lives, causing us to act out our gratitude and obedience by treating others the way *you* treat them. Jesus, we are thankful for this food and for our family, gathered here around this table. Amen.

Grace notes

A friend is a very special person. (We're not talking about the Facebook-only kind of friend.) Friendship is a two-way street. A friend is someone whose laughter you can hear, whose smile you can see, and with whom you can share your thoughts and feelings. A friend is someone who can cheer you up or share your best moments. A friend is someone you care for and who cares for you. How many true friends can you say those things about? Probably no more than one or two. One of A. A. Milne's Winnie-the-Pooh stories shows what real friendship is like: "'I don't feel very much like Pooh today,' said Pooh. 'There there,' said Piglet. 'I'll bring you tea and honey until you do.'"

Scripture

[Paul is asking his friend Philemon to forgive Philemon's slave named Onesimus (ō-NES-e-muss)], who works for Philemon. He says, "So if you consider me your partner, welcome [back] Onesimus as you would welcome me. If he has done anything wrong to you or if he owes you anything, charge that to me."—Philemon 17–18 (NCV)

Grace

Gracious Father, you teach us that being sorry means being willing to make wrong things right again. Teach us that sometimes, when a friend is truly sorry, it's okay to help them get through their deserved punishment (without expecting anything in return). Thank you for your Word to nourish our souls and for this food to nourish our bodies. Please bless those who are too angry to forgive or too afraid to ask for forgiveness, because they need you during this hard time more than ever. Amen.

Grace notes

When you are in a position to help someone, do so. Listen to their troubles; take them seriously; and, if it would be helpful, encourage them to talk to a trusted adult friend. In today's Scripture Paul is offering to take on the burden of someone else's guilt. Does that remind you of anyone else? Isn't that what Jesus did? He took the blame, pain, and punishment for all our sins so that we can stand, forgiven and clean, in God's presence. Jesus loves you (and everyone else) that much. "God has piled all our sins, everything we've done wrong, on him, on him," said the prophet Isaiah.* Isaiah wrote these words long before Jesus was even born, but his prophecy from the Holy Spirit was right on target! One other point of information: slaves in Bible times were not slaves because of the color of their skin or because anyone thought them inferior. People became slaves for several reasons: they might have been captured in a war, or they might have volunteered for slavery to pay off a debt, learn a trade, or be taken care of. The Bible accepted slavery as a fact of life and didn't speak out against it, but Christianity sowed the seeds of its eventual abolishment.

*Isaiah 53:6(b) (MSG)

Scripture

"Everything is clean to the clean-minded; nothing is clean to dirty-minded unbelievers. They leave their dirty fingerprints on every thought and act. They say they know God, but their actions speak louder than their words. They're real creeps, disobedient good-for-nothings."—Titus 1:15–16 (MSG)

Grace

Dear Jesus, thank you for reminding us of the importance of our actions. Inspire us to be good examples so we can earn the right to be heard. Encourage us to act in ways that reflect your teachings. Thank you for our family and for your many other blessings, including this food. Amen.

Grace notes

This Scripture doesn't mean that you will never have bad thoughts—you will, because they're part of being human. It's about the importance of your actions representing God's good name to a watching world. It's also good advice to keep your distance from bad situations that could cause you to have bad or impure thoughts. Have you heard the saying "Walk your talk and talk your walk"? What's that about? Or, as the American poet Ralph Waldo Emerson put it: "What you do speaks so loud that I cannot hear you speak."

sage

Scripture

"This is what the Lord says: The wise man must not boast in his wisdom; the strong man must not boast in his strength; the wealthy man must not boast in his wealth. But the one who boasts should boast in this, that he understands and knows Me—that I am Yahweh, showing faithful love, justice, and righteousness on the earth, for I delight in these things. This is the Lord's declaration."—Jeremiah 9:23–24 (HCSB)

Grace

Almighty God, we praise your holy name, asking your blessing upon our family and on this food. We're happy you are here with us; fill us with your Spirit, Lord. Help us to always remember that our talents and achievements come from you. Remind us to tell others how wonderful you are, God-boasting to everyone. We bow our heads in thanks for your blessings and boast of your faithful love. We like to say, "God is good, all the time. All the time, God is good." Amen.

Grace notes

To admit that your talents and abilities come from God is a huge step toward becoming even more gifted. But to boast about your accomplishments as though you're the reason for this success gets in God's way and hurts his heart; it's called pride. And once pride works its way into your brain it's really hard to whack it back down. Recognizing and accepting God's role in your life requires humility, prayer, and praise. "Every human activity, except sin, can be done for God's pleasure, if you do it with an attitude of praise," said the American pastor and author Rick Warren.

mint

Scripture

"May Jesus himself and God our Father, who reached out in love and surprised you with gifts of unending help and confidence, put a fresh heart in you, invigorate your work, enliven your speech." —2 Thessalonians 2:16–17 (MSG)

Grace

Oh Lord, we can't help but be surprised and encouraged by your unending love. Show us that though we may stumble and fall you are always there to pick us up and brush us off. Be with us when the task is hard. Help us remember that you are right there with us, cheering us on. Thank you for our family, our friends, and this food we're so hungry for. Jesus, you rock! Amen.

Grace notes

In the same way that you train hard to win a track and field event, practice your music scales over and over again, or study for a math test, getting closer to Jesus through his Word takes training and discipline. Keep your eye on the prize, Jesus Christ; start and end with him and you'll always be on the winning side. Even though your best efforts will never be perfect, Jesus asks for your heart, not your perfection, and he has picked you for his team. "A man does not have to be an angel to be a saint," said the Nobel prize winner Dr. Albert Schweitzer. Now that's a prize-winning thought!

Scripture

"Rejoice, O people of Zion! Shout in triumph, O people of Jerusalem! Look, your king is coming to you. He is righteous and victorious, yet he is humble, riding on a donkey—riding on a donkey's colt." —Zechariah 9:9 (NLT)

Grace

Lord Jesus, thank you for this food and for all your blessings. Remind us that from the beginning of time your perfect plan was planned perfectly. Help us to see through the eyes of the prophet Zechariah, who wrote about you, Jesus, riding into Jerusalem on a donkey—500 years before you were born! May we praise your name, Jesus, calling out what the crowds were shouting as you rode humbly into town on the back of that gentle donkey: "Hosanna! Blessed is he who comes in the name of the Lord!"* Amen.

*Matthew 21:9

Grace notes

Zechariah lived in a time when a king on parade was expected to act so high and mighty—so full of himself and of his own importance—that his arrival would strike fear and awe into the hearts of everyone along the route. Standard practice. So for Zechariah to predict that the Messiah would come in peace, approachable to all, was a revolutionary idea. Jesus did a lot of that—surprising people with radically new and different ideas—all of them grounded in humility and love. "All you need is love," said Charles Schulz, the creator of the Peanuts cartoons, "but a little chocolate now and then doesn't hurt." Ha ha! What kind of sweets do you think Jesus liked best?

bay

Scripture

"Then the Lord sent this message through the prophet Haggai: 'Why are you living in luxurious houses while my house lies in ruins? This is what the Lord of Heaven's Armies says: Look at what's happening to you! You have planted much but harvest little. You eat but are not satisfied. You drink but are still thirsty. You put on clothes but cannot keep warm. Your wages disappear as though you were putting them in pockets filled with holes!'"—Haggai 1:3–6 (NLT)

Grace

Mighty God, we lift up our hearts to you. May we always remember this: it matters how we live. Help us see that sometimes, though we don't mean to, we give you only our leftovers—leftover time, leftover energy, and leftover money. Teach us that by straightening out our priorities we crowd out troubles from our hearts to make room for joy. Before we eat, we do what is more important: ask for your blessing, thank you for this food, and joyfully greet you in our hearts. Amen.

Grace notes

Are your days really busy? Are tons of things grabbing your attention? Like school, homework, sports, chores, . . . oh, yes, and God. Oops, shouldn't God be at the top? Does he get only your leftovers? If you want to fix that, give it some serious thoughts and then put those thoughts into action. (Things don't get done by themselves.) What will you discover when you put God first on your list? Lean on him and find out. One thing is for sure: your joy will increase. Putting God first won't always be easy, but the rewards will be big. "Action expresses priorities," said Mahatma Gandhi, a leader in India. And neither the actions nor the priorities behind them happen by themselves.

parsley

Scripture

"I'm singing joyful praise to God. I'm turning cartwheels of joy to my Savior God. Counting on God's Rule to prevail, I take heart and gain strength. I run like a deer. I feel like I'm king of the mountain!" —Habakkuk 3:18–19 (MSG)

Grace

Lord, thank you for the food that gives us strength and for your Word that brings us closer to you (that gives us strength, too, we know!). Remind us, Lord, to praise you even when life seems too hard, too much, and too complicated. We can't know in advance just how or when or where you will work in our lives. Encourage us to trust you, Lord. Even though our joy makes us feel like king of the mountain, we know that you, the one who fills us with that joy, are the real King! Thank you for blessing us and caring for us. Thank you, too, for hearing our prayers. Amen.

Grace notes

Learning to be grateful is one of the best gifts you can give yourself—and, of course, that you can give God. Research shows that, over time, habits of gratitude (how about saying, out loud every day, something you are grateful for?) will make you happier than the best ever birthday present. From gratitude comes more appreciation, and from more appreciation comes more thankfulness—both keep getting bigger and better. "When you rise in the morning, give thanks for the light, for your life, for your strength. Give thanks for your food and for the joy of living. If you see no reason to give thanks, the fault lies in yourself," said the Shawnee chief Tecumseh.

Scripture

"And the kingdom will be the LORD's."—Obadiah 21(b) (NIV)

Grace

Dear Father, you are our Lord and Savior. Thank you for reminding us that everything really does belong to you, that you control our history and our destiny, and that your goodness will always win the day. Teach us to be calm in the face of trouble, for you are with us and love us. We give thanks, Lord, for this food and for our family. Make us your willing, grateful servants. Amen.

Grace notes

The book of Obadiah in the Old Testament was written at least 500 years before Jesus was born. Obadiah was saying that the kingdom, or kingship, would belong to the promised Messiah when he came. Fast forward, and we find Jesus telling the Pharisees (Jewish religious leaders): "The kingdom of God is within you" (Luke 17:21). Jesus was telling these leaders not to look to the sky for some great sign that the Messiah was coming because he was already there among them—already in their midst. He still is! The American Bible scholar Walter Wink said this about Christ's kingdom: "To worship is to remember who owns the house."

mint

Scripture

"Create in me a clean heart, O God. Renew a loyal spirit within me."—Psalm 51:10 (NLT)

"Soak me in your laundry and I'll come out clean, scrub me and I'll have a snow-white life."—Psalm 51:10 (MSG)

Grace

Dear Father, when we don't get it right please help us see the light. Press the restart button on our hearts and renew our spirits. Teach us that a forgiven person is more than just the same person spruced up or cleaned up but a brand new person! A new and updated version. We thank you for this food, Lord. Encourage cravings in us for food that is healthy, too, knowing that you have charged us with taking care of the bodies you gave us. Amen.

Grace notes

God knows you'll never be perfect—at least not while you're here on this earth. That would be impossible; that's just how it is in the world we live in. A word of caution here, though: don't let any guilt feelings destroy what God loves in you. He has loved you, after all, before you sinned, while you sinned, and after you sinned. He understands what it's like to be human because Jesus made the choice to become a man. All Jesus asks is that you maintain a relationship with him by loving and trusting him and by loving others. Prayer is the way to keep that connection strong. "Prayer is not asking. It is a longing of the soul. It is daily admission of one's weakness. It is better in prayer to have a heart without words than words without a heart," said Mahatma Gandhi, a leader in India. How can a heart without words be a kind of prayer?

Scripture

"The LORD does not easily become angry, but he is powerful and never lets the guilty go unpunished. Where the LORD walks, storms arise; the clouds are the dust raised by his feet!"—Nahum 1:3 (GNT)

Grace

Heavenly Father, we ask your blessing on this food, and in our hearts we sing of your glory. Let us be strong in your mighty power. Remind us that we can trust in your fair and perfect justice, that you will right every wrong—even if we're not around to see you do it. Remind us, too, that you give everyone time to become right with you—to ask for forgiveness. Amen.

Grace notes

God is slow to anger; that means he's very patient. He wants to give you time to see things his way. If you stiffen up at the thought of having to give up your ways—or else—know that someday you'll be very glad about his patience. A good thing about growing up is that the process allows you to *grow into* thoughts and habits that will help you get along in the world. "The greatest thing in this world is not so much where we are, but in what direction we are moving," said the American Supreme Court justice Oliver Wendell Holmes Jr. You yourself may be young, but you're already moving in one direction or the other. It's not where you start that matters but where you end up. How true is that!?

bay

Scripture

"You stood there and watched. You were as bad as [Israel's enemies] were. You shouldn't have gloated over your brother when he was down-and-out. You shouldn't have laughed and joked at Judah's sons when they were face down in the mud. You shouldn't have talked so big when everything was so bad."—Obadiah 12 (MSG)

Grace

Father God, bless our food and our time here together. Thank you for your Word that helps us to better live with you at our center. Lord, remind us never to excuse a bullying or mocking kind of behavior. Help us see that laughing at someone who is being bullied makes us as guilty as the bully. Please Lord, remind us of your two greatest commandments: to love you most of all and to love other people as much as we love ourselves.* May your words open our eyes and lift our hearts. Amen.

*Matthew 22:36–40

Grace notes

Do you know what a bystander is? It's someone who is there at the scene of a crime or accident but doesn't get involved. In the case of bullying, if you watch it happening but do nothing you are contributing to the problem. You're giving the bully an audience, which is exactly what bullies want. You have the power to stop the bullying, though, even if you don't feel confident stepping in yourself to confront the bully. Go and get help. If you don't, at the best you'll feel guilty and at the worst you might become the next victim. "If you are neutral in situations of injustice, you have chosen the side of the oppressor," said the South African social rights leader Desmond Tutu. "If an elephant has its foot on the tail of a mouse and you say that you are neutral, the mouse will not appreciate your neutrality," he said. Neither would you!

Scripture

"What can I offer the Lord for all his goodness to me?"—Psalm 116:12 (GNT)

"Being cheerful keeps you healthy. It is slow death to be gloomy all the time."—Proverbs 17:22 (GNT)

Grace

Heavenly Father, it makes us happy to say grace, to be together, and to talk about things that matter. Give us a craving for your Word that feeds our soul and from which goodness flows. Help us to see how important it is to be grateful—that without gratitude we cannot be either happy or pleasing to you. Amen.

Grace notes

God wants you to be thankful because the more thankful you are the happier and fuller your life will become. So why not be full of grateful? Next time you appreciate something your mom does for you, for example, instead of just saying an ordinary, routine-type "thanks," how about something like "You made my day, Mom—thanks!" Not only does that make God happy (a really big deal), but just imagine how big Mom's smile (and yours) could get? "You are much happier when you are happy than when you ain't," said the American poet Ogden Nash. *Hmmm!* Ain't that the truth!

Scripture

"'I am the one who answers your prayers and watches over you. I am like a fir tree that is always green. Your fruit comes from me.' A wise person understands these things, and a smart person should learn them. The Lord's ways are right. Good people will live by them. Sinners will die by them."—Hosea 14: 8(b)–9 (ERV)

Grace

Merciful Father, thank you so much for this food and for your Word that tells us the secrets of a good and happy life. Help us with your strong and loving reminders of how full a life we can have when we're right with you, the one and only true God. Help us to be thankful, too, that one step at a time is just fine with you—we crawl first, and then we walk. We remember, too, that you are always the God of Second Chances. Praises again and again for that! Amen.

Grace notes

God loves you, even when you've done something wrong. He understands that you are human and yearns to give you a second chance. Sinners who never learn or regret what they do, but instead keep on committing the same sins over and over again, bring negative consequences on themselves. God wants you to be wiser today than you were yesterday. "We all have big changes in our lives that are more or less a second chance," said the actor Harrison Ford. Any you'd care to share?

Scripture

"Yes, God's riches are very great! His wisdom and knowledge have no end! No one can explain what God decides. No one can understand his ways. As the Scriptures say, 'Who can know what is on the Lord's mind? Who is able to give him advice?' 'Who has ever given God anything? God owes nothing to anyone.' Yes, God made all things. And everything continues through him and for him. To God be the glory forever! Amen."—Romans 11:33–36 (NCV)

Grace

Wonderful Counselor and Father, we bow our heads in wonder at your majesty. Thank you for our family, our friends, and this meal. Please bless the sick and poor and the people in trouble and give them strength. May we always remember that your ways are immeasurably higher than our ways, Lord, but that you still understand us, because we're the creatures you made. Give us the wisdom to depend on your mysterious ways. Help us listen to and follow your words to grow our character, to become the people you meant us to be, and to let your light shine through us so that we may, with your Spirit's help, accomplish good things in your name and for your kingdom. Alleluia! Amen.

Grace notes

God is on your side, working to transform you into a better and better person. And the more you learn about God, the more you'll understand his ways. Of course, none of us will ever know him completely, but the effort you make to do so is called progress. "Progress always involves risk; you can't steal second base and keep your foot on first," said the American journalist Robert Quillen. Progress—learning new things—also means stepping out of your comfort zone. Do you know what a comfort zone is? It's a feeling that life—all the things you regularly do—is familiar and easy. If you've picked up some new skills your comfort zone is bigger than it used to be. That time and effort it took to acquire those new skills and new ways of looking at things—they're all about your comfort zone growing and expanding, plopping you into a new world of bigger possibilities. That's the run between first and second. That's the tapping into God's riches!

thyme

Scripture

"I'll give you a new heart, put a new spirit in you. I'll remove the stone heart from your body and replace it with a heart that's God-willed, not self-willed."—Ezekiel 36:26 (MSG)

"If you can?" said Jesus. "Everything is possible for the one who believes."—Mark 9:23 (NIrV)

Grace

Lord, we are grateful that we can be a part of your family. Please bless this food before us. We are grateful for your forgiveness, your mercy, and your grace. Please bless us so that we can be fruitful in your sight. We pray that our will may line up with your will because that's when the impossible becomes possible. We believe in you. Amen.

Grace notes

Watch what happens when someone becomes a follower of Jesus. Sooner or later you'll see changes in that person. They'll become different somehow. Rough edges will be smoothed, they won't be so quick to get mad, and their outlook will be more positive and more grateful. *Hmmm*—could that person you're watching just be *you*? "Impossible is just a big word thrown around by small men who find it easier to live in the world they've been given than to explore the power they have to change it," said the boxing great Mohammed Ali. He went on, "Impossible is not a fact. It's an opinion. Impossible is not a declaration. It's a dare. Impossible is potential. Impossible is temporary. Impossible is nothing." What "impossible" thing is in your heart?

Scripture

"The Lord is good to those who hope in him, to those who seek him. It is good to wait quietly for the Lord to save. It is good for someone to work hard while he is young."—Lamentations 3:25–27 (NCV)

Grace

Heavenly Father, thank you for this food, our family, and our friends. Thank you for our teachers who are patient with us and encourage us to work hard. Inspire in us the confidence that paying attention, doing our work, and studying will pay off. Help us to grow up not only smart but also wise about how we can best use our smarts. Watch over us as we learn the important lessons in life, like common sense, self-control, patience, determination, and the importance of knowing your Word. All of these good things come with practice—and with you by our side. Amen.

Grace notes

God is good to those who put their hope in him. He wants you to develop positive moral habits while you're young so that you can live your whole life fully and well. "Would you like to swing on a star? Carry moonbeams home in a jar? And be better off than you are? Or would you rather be a mule?" Your mom and dad may know the rest of the words to "Swinging on a Star" by the American songwriter Johnny Burke. If not, find it on YouTube. Such fun!

Scripture

"Love can't be bought, love can't be sold—it's not to be found in the marketplace."—Song of Songs 8:7 (MSG)

Grace

Heavenly Father, thank you for this food. Please bless our families—as well as those in our world who feel lonely or unloved. May we always remember that your love comes freely, without a price tag. Fill us with thankfulness that each of us is Number 1 in your book. *El Shaddai*, we love *this* sound of your holy name. Praise be to you. Amen.

Grace notes

Jesus' love for you cannot be bought at any price. No matter how good you are, no matter what you do or don't do—God loves you just the same. And if you love him right back you will show it by the kind of person you become. Getting to know God's different names helps you see the different sides to his character, to who he is. *El Shaddai*, for instance, means God Almighty. In a prayer tell God what it means to you that he is not only absolutely powerful but also your friend. The process will bring you closer to him, and isn't that a great way to become a better person? The professional baseball player turned evangelist preacher Billy Sunday changed thousands of lives. "There are 256 names given in the Bible for the Lord Jesus Christ," he said, "and I suppose this was because he was infinitely beyond all that any one name could express." Of all his traits, none is more important than his changeless love. God *is* love, the Bible tells us.* "Love" is so much a part of him that it's like one of his names, then, right? Praise him!

*1 John 4:8

Scripture

"I intend to build a great temple, because our God is greater than any other god. Yet no one can really build a temple for God, because even all the vastness of heaven cannot contain him. How then can I build a temple that would be anything more than a place to burn incense to God?"—2 Chronicles 2:5–6 (GNT)

Grace

Thank you, Lord, for blessing us with your gifts, for this food, and for our family; we don't want to take any of your gifts for granted. We know we couldn't begin to build a temple or a house big enough, strong enough, or splendid enough to honor you—even your awesome universe can't contain you, and yet you choose to make your home in each of our hearts.* Now *there's* a Wow! Help us to show those around us by our actions that you've made yourself at home in us. We are amazed by your blessings. Amen.

*1 Corinthians 6:19

Grace notes

In Hebrew times parents' hopes for their new baby and for his or her personal qualities and reputation were reflected in the name they chose to give to him or her. Solomon wanted to build a temple to enhance the power and influence of God's *name*—to show the surrounding nations that God was almighty, holy, and everywhere present. This temple wasn't built for God himself but for God's *name*—that's an important difference. A temple built for God would have suggested that God could have been contained—that he would have fit—within its walls. Solomon knew that would have been impossible. "God is great not just because nothing is too big for Him," said the American pastor Mark Batterson. "God is great because nothing is too small for Him, either."

Scripture

"With God's help I can jump over a wall."—Psalm 18:29(b) (NCV)

Grace

Almighty God, you are our rock, our great protector. Keep us safe, and help us to grow up strong in the ways that count. Show us the power of your Word, Lord, for all our strength comes from you. Guide us in your mighty ways; light our path with wisdom and understanding so that we too can confidently face any obstacle, climb any mountain, jump over any obstacle. With you, God, nothing is impossible.* Amen.

*Luke 1:37

Grace notes

Sometimes God won't let you jump over that wall—for reasons he chooses not to share. Is that a bad thing? It depends on how you look at it. It just might be that on the other side of that wall—that humungous challenge or risk—waits great danger. Allow God to use all your life experiences to prepare you for greater and greater things. Let him use everything that happens in your life to teach you what you need—qualities like never giving up, humility, and fairness. "Sometimes you come up against a mountain and you end up making the mountain seem bigger than God," said the NBA star Jeremy Lin. Mountains are like anthills to God, aren't they?

Scripture

"Jesus is the One whom God raised from the dead. And we are all witnesses to this. Jesus was lifted up to heaven and is now at God's right side. The Father has given the Holy Spirit to Jesus as he promised. So Jesus has poured out that Spirit, and this is what you now see and hear."—Acts 2:32–34 (NCV)

Grace

Dear Jesus, thank you for loving us, for making your home in our hearts, and for our family gathered here. Please bless our food. Lord, remind us that you live in each of us through the Holy Spirit. Help us understand and remember that you are so close we can hear you speak to us if we're only willing to listen. Guide us and direct our way, Lord, for we believe in your love. Plant in us the desire to be ever closer to you. Watch over us, and bless us as a family. Amen.

Grace notes

Imagine what it would have been like to see Jesus walk up to you after you'd witnessed his death. When the time came, like in that room where God sent the Holy Spirit into his disciples, there would have been no doubt in your mind that the Holy Spirit, God himself, had poured himself into you. Now, today, believe that that very same Holy Spirit needs only an invitation to move in with you. The wise pastor and author Max Lucado said, "The Wizard of Oz says look inside yourself and find self. God says look inside yourself and find the Holy Spirit. The first will get you to Kansas. The latter will get you to heaven. Take your pick."

bay

Scripture

"Come to the Lord, all you who are not proud, who obey his laws. Do what is right. Learn to be humble."—Zephaniah 2:3(a) (NCV)

"The Lord your God is with you; the mighty One will save you. He will rejoice over you. You will rest in his love; he will sing and be joyful about you."—Zephaniah 3:17 (NCV)

Grace

Our great God in heaven, we humbly come before you, asking your blessing in every way. Thank you for this food and for our time together. Encourage us, Lord, to live in your ways, to seek you, to be right with you, and to rest in your unchanging love, through good times and bad. Help us to be excited about you, because it's only in your light that we can bloom like the unfolding petals of flowers in the sun. Lord, we long to hear your joyful laughter as you appreciate just being with us, your beloved children. Amen.

Grace notes

God loves you so much. Did you know that *you* have his undivided attention, now and always? He's the ultimate multi-tasker; he can pay attention to everyone at the same time! He doesn't expect perfection; he knows you're a work in progress. Just as you can't see the wind but know it's there, you can trust in Jesus; he's as real as can be. "God has editing rights over our prayers. He will edit them, correct them, bring them in line with His will and then hand them back to us to be resubmitted," said the American pastor Stephen Crotts. Now that's *some parenting!*

Scripture

"The people [of Israel] will throw their silver into the streets, and their gold will be like trash. Their silver and gold will not save them from the Lord's anger. It will not satisfy their hunger or fill their stomachs, because it caused them to fall into sin. They were proud of their beautiful jewelry and used it to make their idols and their evil statues, which I hate. So I will turn their wealth into trash."—Ezekiel 7:19–20 (NCV)

Grace

Almighty God, we come before you with grateful hearts for your goodness and generosity. We thank you for all your blessings. May we understand that money itself isn't bad—it's *the love of it*, not the good it can do, that causes the problem. Help us to remember that you're the one who gives us the talents that gain for us the wealth we enjoy. Inspire us to worship you and not the things of this world. Lord, we thank you for this food, our family, and all the important things *money cannot buy*. Create in our hearts an attitude of gratitude. Amen.

Grace notes

Sometimes it seems as though some truckloads of money would solve all your family's problems, doesn't it? If you're thinking that way, though, you might want to think again. Most lottery winners will tell you that the mounds of gold have ruined their lives and that they now wish they had torn up that winning ticket. Seven of every ten people who receive what we call "windfall cash" lose it within a few years. Like anything else in this world, if you're not ready to handle great wealth it will handle you. "Let us more and more insist on raising funds of love, of kindness, of understanding, of peace. Money will come if we seek first the Kingdom of God—the rest will be given," said the unselfish Catholic nun known to the world as Mother Teresa.

Scripture

"Do you want to enjoy life? Do you want to have many happy days? Then avoid saying anything hurtful, and never let a lie come out of your mouth. Stop doing anything evil, and do good. Look for peace, and do all you can to help people live peacefully."—Psalm 34:12–14 (ERV)

Grace

Heavenly Father, we hear your words of wisdom—they are like the best, sweetest-tasting desserts. You give us many reasons to be kind to others. Inspire us to remember how much good comes from having you in our life—from living in the same way you would. Give us the wisdom to see that showing goodness to others is good for us, honors you, and makes everyone happy. We want to be happy. Thank you for this meal, and please bless our family. Amen.

Grace notes

It's good to have rules—for the other guy, right? Sometimes it feels that way—there are so many do's and don'ts for kids that it can be hard to keep track. You may be surprised to learn that it's the same way for grown-ups. All of us are social beings who need rules in order to get along and to cooperate with one another. The people around us can be a pain sometimes, but imagine the chaos if there were no rules, for example, about driving along the road. One of the best rules going is to be kind to others—in Jesus' words, to love others just as much as we love our own selves. God has been around for a long, long time (that's certainly true, since he *created* time!), and he knows what will allow you to be the happiest. "Kindness is the language which the deaf can hear and the blind can see," said the American author Mark Twain. *Nobody* fails to notice and appreciate kindness!

Scripture

"The Lord's teachings are perfect. They give strength to his people. The Lord's rules can be trusted. They help even the foolish become wise. The Lord's laws are right. They make people happy. The Lord's commands are good. They show people the right way to live."—Psalm 19:7–8 (ERV)

Grace

Gracious Father, thank you for this day, for your blessings, and for this food. Please bless our family and friends. Grant us good judgment, Lord, to let the Bible teach us what is right and wrong. Remind us to pray for guidance. Remind us, too, that you know everything about us and can see the road ahead, even when we can't. Teach us not to worry about where the path will take us, but instead to just follow you, watching for your footprints with confidence that you will lead us along the right path. Amen.

Grace notes

Following Jesus will give shape, purpose, and character to your life. As Dr. Mark L. Strauss reminds us: "God doesn't give you rules to control your life. He gives you rules to protect you. Look at God's heart behind the commands." If you do, you'll see the spirit of the law. All you have to do is let him lead. Look to Jesus, and he will make your path smooth and straight.* "God helps those who help themselves," said Ben Franklin. Many people think those words come from the Bible, but they don't. They're true *only*, we might want to say to Ben, if you throw in a heaping helping of God's grace and mercy.

*Proverbs 3:6

Scripture

"The temptations in your life are no different from what others experience. And God is faithful. He will not allow the temptation to be more than you can stand. When you are tempted, he will show you a way out so that you can endure."—1 Corinthians 10:13 (NLT)

Grace

Heavenly Father, please bless our dinner, and thank you for your promise to be with us always. We pray for guidance, for help in understanding that you will be stronger than any temptation if we will only seek you out. Remind us to call on you through prayer and when we are tempted, to do this: RUN! Father, you see the good in us in spite of the bad; you know our limits, and you still love us more than we could ever imagine. We are humbled by your protection and love. Blessed be your name, dear God. Amen.

Grace notes

Many people mistakenly think this verse means that God will never give you more pain or heartache than you can handle. It doesn't mean that at all. What it does say is that God will not allow you to be tempted to do wrong beyond your *ability* to say no. In other words, whatever it is that's tempting you, Jesus has already decided that, with his help, you're strong enough to walk the other way. Now, whether you choose to live up to that ability is your choice. (If you have trouble telling the difference between a temptation and a test, maybe this will help: a temptation might start out as a one-time test, but it could lead to a pattern of bad behavior—an example: being dishonest gets easier every time you tell a lie. A true test—you'll know this only after you've come out on the other side successfully—is a God-inspired event that will mature you and make you stronger. Remember that, unlike tests, temptations never come from God.) "We gain the strength of the temptation we resist," said the American poet Ralph Waldo Emerson. It's the saying no, not the temptation itself, that gives us that power. Choose truth!

bay

249

Scripture

"The eye cannot say to the hand, 'I don't need you!' And the head cannot say to the foot, 'I don't need you!'"—1 Corinthians 12:21 (NCV)

Grace

Wonderful Father, thank you for this food and for our family. Thank you, too, for this day. Remind us that you've chosen for each of us special gifts we call talents. Encourage us to value what we've been given and not be jealous of others and their gifts. Remind us that everybody's abilities and offerings contribute to your kingdom work—just as our eyes, hands, and ears all work together for each of us. Remind us we can't have a baseball game if everyone wants to be the pitcher. Amen.

Grace notes

The worst team players are the great athletes who insist on being the stars, who play for themselves only. Being a team player is actually great fun, even if, for instance, you have to bunt out in order to help your teammates move around the bases. "Finding good players is easy," said the Hall of Fame baseball coach Casey Stengel. "Getting them to play as a team is another story." "I scratch your back and you scratch mine" is another way of saying "Let's help each other get the job done."

parsley

Scripture

"My children, our love should not be just words and talk; it must be true love, which shows itself in action."—1 John 3:18 (GNT)

Grace

Wonderful Jesus, thank you for your love for us. Thank you for this food and for our family—we love each other, too. Give us each a desire to always follow up our good promises with action. Teach us that being true to our word gives us a reputation for goodness. Teach us to be joyful givers—forces of action that will make a difference in this "*Me! me!*" world. Amen.

Grace notes

Have you had enough of people who say one thing but do another? Just make sure you don't fall into the same trap. It's a good idea, every once in a while, to ask yourself how big a helper you've been: "What have I done for someone lately?" The actor Will Smith had this to say: "If you're not making someone else's life better, then you're wasting your time. Your life will become better by making other lives better." Oh, he does know his lines!

Scripture

"Be content with who you are, and don't put on airs. God's strong hand is on you; he'll promote you at the right time. Live carefree before God; he is most careful with you."—1 Peter 5:6–7 (MSG)

Grace

Father God, please bless this food and our family. We love being with each other, so help us to be loving. Teach us to trust and believe in you, because that is how we grow strong. Inspire us to be happy in your love and goodness—in knowing that we are your handiwork. And what an artist you are, God . . . Help us to remember that, since you are the artist and we are the art, all the glory belongs to you. Amen.

Grace notes

Get ahead of God and you'll find yourself in trouble. In other words, pride in your own accomplishments will put you in quicksand faster than Superman can leap a tall building. "The proud person always wants to do the right thing, the great thing," said the Danish philosopher Søren Kierkegaard. "But because he wants to do it in his own strength, he is fighting not with man, but with God."

mint

Scripture

"The master [said to the servant], 'You did well. You are a good and loyal servant. Because you were loyal with small things, I will let you care for much greater things. Come and share my joy with me.'" —Matthew 25:21 (NCV)

Grace

Dear Jesus, we are thankful for all you give us, especially right now for this delicious-smelling meal and the togetherness with those we love. Please bless our food. Remind us that being faithful to you and believing in your plans for us allow us to grow into good people. Help us to show our loyalty to you in all things, Lord. Amen.

Grace notes

If you prove yourself dependable in the little things, you'll graduate to bigger and bigger responsibilities as time goes by. That means listening well and following instructions. What does *listening well* look like? It means not looking at your phone or video game when someone is talking to you—look into their eyes instead. Use body language, like nodding your head, to show that you're listening. Don't think about your response while they're still talking—wait and listen. Do those things and you'll be amazed at how much less trouble you'll get into. "As I learned from growing up, you don't mess with your grandmother," said Prince William, Duke of Cambridge. Good advice for everyone, even if your grandmother isn't the Queen of England.

Scripture

"The Holy Spirit produces this kind of fruit in our lives: love, joy, peace, patience, kindness, goodness, faithfulness, gentleness, and self-control."—Galatians 5:22–23(a) (NLT)

Grace

Loving Father, we thank you for your blessings, including this food, our family, and our friends. We thank you for the joy and peace in our hearts when we think of you. We thank you for reminding us that patience, kindness, and goodness come with practice. We thank you for your grace that saves us and for teaching us the wisdom of self-discipline. We thank you for teaching us to live in your way, because that's the way your gifts come to us. Amen.

Grace notes

If you ever hear someone say something like "You can tell that so-and-so is a good person by the *fruit* they produce," you'll know now what that means. *Fruit* sums up the nine qualities that Paul talked about: love, joy, peace, patience, kindness, goodness, faithfulness, gentleness, and self-control. These *fruits* come through the Holy Spirit when you develop a relationship with Jesus. The Holy Spirit places this fruit in you as you draw closer to him, and developing that relationship involves prayer, worship, and doing what God tells you to do. Also, the more you develop these qualities the more courage you'll have to do or say what is right, even when other people disagree. For example, it took great courage for the Italian explorer Christopher Columbus to set sail across the huge, unknown ocean. Listen to his words: "It was the Lord who put into my mind that fact that it would be possible to sail from here to the Indies. All who heard of my project rejected it with laughter, ridiculing me. There is no question that the inspiration was from the Holy Spirit because He comforted me with rays of marvelous inspiration from the Holy Scriptures." If Columbus had not first developed the qualities of self-control, patience, and faithfulness, among other things, do you think he could have done what he did?

Scripture

"With a loud cry Jesus died. The curtain hanging in the Temple was torn in two, from top to bottom. The army officer who was standing there in front of the cross saw how Jesus had died. 'This man was really the Son of God!' he said."—Mark 15:37–39 (GNT)

Grace

Dear Jesus, thank you for the food that gives our bodies fuel. Thank you for your sacrificial death and resurrection that give our lives meaning. May the richness of your glory shine on us and guide us as we grow. Help us to love others in the same way you love us. Teach us that ripping apart the temple curtain was your Father's way of saying that nothing can ever again come between us and you. Jesus, you offer us a whole new way of life,* but it's up to us to accept your sacrifice, ask your forgiveness, invite you into our hearts, and put our faith in you. You died to change our lives, but we have to give you permission to do so. We are so grateful for your unbelievable love. Amen.

*See John 14:6

Grace notes

Before Jesus made the perfect sacrifice for our sins that allowed us to be in God's presence, no one could look upon the face of God and live.* That was because God is holy—perfectly holy—and sin cannot exist in his presence. God gave instructions to build that giant curtain to keep people (other than the high priest) from entering the holiest of holy places; he wanted to protect them. At the exact moment of Jesus' death, though, God ripped the curtain in half to show that Jesus' sacrifice made it possible for anyone to "walk through the curtain" to him (God). This was not just any curtain, mind you; it was 83 feet high, and it took the strength of 300 priests to lift it into place. (Jewish literature—called the Mishnah—said that this curtain was as thick as a man's hand, although this could have been an exaggeration. Think of a huge, thick hanging carpet.) Could anyone other than God have ripped it from top to bottom, right down the middle? God ripped the curtain to point our eyes to the cross, declaring that Jesus is the only way to him. "Jesus didn't die to save me from God. Jesus died to save me from myself," said the American author Ricky Maye. The curtain was there until the time that our sins could be wiped away. Do you see how the tearing of the curtain showed us that God isn't some angry force to be afraid of?

*Exodus 33:20

Scripture

"Those who cause trouble for their families will inherit nothing but the wind. A foolish person will end up as a servant to one who is wise."—Proverbs 11:29 (ERV)

Grace

Gracious Father, we thank you for your blessings, for this food, and for this day. Keep us from getting into trouble, like following the wrong crowd, so we can enjoy a life of peace and fulfillment under your care. Lord, guide us in choosing ways that are wise; we want Mom and Dad to be pleased with us and really want to avoid causing them heartache or problems. We pray for your guidance and strength, Lord. Amen.

Grace notes

You know what a troublemaker is, right? It's that person who's always causing problems, who loves more than anything else to do exactly what a grown-up tells them not to do. When someone deliberately refuses to do what they know is right you have to wonder why. You do know, don't you, that down the line they won't prosper; unless they change their ways they'll run a good chance of ending up in a dead-end job, with no one particularly happy to be around them. "While we are free to choose our actions, we are not free to choose the consequences of our actions," pointed out the author Stephen R. Covey. When have you had to face the consequences for a foolish action? Learn something from it, because experience is one of the best ways to gain wisdom.

Scripture

"'The most important [commandment],' answered Jesus, 'is this: "Hear, O Israel, the Lord our God, the Lord is one. Love the Lord your God with all your heart and with all your soul and with all your mind and with all your strength." The second is this: "Love your neighbor as yourself." There is no commandment greater than these.'"—Mark 12:29–31 (NIV)

Grace

Dear Jesus, thank you for this food and for being part of our lives. Hear ye, hear ye, everyone—we love God. *We love God!* And we love it that you loved us first! Teach us the best way to show what it means to love others, just as you say, Lord. We understand that you are asking us to love other people *not more than* but *as much as* we love ourselves—to love and value all people, including ourselves, equally, as you do. Help us see that your words come right out of the playbook for the most important "game" ever: a life of meaning and purpose. Remind us that the first step in a good life is to faithfully follow your teachings. You are our coach, Jesus, and we trust you. Amen.

Grace notes

You love God because he loves you. This isn't a part-time love meant only for days at church. It's a full-time job. And it's impossible to truly love him without also loving the other people he has created. To love him means that you treat others with love and consideration; it's his world and we play by his rules. The Washington Redskins Coach Joe Gibbs said it this way: "You and I are players, God's our coach, and we're playing the biggest game of all. We have a loving God that made us. We need to get on His team. It says in His word, there's only one way to Him and that's through Jesus Christ." No, life isn't all fun and games; loving God and others is serious business for his kingdom. But that doesn't mean it can't be the most joyful and exciting experience ever!

mint

Scripture

"Do you want to enjoy life? Do you want to have many happy days? Then avoid saying anything hurtful, and never let a lie come out of your mouth. Stop doing anything evil, and do good. Look for peace, and do all you can to help people live peacefully. The Lord watches over those who do what is right, and he hears their prayers."—Psalm 34:12–15 (ERV)

Grace

Father in Heaven, we're amazed by you. We love that you protect us and care about us, that you give us food for our bodies and joy in our hearts. Inspire us to stand with you, Lord, so that your light can shine through us in every direction, covering the world and pointing all people in your direction. Give us delight in doing good and helping others, for that makes you happy. Thank you for hearing our prayers—every one of them. We want what you want for our lives. Amen.

Grace notes

You could do all that the psalm writer says and still have bad days; they happen in a sinful world. But God will always be with you. Sometimes God may seem closer when things are going well, but that's not true at all. Could it be that your happy feelings just make it feel that way? Become more aware of God's presence and see whether your problems don't get smaller and your spiritual rewards get bigger. As today's Scripture reminds us, life *will* be smoother for everybody when our actions are spreading around the happiness and peace that come from him. That's just natural, because happiness and peace are catching. Here's something right you can do: between now and tomorrow evening's dinner, do something kind for someone. Then tomorrow around the table take turns describing what you did and what response you got. The motivational speaker Brian Tracy looks at it this way: "Successful people are always looking for opportunities to help others. Unsuccessful people are always asking, 'What's in it for me?'"

Scripture

"Do your best to improve your faith. You can do this by adding goodness, understanding, self-control, patience, devotion to God, concern for others, and love. If you keep growing in this way, it will show that what you know about our Lord Jesus Christ has made your lives useful and meaningful. But if you don't grow, you are like someone who is nearsighted or blind, and you have forgotten that your past sins are forgiven."—2 Peter 1:5–9 (CEV)

Grace

Heavenly Father, teach us of your love for all creation, that you have invited us to love you, and that you are slow to anger and rich in kindness and truth. Teach us that through Jesus' sacrifice on the cross our sins have been forgiven. Thank you, Lord, for this food. You are the one we serve. Amen.

Grace notes

God gives you the power to live a good life and to help others. Working on that good life won't save you (Jesus already did that), but it will prove to God and others that your faith really means something. You might think that living that way will take too much effort. Never fear—Jesus says that the Holy Spirit is at work in your life. Ask him for the strength and guidance to add to your faith those qualities of goodness, understanding, self-control, patience, devotion to God, and love and concern for others. Pretty soon you'll find it easier than you think, and your life will be more meaningful. Can you see how that works?

Scripture

"God said, in effect, 'If that's what you want, that's what you get.' It wasn't long before [the godless and wicked people] were living in a pigpen, smeared with filth, filthy inside and out. And all this because they traded the true God for a fake god, and worshiped the god they made instead of the God who made them—the God we bless, the God who blesses us. Oh, yes!"—Romans 1:24–25 (MSG)

Grace

Father God, thank you for this food and for our family. Please bless us with a thirst for knowing more about you, the one true God—the God we praise and the God who blesses us. (Actually, Lord, please make that a thirst for knowing *you* better, too—knowing *about* you only takes us so far.) Teach us that the gift of free will you have given to all human beings—the ability to think, feel, and do whatever we want—can have bad results if we don't pay attention first to what YOU want. Lord, it is you who gave us life and you who love us, and that means that you want the best for us. Remind us that you are a forgiving God, the God of Second Chances. Lord, we'd like to learn our lessons sooner rather than later. Amen.

Grace notes

The picture this verse paints isn't pretty, is it? Take the time to read it again, and picture it as a painting. You probably wouldn't want it on your bedroom wall. This is what happens when people trade human wisdom for God's wisdom. Did you know that when people devote all their time and energy to one thing they, in a sense, begin to worship it? It becomes a god (with a small *g*), but it definitely isn't our big-g God. Back in Bible days (in many places in our day, too) people often worshiped idols made of metals like gold or bronze. Today we are more likely to "worship" a video game, Facebook, or texting—anything other than God—if we let our fascination with it get out of hand. Whom do people think they are kidding, anyway? Not God!

Scripture

"All of you should live together in peace. Try to understand each other. Love each other like brothers and sisters. Be kind and humble. Don't do wrong to anyone to pay them back for doing wrong to you. Or don't insult anyone to pay them back for insulting you. But ask God to bless them. Do this because you yourselves were chosen to receive a blessing."—1 Peter 3:8–9 (ERV)

Grace

Dear Jesus, thank you for bringing us together to share good food and to talk about good things. We are grateful for our meal and for each other. Teach us that when we act with kindness—an on-purpose, genuine kindness—it makes you smile, Lord. Remind us that responding to bad behavior with more bad behavior is never helpful, because two wrongs don't make a right. Remind us that you stand with us as we try to live life your way and that you give us the strength to succeed. Bless us all—and by this we mean *all* people, even those we might not think deserve it. Amen.

Grace notes

Do you think your personal growth has anything to do with how you get along with others? What values do you learn when you have to interact with other people? You might right away mention sharing, kindness, and manners—and these are right on. But what else? Sometimes you have to act in certain ways when you don't want to, for the sake of what we call common courtesy or common decency. Examples might be dressing up to go visit someone when you don't want to go, being polite and talking rather than keeping your ear buds in, shaking hands firmly when people hold them out to you at church or in other public places, or letting Mom talk on the phone without interrupting her. This kind of decent behavior helps the wheels of everyday life turn smoothly. As an unknown author said, "If you don't believe in cooperation, look what happens when a car loses one of its wheels."

sage

Scripture

"So God created human beings in his image. In the image of God he created them. He created them male and female. God blessed them and said, 'Have many children and grow in number. Fill the earth and be its master. Rule over the fish in the sea and over the birds in the sky and over every living thing that moves on the earth."—Genesis 1:27–28 (NCV)

Grace

"Dear God, thank you for building all the people."* Thank you for making people of all different kinds and with all different shapes, faces, and colors—but always like you. Teach us to treat everyone as though they are your favorite, because we all are! Help us to "help" you create a world of loving and happy people, caring for each other and for the animals and fish and birds, too—for everything! Thank you for giving us food, especially for what we're about to eat now. Amen.

*Thank you to four-year-old Wyatt for this contribution.

Grace notes

God created you in his image. Imagine being like the God who, in a single breath, could create the heavens and the earth! Don't worry that you might grow up looking like everyone else—it's the spiritual image (who you are on the inside) that Moses, the writer of Genesis, was talking about. Like God, you can be kind and loving and good. For example, God created you with intelligence, a personality, morality, spirituality—and whether or not you'll ever understand how he did it, know that he created you out of love. He didn't create you because he needed something from you or because he was lonely; he created you because he wanted a loving relationship with a free-thinking person just like you who can love him back because you want to. You love him—and others—because he loved you first.* With God loving you like that, anything—and everything—is possible, as long as you let him call the shots.**

*1 John 4:19 **Matthew 19:26, Mark 9:23; 10:27; Luke 1:37; 18:27

mint

Scripture

"Be careful what you think, because your thoughts run your life. Don't use your mouth to tell lies; don't ever say things that are not true. Keep your eyes focused on what is right, and look straight ahead to what is good. Be careful what you do, and always do what is right. Don't turn off the road of goodness; keep away from evil paths."—Proverbs 4:23–27 (NCV)

Grace

Dear Jesus, our teacher, you guide us with your straightforward advice. We pray for hearts that want to do the right things. Remind us that you will support us even when we blow it, even when we don't feel or act like Miss Nice Girl or Mr. Nice Guy. Remind us that temptation has a sneaky way of getting to us, and then of getting the better of us. Teach us that *Just this once* can easily turn into *just one more time* and pretty soon becomes *all the time*. Remind us that it's better to starve the temptation monster when it's little, before it has a chance to get us! Thank you, Lord, for this food for nutrition and this food for thought. Amen.

Grace notes

It can be difficult to see how something we think or do today can have a lasting negative effect on our future, but that's exactly what can happen when we give in to temptation. Temptation is a short-term desire that can mess up our long-term goals. Imagine yourself as a future grown-up looking back at the now-sized you. How has your life turned out? Has giving in to temptation as a kid been the beginning of bad habits that are messing up your adult life? "Your capacity to say 'No' determines your capacity to say 'Yes' to greater things," said the American missionary to India E. Stanley Jones. What greater things do you look forward to doing in your life? Does that change the way you act now? Should it?

Scripture

"Jesus said, "I am the bread of life. No one who comes to me will ever go hungry. And no one who believes in me will ever be thirsty." —John 6:35 (NIrV)

Grace

Everlasting Christ, thank you for the food that nourishes our bodies and the food that nourishes our souls. Feed us, Jesus, for you alone have the words of eternal life.* Give us eyes to see that through you our Father God teaches us the truth. Fill us with a desire to fulfill your purpose in our lives. Amen

*John 6:68

Grace notes

"I am the bread of life" was quite a declaration from Jesus to the people of Galilee. Bread and water were essential for their lives; they also understood that Jesus was making a comparison to spiritual life. But do you think they really understood who it was they were talking to, or that Jesus was offering the nourishment that would let them live forever? That would be a huge, wonderful mouthful, wouldn't it! Today our spiritual lives are fed by God's Word. Author Albert F. Schmid said it well: "A well-read Bible is a sign of a well-fed soul." Now *that's* some soul food!

Scripture

"[God] has set the right time for everything. He has given us a desire to know the future, but never gives us the satisfaction of fully understanding what he does. So I realized that all we can do is be happy and do the best we can while we are still alive. All of us should eat and drink and enjoy what we have worked for. It is God's gift."—Ecclesiastes 3:11–13 (GNT)

Grace

Heavenly Father, thank you for the gift of curiosity. Teach us to use it to find excitement in life, but don't let our curiosity over mysteries we can't solve in this life cause us worry or frustration. Create in us a desire to find enjoyment in your gifts rather than in the false gifts of the world. Help us understand, too, that life without problems is impossible, since the life we now know is in and of this sinful world. Teach us that even though we don't always understand why things happen the way they do, you do have the answers. Help us to rest in you, Lord, knowing that you alone see the big picture and have everything under control. We give you thanks for the nourishing food you've set before us. Amen.

Grace notes

The Teacher who wrote Ecclesiastes is telling us to be happy in this life; it makes no sense for us to worry about what we cannot know or control. So find enjoyment in God's gifts, but never think that "normal" applies only to times when nothing is going wrong. The enjoyment in life is the character you build as a result of "normal." God wants you to be content, to take life's ups and downs as they come. The American First Lady Eleanor Roosevelt said this about her husband, President Franklin D. Roosevelt, who became unable to walk and was wheelchair bound because of a disease called polio: "I think probably the thing that took most courage in his life was his mastery and his meeting of polio [his coming down with and learning to deal with this disease]. I never heard him complain. . . . He just accepted it as one of those things that was given you as discipline in life." He knew, too, that each victory left him stronger—stronger in mind and body—than he had been before. President Roosevelt's son Elliott called his father a pastor in disguise because of his strong faith. Roosevelt's faith served him well—very well—don't you think?

Scripture

"For I know the plans I have for you, declares the Lord, "plans to prosper you and not to harm you, plans to give you hope and a future. Then you will call on me and come and pray to me, and I will listen to you."—Jeremiah 29:11–12 (NIV)

Grace

Almighty God, we thank you for the blessings you give us when we seek you. Create in us a desire to live happy lives, knowing that an amazing, not-of-this-world joy awaits us. Teach us that as much as we like material things, that kind of prosperity is nothing compared to what we'll find in heaven. Thank you for the eats, Lord. We praise your wonderful name. Amen.

Grace notes

Jeremiah was talking here to the people of Israel, not to us as individual Christians. In the verse just before this one the prophet Jeremiah told God's Old Testament people that they would be in exile for 70 years but that after that time their nation would become strong once again. That's what Jeremiah meant when he said that the Lord had great plans for them. Jeremiah also told those saddened people something that comforts us still today: "You will find me if you seek me with all your heart." Hundreds of years ago a great man named Thomas à Kempis said this: "For a little reward, men make a long journey; for eternal life many will scarce lift a foot once from the ground." Why do you suppose that is true?

sage

Scripture

Who has scooped up the ocean in his two hands, or measured the sky between his thumb and little finger? Who has put all the earth's dirt in one of his baskets, weighed each mountain and hill? Who could ever have told God what to do or taught him his business? What expert would he have gone to for advice, what school would he attend to learn justice? What god do you suppose might have taught him what he knows, showed him how things work? Why, the nations are but a drop in a bucket, a mere smudge on a window. Watch [God] sweep up the islands like so much dust off the floor!"—Isaiah 40:13–14 (MSG)

Grace

Almighty God, how holy you are! Your glory fills the world.* Teach us, Lord, to be in awe of what you have done and to remember that you can do just as many extraordinary things in our lives. Strengthen our faith, for you alone are all powerful, all knowing, all loving, and everywhere at the same time. Thank you for our family and for those we love and who love us. Teach us to reach out to all people with love and kindness, knowing that your unfailing love protects us, and them, even when life gets scary. Thank you for this food; may it give us the energy we need to accomplish your purpose in our lives. Holy is your Name. Amen.

*From Isaiah 6:3

Grace notes

God's power is unlimited and his wisdom unknowable. He is everywhere throughout the universe at the same time. The most amazing thing is that, big and powerful as he is, he loves you enough to care about everything in your life. He can give you his undivided attention when you talk to him. You can talk to him even about little things, like hard math problems or a friend who doesn't want to play at recess. You can talk to him about big things, too, like what to be when you grow up. You can talk about things that scare you—and about things that make you happy. If they're important to you, they're important to him. "When you speak of heaven," says the British preacher Charles Hadden Spurgeon, "let your face light up."

Scripture

"Make swords from your plows, and make spears from your hooks for trimming trees. Let even the weak person say, 'I am a soldier.'"—Joel 3:9–10 (NCV)

"[God] will settle disputes among great nations. They will hammer their swords into plows and their spears into pruning knives. Nations will never again go to war, never prepare for battle again."—Isaiah 2:4 (GNT)

Grace

Heavenly Father, please bless our food, our family, and all who defend our country. Teach us to understand that though peace is always our goal, it's only in heaven that total peace rules. Remind us, too, that until then you don't want us to stand by and do nothing in the face of evil. Remind us of your command to hate what is evil and cling to what is good.* Lord, please keep safe those who protect our freedom and those who make it possible for us to love you freely, without persecution. God, you are almighty, and we rely on your love and protection! Amen.

*Romans 12:9

Grace notes

Is God a God of peace or a God of war? These verses might suggest that the Bible makes opposing statements (as though Joel is for war and Isaiah is for peace). It's true that confusing thoughts come up when you pull something out of its surrounding passage or circumstances (we call that context). (People do that a lot—innocently or not—in their attempts to prove a point about their beliefs.) Here the prophet Joel foretells a time when we will have to fight, either to protect ourselves or to protect innocent people in faraway lands. In the book of Isaiah, however, God promises that at some future time there will be no more war because he will intervene and settle *all* disputes—forever. In the words of a song written by Pete Seeger, borrowing words from Ecclesiastes 3:1–8, "To everything—turn, turn, turn. There is a season—turn, turn, turn. A time for every purpose under heaven. A time to love, and a time to hate; a time of war, and a time of peace." Why do you think Pete Seeger's song says "turn, turn, turn"? What does this songwriter want people to do? Do you think he might be calling you to turn down the peace path whenever you can?

Scripture

[Jesus said,] "'My purpose is to give life in all its fullness.'"—John 10:10 (NLT)

Grace

Dear Jesus, thank you for your many blessings. Thank you for our family and friends. Thank you for feeding us, and for being our shepherd and watching over us. Open our hearts, Lord, to know that your words of hope will mean more to us as we grow and understand things better. Show us what it is that makes life full and meaning-full. May we always rejoice in your care and love for us. Amen.

Grace notes

Your choices have a lot to do with how your life will turn out: full or empty; creative or boring; forgiving or resentful and angry. It'll take effort no matter what you choose, so choose the goodness in life (your rewards will be full). Pursue Jesus and he will pursue you. "I read the Bible every day," said the Academy Award recipient Denzel Washington. That's one of the best ways to pursue Jesus, isn't it?

Scripture

"Joash became king of Judah in Jehu's seventh year as king of Israel, and he ruled for forty years in Jerusalem. His mother's name was Zibiah, and she was from Beersheba. Joash did what the LORD said was right as long as Jehoiada the priest taught him."—2 Kings 12:1–2 (NCV)

Grace

Wonderful Counselor, thank you for our family and friends, and especially for those who give us good, godly advice. Thank you for our parents, who love us and instruct us in your Word. Give us a strong faith, a sure confidence that we're never *really* alone because you're always with us. Lord, please bring people into our lives who will teach us how to think wisely. And help us to keep thinking wisely even when they aren't watching. Thank you for this food you have provided. Amen.

Grace notes

Joash, who was only seven years old when he became king, was a good ruler as long as he had a good uncle, the high priest Jehoiada, to advise him. But after Jehoiada died Joash became cruel and evil, throwing all that good advice right out the palace window. What can we learn from Joash's mistakes? The American author Jim George had some wise words to say: "A good leader will seek the wisdom of others. After all, no man is an island!" No boy or girl, either!

parsley

Scripture

"Then the Lord said to Moses, 'Tell Aaron and his sons to bless the people of Israel with this special blessing: "May the Lord bless you and protect you. May the Lord smile on you and be gracious to you. May the Lord show you his favor and give you his peace."'—Numbers 6:22–26 (NLT)

Grace

Loving Father, we are in awe of your might and faithfulness and that you have loved us from the beginning. May we always remember that through Jesus your blessing extends to all of us. Remind us that you created us to be in a relationship with you, to love you as you love us. Keep us safe, encourage our heart to obey your commandments, and create in us the knowledge that true joy and happiness come when we walk with you. When we do, turn your face to us, Lord, and show us your smile. Thanks for our meal and for our family. Amen.

Grace notes

Imagine Jesus looking at you and saying the blessing in this Scripture out loud, just to and for you. Imagine a wave of love coming over him as he looks at you, directly into your eyes—because that's just what happens. That feeling he has for you is all about love and joy. A well-loved line from the book *A Christmas Carol* by Charles Dickens fits well here: "God bless us, every one!"

sage

Scripture

"When God approves of your life, even your enemies will end up shaking your hand."—Proverbs 16:7 (MSG)

Grace

Heavenly Father, we are grateful for your love, your grace, and your protection. Help us remember that pleasing you is what's important, and from that can come only good in our lives. Help us realize that your power can make anything happen, that you hold our hearts and our futures in your hand and can transform any circumstance for our benefit. Thank you for our food, and we pray that you will grant us peace in our family. Amen.

Grace notes

Make peace first with God and then with your enemies. That's the best way to deal with those "problem" people in your life. You know the ones—those who always want to argue with you—and you know that those arguments never seem to end well. God can put peace in your heart where there was once anger. Ask him for guidance; he delights in helping you. Chances are those "problem" people could use a little love in their lives, too. "If you want those around you to accept God and His many gifts," said the writer and mathematician David Mangan, "first accept His love for you." Those angry people will see and like the change in you.

mint

Scripture

"You have not seen Christ, but still you love him. You cannot see him now, but you believe in him. So you are filled with a joy that cannot be explained, a joy full of glory."—1 Peter 1:8 (NCV)

Grace

Heavenly Father, you fill us up with love and goodness. We ask that our being here together and knowing you are with us (even though we can't see you) give us the opportunity to talk about the day's blessings. Help us to leave the table filled up not only with this good food but also with your love, goodness, and joy. We hold on to you first but also to each other. Help us to believe in you and to remember to keep you always in our thoughts. Our thought now is to thank you for the food and for each other. Amen.

Grace notes

Do you know the difference between joy and happiness? Often they overlap, but happiness comes from the world, while joy comes from God. Happiness is temporary—it doesn't last that long and comes and goes, depending on how things are going in your life or in your day. Can you think of some things that used to make you happy—maybe even very happy—but no longer interest you? Joy is everlasting because it comes from God, and it will carry you through all of your days, either good, bad, or somewhere in between. "Joy is the infallible [the unfailing] sign of the presence of God," said the French novelist Leon Bloy.

Scripture

"This is how much God loved the world [if you want to make it personal, you can read "the world" as "you"]: He gave his Son, his one and only Son. And this is why: so that no one need be destroyed; by believing in him, anyone can have a whole and lasting life. God didn't go to all the trouble of sending his Son merely to point an accusing finger, telling the world how bad it was. He came to help, to put the world right again."—John 3:16–17 (MSG)

Grace

Dear Father, we love your Son, Jesus, and all that he has done for us. We know that, through Jesus and the Holy Spirit, you will be with us always. Remind us that Jesus will be with us as we grow and learn more about you. We pray for guidance and help each day and each hour. Give us wisdom to surrender everything to you—to put you first in our lives—just as you sacrificed your all for us. Thank you for the many blessings you give us, including this food and our family and friends. Amen.

Grace notes

If the message of the Bible could be stated in two verses, many people would name the two in today's reading. God loves you—with everything that's in him. He knows your name and everything about you. He knows your smallest problems and your biggest dreams. And his message—his love—is for everyone. No one on this planet is excluded; there is hope for every last person. There are no rules or requirements beyond a desire to know the Lord. "If Christ has not been raised, then all our preaching is useless, and your faith is useless," said the apostle Paul in 1 Corinthians 15:14.

bay

Scripture

"See how much the Father has loved us! His love is so great that we are called God's children—and so, in fact, we are."—1 John 3:1(a) (GNT)

Grace

Dear Jesus, Wonderful Counselor, thank you for our food and family. Help us see how very much you want to be with us (*Wow!*). Teach us that, in just the way Mom and Dad always love us and we never stop loving them, you love us forever and always. We love you, too, God. (Ditto for Mom and Dad.) Yay, God! Amen.

Grace notes

The American songwriter Anna Bartlett Warner wrote this verse almost everyone knows: "Jesus loves me—this I know, for the Bible tells me so. Little ones to Him belong—they are weak, but He is strong." It isn't only young people who sing this song. In 1943, long before John F. Kennedy became an American president, his torpedo boat, PT-109, was rammed in an attack during World War II. While waiting for rescue he and the other sailors prayed and sang this very song. Here's a surprising fact: "Jesus Loves Me" is also known as "the Favorite Hymn of China." All of those people in faraway China (and everywhere else) who know and love God are his children, too.

Scripture

"The heavens declare the glory of God, and the skies announce what his hands have made. Day after day they tell the story; night after night they tell it again. They have no speech or words; they have no voice to be heard. But their message goes out through all the world; their words go everywhere on earth. The sky is like a home for the sun."—Psalm 19:1–4 (NCV)

Grace

Lord God, how majestic is your name in all the earth!* Remind us that just as you made the heavens you made us—wonderfully!** We worship you in the beauty of your holiness, for you are God.*** Lord, we give you our hearts. You are our strength, and to you belongs the glory for everything under the heavens. Thank you, God, for giving us life. Thank you for this food, and may it nourish our bodies. And thank you for our family. Amen.

*Psalm 8:1; **Psalm 139:4; ***Psalm 29:2

Grace notes

In a time when pagans (idol worshipers) made (small-g) gods of many things, including the sun, moon and stars, the writer of this psalm proclaimed that the heavens and everything in them are the work of the one true God. The heavens speak of the eternal endurance of God, the fact that he has always been and always will be here for us. It's hard to imagine not believing in God when we look at the beauty all around us on the earth and in the sky, isn't it? "Whenever I see sunbeams coming through clouds, it always looks to me like God shining himself down onto us," said Terri Guillemets, the woman who created the "Quote Garden" website. "The thing about sunbeams," she went on to say, "is they're always there even though we can't always see them. Same with God." There are other things you can't see, but you know they're there, right? Gravity, for instance. Or air or wind. Can you think of other examples?

sage

Scripture

"Let me shout God's name with a praising song. Let me tell his greatness in a prayer of thanks. For God, this is better than oxen on the altar, far better than blue-ribbon bulls."—Psalm 69:30-31 (MSG)

Grace

Father in heaven, thank you for our family, our food, and the reality that you are with us. We pray for grateful hearts; how we appreciate what we have—every day and in every way! Just as the dawn promises the sunshine and fills the day with light, teach us that the more we get to know you the more heaven sheds its light into our lives. Amen.

Grace notes

This Scripture foretells of a coming time when sacrifices on the altar would never again be needed. The idea that God would be happier with their prayers, their truly felt "I'm sorries," their loving hearts, and their kind and grateful actions would have seemed very strange to God's people back then. They followed God's law for their day by sacrificing oxen, bulls, goats, and birds, but this was a temporary fix; the sacrifices covered short time periods, individual sins, and had to be made over and over again. Jesus died on the cross to pay for our sins once and for all. All we have to do to take advantage of that sacrifice (to accept his forgiveness) is to ask Jesus into our hearts and lives. With the sacrifice of Jesus God showed the world that we can have complete trust in him and his promises. That's called faith. As an unknown smart person once said: "Sometimes I just look up, smile and say, 'I know that was you GOD. Thanks!'"

Scripture

"Come, let's shout praises to God, raise the roof for the Rock who saved us! Let's march into his presence singing praises, lifting the rafters with our hymns! And why? Because God is the best, High King over all the gods. In one hand he holds deep caves and caverns, in the other hand grasps the high mountains. He made Ocean—he owns it! His hands sculpted Earth!"—Psalm 95:1–5 (MSG)

Grace

Heavenly Father, inspire us to stand with you so that your light can shine through us. Remind us that though you are powerful enough to create everything, you never lose sight of us—better yet, you are *in* us. God, you can't be outdone! Lord, you are awesome! Thank you for our blessings, today and always. Thank you for this food, for family, and for creating us and giving us life. Amen.

Grace notes

Begin your day with prayer; it's the best way to say hello to another day of life. If you can get in the habit of saying a prayer before you get out of bed, you'll be way ahead of the day. The Creator of the world is just waiting for you to wake up and greet him and then to walk to school with you! Now *that's* a big deal. "Do not have your concert first, and then tune your instrument afterwards. Begin the day with the Word of God and prayer, and get first of all into harmony with Him," said the British missionary to China J. Hudson Taylor. Once you're all tuned up you can play a tune worthy of the Hit Parade!

Scripture

"Live creatively, friends. If someone falls into sin, forgivingly restore him, saving your critical comments for yourself. You might be needing forgiveness before the day's out. Stoop down and reach out to those who are oppressed. Share their burdens, and so complete Christ's law. If you think you are too good for that, you are badly deceived."—Galatians 6:1–3 (MSG)

Grace

Dear Jesus, thank you for our friends, our food, and our family. Help us to remember how important it is to love and take care of one another. Show us how to help and encourage those who are struggling—to give them encouragement. Teach us to share, not lecture. Teach us to understand that helping someone can change their world! Amen.

Grace notes

When in doubt about how to act in any situation, choose the way that is gentle and kind. Do not judge; that's God's job, and besides, that introduces pride and conceit into the mix. Realize before you criticize someone about their behavior that none of us is perfect. Think of yourself as a coach or helper, full of encouragement and enthusiasm. And here's an idea: when you find yourself having to correct someone, do it with a sandwich! A sandwich approach, that is: put the "meat"—the part that needs changing—between two pieces of bread—two positive things that they already do well. "A coach," said the UCLA basketball coach John Wooden, "is someone who can give correction without causing resentment." Why not practice this kind of coaching with someone in your family? What words could help the person without hurting their feelings?

Scripture

"Whatever you have said in the dark will be heard in the light, and what you have whispered behind closed doors will be shouted from the housetops for all to hear!"—Luke 12:3 (NLT)

Grace

Gracious Father, we are grateful for your blessings, for our family, and for this food. Thank you for reminding us that bad talkers will soon get exposed. Please forgive us, Lord, when we act as though you're not there. Do we really think you're not looking or that your ears aren't working? Amen.

Grace notes

This verse is about sinning with our words. An example of this is something called hypocrisy. A famous American leader named Adlai E. Stevenson II once said, "A hypocrite is the kind of politician who would cut down a redwood tree, then mount the stump and make a speech for conservation [to protect the trees]." The bad news about hypocrisy—about criticizing someone else for the very same thing *you* do, even if in private—is that God doesn't want you to do it. Here's the good news: when God looks at those who love him and try to please him, he sees none of their faults; what he does see is Jesus and you, standing side by side as a team. God isn't out to get you—to shout your faults from the rooftop for everyone to hear. Oh, what a relief *that* is!

parsley

Scripture

"Here I am! I stand at the door and knock. If any of you hears my voice and opens the door, I will come in and eat with you. And you will eat with me."—Revelation 3:20 (NIrV)

Grace

Everlasting Father, we are so thankful for your unending love. Help us to listen for your knock and invite you to come on in and join us. Inspire us to throw open the door excitedly, opening our hearts to learn more about the qualities we really need: love, joy, peace, and an eagerness to serve each other.* We thank you for the food you provide, Lord. May Mom's good cooking and the good company around this table please you so much that you ask for seconds! We really welcome you into our lives. Amen.

*See Galatians 5:22–23(a)

Grace notes

Hospitality was extremely important in Bible days since there were very few inns or restaurants for travelers. If someone, even a stranger, knocked on your door, you would welcome the traveler in for a meal and probably even for a place to sleep. Have you invited Jesus into your heart? He desires closeness with you and is just waiting for your invitation. What have you got to lose? The answer is nothing—and everything. (Become dependent on Jesus and you'll gain much. Remain independent and gain nothing.) One time Jesus told his disciples that the tired and hungry stranger at their door might be an angel in disguise.* Another time he said that giving a cup of cold water to a thirsty someone is the same as giving it to him.** Impossible, you might think? Think again. "We have a God who delights in impossibilities," said Billy Sunday.

*Hebrews 13:2; **Matthew 10:42

Scripture

"How can a young person keep his life pure? By living in keeping with your word. I trust in you with all my heart. Don't let me wander away from your commands. I have hidden your word in my heart so that I won't sin against you. LORD, I give praise to you."—Psalm 119:9–12(a) (NIrV)

Grace

Heavenly Father, open our eyes to what is pleasing to you. Remind us how good it feels to be good. Remind us that your smile is for us, that your hands rest on our shoulders to encourage us, and that all you ask in return is our whole hearts. Teach us that you want us to be happy. Father, we thank you for your Word, for our family, and for this meal. Lord, we give you praise. Amen.

Grace notes

Maybe Mom or Dad or a grandparent can help you memorize a special verse to keep in your heart. Did you know that the shortest verse in the Bible has only two words? See if you can find it. (Hint: it's in the Gospel of John. Even this very short verse can mean a lot if you know the story around it.) Today's verse would be a good choice to memorize (especially the part that begins with "I trust . . ."). "The scriptures are given not to increase our knowledge," said the American evangelist Dwight L. Moody, "but to change our lives."

mint

Scripture

"Let other people praise you—even strangers; never do it yourself." —Proverbs 27:2 (GNT)

Grace

Father God, thank you for blessing us with food and family. Thank you for helping us to think things through. Teach us to accept praise carefully, for you are responsible for our talents. Teach us also to appreciate and thank all the people who help us develop those gifts. Teach us to live with grateful hearts for all the good things in life. You are the Almighty God, the Creator of the universe and of everything good. Amen.

Grace notes

Ever find yourself telling people how good you are—bragging? It gets old really fast. People may be polite on the outside, but on the inside they're screaming for you to stop. Take a moment to think about why you might be doing that. Is it to feel better about yourself or to make yourself seem better or more important to the person you're talking to? It's important to ask yourself these questions. Let your good works do their own boasting. If you're going to boast, boast about Jesus!* "The trouble with most of us is that we'd rather be ruined by praise than saved by criticism," said the famous American preacher Norman Vincent Peale. Talk about these words with your family. How could praise ruin us or criticism save us?

*1 Corinthians 1:31

Scripture

"A stone is heavy, and sand is hard to carry, but the irritation caused by a fool is much harder to bear."—Proverbs 27:3 (ERV)

Grace

Wonderful Teacher, thank you for this day, for our food, and for those we love. Teach us not to let a fool's behavior make us crazy, because anger never helps. Teach us the harder but better way: the way of patience. Remind us that sometimes we too act as though you're not around. Help us not to give in to temptation, for isn't that where foolish behavior starts? Your Word gives us a lot to think about, Lord. Amen.

Grace notes

When the Bible talks about a fool, it's not talking about someone who is silly or not so smart but about someone with a weak will who has a hard time choosing the right way. The "fool" here is the stubborn person who has never learned self-control, who loves to annoy people or who gets mad at the slightest thing—over and over again. Ignore them if you can. Pray for them, definitely. "Any fool can criticize, condemn and complain—and most fools do," said Benjamin Franklin. So what does that make *us* when we react in those ways? Wise or foolish? *Hmmm*—you get to choose!

bay

Scripture

"Become wise, dear child, and make me happy; then nothing the world throws my way will upset me."—Proverbs 27:11 (MSG)

Grace

Father in heaven, we praise you for who you are and thank you for our food. Teach us that the riches Mom and Dad desire for us, the one thing that will make them shout with happiness, is knowing we're headed in the right direction. Show us the way, Lord, from your Word. Give us the desire to know you and to honor our parents. Halleluiah! Amen.

Grace notes

It doesn't take a detective to see the truth in this verse. Your mom and dad show their love for you in many ways. Sometimes it comes down to the little things, like making your lunch; tucking you in at night; going to your games; or, if you're old enough to go out with friends in the evening, waiting up for you at night. Sometimes they show their love in bigger ways, too: saving money for your lessons, being there when you need to talk to them, and even getting you out of trouble. (A harder choice for them might be to let you learn your own lessons by *not* getting you out of trouble.) Name as many ways as you can in which your mom and dad show their love for you. Now for the bigger question, the question of this verse: How do you show your love for them? In what ways are you becoming wise? "I have frequently gained my first real insight into the character of parents by studying their children," said Sir Arthur Conan Doyle (author of the Sherlock Holmes stories). Sir Arthur Conan Doyle was a clever man.

Scripture

"A prudent person sees trouble coming and ducks; a simpleton walks in blindly and is clobbered."—Proverbs 27:12 (MSG)

Grace

Dear Jesus, it is so wise for us to recognize how important you are in our lives and to thank you for your blessings—right now at mealtime, definitely for this food. Watch over us and protect us in times of trouble. Keep us safe, and teach us to be aware of what's going on around us. Teach us to think of the results of what we're thinking of doing before we do it. Our very lives—spiritually, mentally, and physically—might depend on it. Amen.

Grace notes

Being aware of your surroundings is a key to avoiding many painful and dangerous situations. Here are some suggestions to train yourself to become more aware: when you walk into a room, look around and see who's there. Find one thing in the room that really catches your eye. Make a game of observing things. At the mall with your friends describe someone who has just walked by (with your back turned so you can't see them). Notice a car in the parking lot. Then look away and remember details like color, make, and license plate. Make a game of it! Your skill will improve. "To acquire knowledge, one must study; but to acquire wisdom, one must observe," said Marilyn vos Savant, who has the highest recorded IQ (a measurement of intelligence or brain power) ever recorded (yes, it's in the Guinness Book of World Records). One kind of trouble to watch out for is temptation. It doesn't have a color or a license plate number, but that doesn't mean you can't be on the lookout for it. Temptation might just be the most dangerous thing around!

Scripture

"If you wake your friend in the early morning by shouting "Rise and shine!" It will sound to him more like a curse than a blessing." —Proverbs 27:14 (MSG)

Grace

Loving Father, we're grateful for all that you teach us, and we ask you to help us remember that the answers to all of life's big questions can be found in your Word. We ask you to help us remember to think before we act. Teach us to treat others the way we ourselves would like to be treated. Guide us in the direction of thoughts, words, and actions that aren't mean, rude, or just plain thoughtless—like being loud when we know our neighbor works at night and sleeps in the daytime. Kindly (and quietly) now we say thanks for the food. Amen.

Grace notes

It's important in a friendship to know who's a morning person and who isn't. Would you ask a person who doesn't wake up bright and cheery for a big favor first thing? Well, only if you wanted a grumpy answer! "If people were meant to pop out of bed, we'd all sleep in toasters," someone once joked. How do you know whether someone is a *morning* person or an *evening* person? Ask them in the middle of the day!

mint

Scripture

"Don't let anyone fool you. 'Bad companions make a good person bad.'"—1 Corinthians 15:33 (NIrV)

Grace

Dear Jesus, our One and Only, thank you for giving us each other, our friends, and this yummy food. Help us to serve you with love and thankfulness, doing your good work as your hands and feet in this world. Remind us that helping or giving good advice to a bad companion can be very tricky and that we ourselves must be strong so that the "bad" doesn't rub off on us. Lord, give us wisdom and strength to deal with these things. Stay with us, right here in our hearts, to guard our ways and guide our decisions. Amen.

Grace notes

Have you ever heard the old saying "Birds of a feather flock together"? The point is to be cautious about the company you choose to keep. Those with bad reputations can suck you in and drag you down. Here's another good saying to think about, this one from Benjamin Franklin: "If you lie down with dogs, you get up with fleas." But wait: Aren't you supposed to be a good example to those who need role models for right behavior? Yes, you are, but influence works in both directions—bad and good. For now, your parents have a lot to say about your friendship choices. Seek their advice. Like the eagle, they have sharp vision.

Scripture

"Praise be to the God and Father of our Lord Jesus Christ. God is the Father who is full of mercy and all comfort. He comforts us every time we have trouble, so when others have trouble, we can comfort them with the same comfort God gives us."—2 Corinthians 1:3–4 (NCV)

Grace

God of comfort, we praise your holy Name and thank you for loving us so much. Give us the patience to spend time with those who need comfort; sometimes they just need a listening ear. Help us see that praying, especially for others, is a way to honor and praise you. Thank you for listening to our prayers. You are so important in our lives and in the lives of those who need our prayer. We pray for everyone here at the table, thanking you for your goodness and for providing this food. In Jesus' great name, Amen.

Grace notes

You know what a hug is, of course. But here's another way to think of it: a hug is a prayer without words. Think about this, too: when you pray out loud with others you enlarge the circle of those who love God; it's like a group hug, with God in the center. Today's Scripture calls God the God of all comfort. What a comforting thought! Think of some good ways you can spread comfort around, starting with your family right here at the table. Then remember to do it again tomorrow, at school or wherever you are. A wise person once said: "God didn't promise days without pain, laughter without sorrow, sun without rain. But He did promise strength for the day, comfort for the tears, and light for the way. If God brings you to it, He will bring you through it." Sounds good, Lord. We get it. Hugs!

Scripture

"When birds are sold, five small birds cost only two pennies. But God does not forget any of them. Yes, God even knows how many hairs you have on your head. Don't be afraid. You are worth much more than many birds."—Luke 12:6–7 (ERV)

Grace

Hello, Jesus! Thank you so much for taking care of us, and for watching over us; we know that our life and our family wouldn't be the same without you. Remind us how important each of us is in your eyes, and to let your light shine through us. Teach us that though we may never realize how much our kind actions may help others, you know—just as you number the hairs on our heads (how caring is that?!). Jesus, we sing your praises; how great you are. Please bless our food. Amen.

Grace notes

It's a fact! Your kindness to others makes you feel good, too. Wouldn't it be great if you could know exactly what difference your kindness was making? Much of the time you can't, especially in situations where the results might not be immediate (like how good it feels to eat when you're really hungry). But don't let that stop you from being kind. We humans tend to mimic behavior; your acts of kindness could lead to a chain reaction! Here's something else to think about: imagine someone coming to you, years after the fact, and telling you about something you did for them and how they still remember and appreciate it. What a grand feeling! And how do you think someone would feel if you did the same thing? Think of the look on your teacher's face if you told her, years later, how grateful you were? Teachers live for that kind of stuff, you know. "Our actions are like ships which we may watch set out to sea, and not know when or with what cargo they will return to port," said the Irish author Dame Iris Murdoch. Make sure your ship sails on winds of love and kindness.

parsley

Scripture

"Hear, O Israel: The Lord our God, the Lord is one. Love the Lord your God with all your heart and with all your soul and with all your strength. These commandments that I give you today are to be on your hearts. Impress them on your children. Talk about them when you sit at home and when you walk along the road, when you lie down and when you get up. Tie them as symbols on your hands and bind them on your foreheads. Write them on the doorframes of your houses and on your gates."—Deuteronomy 6:4–9 (NIV)

Grace

Almighty God, we know you are the One and Only, and we honor you for all that you are. Teach us that praying and thinking and learning more about you aren't just for in-church time but for anytime and all time. Thank you for a mom and dad who know and care about this. Inspire us to see you in all of creation: the brilliant red flower, the sleeping puppy, the twinkling night sky, and the roar of thunder. Assure us that we can practice your commandments through the kindness, patience, and love we show others. We ask your blessings now on our food and family. Amen.

Grace notes

In the Hebrew language this Bible passage is called the *Shema*, which means "to hear." Recited twice a day by many Jews, it's the most important prayer in the Jewish religion. Most of the time it's sung, not spoken. The instruction to tie these commands on their foreheads was followed exactly by Jewish men. Many Israelite men wrote verses from the Torah (the first five books of the Bible) on parchment (a kind of paper) and put them in a little black box called a tefillin. They tied the tefillin around their foreheads to remind them of God leading the children of Israel out of Egypt. Prayers help you to be a better, stronger Christian, and reminders are always good, too. What, or who, reminds you to pray? In the words of a Jewish teacher, Rebbe Nachman of Breslov: "If you are not a better person tomorrow than you are today, what need have you for a tomorrow?"

Scripture

"All Scripture is inspired by God and is useful to teach us what is true and to make us realize what is wrong in our lives. It corrects us when we are wrong and teaches us to do what is right. God uses it to prepare and equip his people to do every good work."—2 Timothy 3:16–17 (NLT)

Grace

Jesus, we are thankful for this day and for this food. We are grateful for all your blessings and we pray for your guidance. Jesus, help us to see your Word for what it is meant to be: a book of living words, alive with truth for us. Teach us that, when we ask the Holy Spirit to read right along with us every time we open the Bible, there will always be something new in it for us. Remind us that Scripture is your best gift because it teaches us to know you better and better—and knowing you is the only way to live well. Remind us of this simple way to remember to put you first: life without you is like an unsharpened pencil—it has no point. Amen.

Grace notes

The Bible is a love story of God's plan for us. He enlisted the help of 40 authors in three continents, in three languages, to write 66 books over a 1600-year period, and yet there are no major contradictions. You might hear some people say there are, but those who do either misunderstand the Bible, haven't read all of it, or haven't read surrounding verses that help explain it. "If you believe what you like in the Gospel, and reject what you don't like, it is not the Gospel you believe, but yourself," said Saint Augustine. Dr. Mark L. Strauss makes another important point: "Though the Bible wasn't written to us, it was written for us." Writing for their audience, the writers didn't include facts their readers already knew. (When you talk about your day, you don't have to identify your school, right?) Remember that so you can ask yourself what else might have been going on that was left unsaid. For example, can you conclude that all women shouldn't speak in church just because Paul told the women of a troubled Corinth church not to? But Paul praised women leaders of a Roman church and referred, elsewhere, to his female co-workers.* Meant to be read, examined, and loved, the Bible has been studied from every angle, looked at through a microscope and a telescope, compared to and contrasted with many other books. And through all of this it has always been the world's bestseller. Face it, we're hungry for the truth in God's Word. Do you think that perhaps God gave us the Bible as a way to make us think and to bring our hearts, minds, and souls ever closer to him?

*Back then, society treated women as inferior; Paul never did. Check out Romans 16.

Scripture

"Dear brothers and sisters, I close my letter with these last words: Be joyful. Grow to maturity. Encourage each other. Live in harmony and peace. May the grace of the Lord Jesus Christ, the love of God, and the fellowship of the Holy Spirit be with you all."—2 Corinthians 13:11, 14 (NLT)

Grace

Jesus, our Lord, may you transform our lives with your nearness. Teach us to see and hear you with our hearts and minds and souls. Guide us. Watch over us. Encourage us. Satisfy us. Remind us to encourage one another and to live together, as your children, in your grace and peace. Praise you, Jesus, for all our blessings, including our family and our dinner. Amen.

Grace notes

Did you know that when you have confidence in God your willingness to do right things with his Spirit's help brings you happiness? With obedience comes everything in life that is right, true, and beautiful. This is an experience of the heart that will help you find God's purpose in your life. "Happy moments, PRAISE GOD. Difficult moments, SEEK GOD. Quiet moments, WORSHIP GOD. Painful moments, TRUST GOD. Every moment, THANK GOD," said Pastor Rick Warren. *Praise*, *seek*, *worship*, *trust*, and *thank*. Great words to live by.

Scripture

"God has made everything beautiful for its own time. He has planted eternity in the human heart, but even so, people cannot see the whole scope of God's work from beginning to end."—Ecclesiastes 3:11 (NLT)

Grace

God Almighty, remind us that you created the universe merely by breathing words*—your power is that awesome! Teach us to trust that you're big enough, loving enough, and wise enough to make everything work out in the end—and we don't need to know how you do it. Teach us that a *normal* life has its ups and downs and that you work in our lives even in the down times for our good. Remind us that you, as great as you are, have all the time in the world for each one of us. May our words breathe life into everything we do for you. Lord, please bless our food and our family. Your goodness and mercy have no end. Amen.

*Genesis 1

Grace notes

If you have any doubt that God is working in your life, it may be that you only need to look backward; the reasons things happen sometimes become obvious after the fact. As you get older and experience more of life, you'll learn to see signs of God's handiwork at work. For example, someone might have to repeat a grade and ends up meeting a lifelong friend he would not have otherwise met. Or someone might not make the team, only to discover that their real talent lies in another sport . . . or in music or art or drama or . . . God has a purpose and a plan for you, and everything will work out if you'll only let him have his way. The great film director Alfred Hitchcock, who always liked to say things with a twist, had this to say: "In feature films the director is God. In documentary films, God is the director." *What?* That was his way of saying that God's in charge—of everything.

bay

Scripture

"David said to the Philistine, 'You come to me using sword, spear, and javelin. But I come to you in the name of the Lord.'"—1 Samuel 17:45 (ERV)

Grace

Father God, help us trust in you as David did. Encourage us to trust you because you are GOD ALMIGHTY. Lead us to a faith that is willing to put our lives in your hands, for there can be no safer place. Lord, may we always keep in mind the blessings you give us and remember to say thank you. We thank you now for this food and for our time together. Amen.

Grace notes

The giant Goliath had just given the frightened Israelite army a war speech filled with hate, scorn, and curses. There was no room at all for God in Goliath's heart, and he was about to pay big time for his pride and disrespect. Even though David was a boy with only a slingshot and five smooth stones from the creek, he used his head to make a plan and called upon God for protection and victory. This story is a favorite with many, and you know already how it ends. "They always win who side with God," said the English hymn writer Frederick William Faber. That doesn't mean everything will always go well for us in this life. This victory was meant to illustrate that God will always triumph. But then, you already know that, too.

Scripture

"Above everything else, guard your heart. Everything you do comes from it. Don't speak with twisted words. Keep evil talk away from your lips. Let your eyes look straight ahead. Keep looking right in front of you. Think carefully about the paths that your feet walk on. Always choose the right ways. Don't turn to the right or left. Keep your feet from the path of evil."—Proverbs 4:23–27 (NIrV)

Grace

Lord Jesus, teach us to hold these words close, for they are big keys to life. Remind us to turn to you first (not last) in prayer when we have a problem. Help us to live by your words, to unlock the treasure of joy that is found in right living, and to remember that you are there for us whenever we need your encouragement. May we come to understand that through you and your Word alone we can find the amazing, indescribable life you reserve for those who choose to trust and obey you. Jesus, we thank you for our food, our family, and our future with you. Amen.

Grace notes

Life flows from the heart, that place in you that guards your intentions and emotions. Did you realize, though, that your heart and mouth are directly connected to each other? Guard your heart—avoid anger and pride; keep your word; and, most importantly, entrust your heart to Jesus—and you will have fewer regrets about the words that come out of your mouth. Let God's truth be your guide as you hike along life's path, making sure not to stray off into the bushes where dangers may lurk. "Anyone who doesn't take truth seriously in small matters," pointed out the famous scientist Albert Einstein, "cannot be trusted in large ones either." How well are you handling God's truth?

Scripture

"Don't copy the behavior and customs of this world, but let God transform you into a new person by changing the way you think. Then you will learn to know God's will for you, which is good and pleasing and perfect."—Romans 12:2 (NLT)

Grace

Father, we're grateful for the privilege of coming together to share this meal. Lord, it's so easy to get caught up in wanting and doing what others want and do—to go along with the crowd. Make us bold enough to say no whenever your good name—and our good reputation, too—may be at stake. Help us see that when we're willing to change the way we think we'll want to change the way we live, too. We thank you for this food, our family, and all our friends. Please be with all who need you tonight—and especially with those who don't know or care about the things that are good and pleasing and perfect in your sight.* Amen.

*Romans 12:2

Grace notes

Do you ever wish you felt cooler at school? Some kids care way too much and go all out, dressing as though they're older, hanging out with older or more popular kids, or doing things to impress the "in" crowd. They run the risk of getting into situations where they find themselves lying, sneaking around, or worse. There's a word for what they become: *posers*. It means being a pretender, people who are trying to pass themselves off as other people, trying to make the world believe in false pictures of themselves. And that is so not cool. God is the only one you need to impress; what you may not realize is that he is already very impressed with you (he values you, just as you are). Oh, what a relief that is! "Popularity isn't just something that happens," said the Canadian author Robert Bringhurst. "You have to give something in exchange for it, and that's the dangerous part of the process." Are you a copycat or an original?

Scripture

"Respected people do not tell lies, and fools have nothing worthwhile to say."—Proverbs 17:7 (GNT)

Grace

Gracious Father, thank you for our family, our food, and our friends. We pray for all those who need your help this evening, in whatever special way. We pray that we may, now and in the future, be people who are respected for our honesty and reliability. Sharpen our minds and point us in the right direction. Remind us that prayer and respect for your Word will keep us close to you and will earn both you and us the respect of others. We see the wisdom of this proverb, Lord, and that's no lie. Amen.

Grace notes

Everyone knows the story of the boy who cried wolf. Its message is so true. Be a *habit*-ual liar (a person in the habit of lying) and when you need help or have something important to share no one will believe you. Can you just see their eyes roll as they walk away? But there's danger in even the occasional lie. "I'm not upset that you lied to me," said the great Germany scholar Friedrich Nietzshe. "I'm upset that from now on I can't believe you." Words and actions have consequences. Aren't you lucky that now you know better!?

thyme

Scripture

"When you look for me with all your heart, you will find me: I will be found by you, announces the Lord."—Jeremiah 29:13–14 (NIrV)

Grace

Heavenly Father, great is your glory and great are you. May we experience the joy of seeking and then finding you. May we find you in the warmth of the sun, in the laughter of friends, and in the pleasure of those people who love us so much. Remind us that worship is not a command from you but a chance for us to *be* with you, our loving Friend and greatest treasure. Thank you for the blessings of this day, for our food, and for those who mean so much to us. Amen.

Grace notes

Does God choose you, or do you choose him? The answer is *yes* to both questions. When you truly seek him—seek him with all your heart—you might be surprised to find out that God chose and claimed *you* as his very own not only before you were born but before he had even created the world.* He's been waiting for you all this time. God hasn't been playing hide-and-seek with you. He was never hiding! "The Bible says that all things work together for the good of those who love the Lord and are called according to his purpose.** I believe that. Because I've seen it all work," said the American actor and director Tyler Perry.

*Ephesians 1:4 **Romans 8:28

Scripture

"You must not hate your fellow citizen in your heart. If your neighbor does something wrong, tell him about it, or you will be partly to blame. Forget about the wrong things people do to you, and do not try to get even. Love your neighbor as you love yourself. I am the Lord." —Leviticus 19:17–18 (NCV)

Grace

Almighty God, you are our Lord. May we always remember how much you love each one of us—keeping in mind that sometimes those who seem to us to least deserve your grace need it the most. Teach us that forgiving means losing any desire to *get back* at others. It isn't our job to teach them a lesson. Instead, teach *us* to help others in a kind—never a preachy—way. Please bless this food, Lord, that it may nourish our bodies as your words nourish our souls. Amen.

Grace notes

Hate is a terrible thing. It will destroy you if you let it. It feeds on itself, getting bigger and *badder* the longer you hang on to it. Sometimes you just want to lash out, hitting at everything and everyone in sight; we all sometimes feel that way. But think about it: Does that ever solve a problem? No, of course not—it might even create a bigger one. Anger messes with your ability to think clearly, making your thinking twisted and exaggerated. So how do you calm down this monster inside you? Deep breathing (you know, counting to 10 . . .) can be an amazing help. Close your eyes if you have to and let out your breath slowly. You're guaranteed to see a difference in your level of anger. Not that it should be necessary to mention this, but prayer helps, too! "Darkness cannot drive out darkness: only light can do that," said the famous preacher Dr. Martin Luther King Jr. "Hate cannot drive out hate: only love can do that," he went on to say.

Scripture

"The wisdom that comes from God is first of all pure, then peaceful, gentle, and easy to please. This wisdom is always ready to help those who are troubled and to do good for others. It is always fair and honest." —James 3:17 (NCV)

Grace

Heavenly Father, thank you for this food and for our family. Bless those who are deep in trouble—even if it's their own doing. Help us to love them, even when our patience runs thin. Help us to remember that everyone could use a little kindness and encouragement at times. Teach us patience, and guide us to find ways to help those in need. Let us remember how much you love all of us. In Jesus' name we pray. Amen.

Grace notes

Here's a little secret: consider a viewpoint other than your own. This habit will help you in so many ways. Decisions become easier, kindness comes more quickly, and people will want to be your friends. *To Kill a Mockingbird* by Harper Lee is a well-loved novel in which a man named Atticus Finch tells his young daughter "If you can learn a simple trick, Scout, you'll get along a lot better with all kinds of folks. You never really understand a person until you consider things from his point of view, until you climb inside of his skin and walk around in it." Try it sometime and see what happens.

Scripture

"'What I'm about to tell you is true,' Jesus answered. 'Before Abraham was born, I am!'"—John 8:58 (NIrV)

Grace

Dear Jesus, we are grateful for this day and for our food. Please bless us and give us understanding of your Word. May we always remember that your love extends to everyone and that the gates of heaven are wide open; all are welcome. We pray to you, Jesus, remembering that you do not just speak *of* God or *for* God; you speak *as* God. You do not just *speak* the truth; you *are* the truth. Jesus, it is because you are God that your words are our way, our truth, and our life.* Teach us to love everyone as you do. Amen.

*John 14:6

Grace notes

Jesus had just told the religious leaders that he had talked to Abraham. That would have been shocking news, since Abraham had lived more than 1800 years before Jesus was even born. When they asked how that could be, he replied with "Before Abraham was born, I am." That was the boldest claim Jesus could have made—telling them that he himself is God. He had already told them he was not of this world,* but they still didn't get it, so he told them the same thing again and again—in seven different ways: "I AM the Bread of Life"; "I AM the Light of the World"; "I AM the Door of the Sheep"; "I AM the Good Shepherd"; and "I AM the Resurrection and the Life." Do you think they got it after all that? The religious leaders saw all the miracles Jesus performed and yet still refused to believe. What did it take for you?

*John 8:23; **John 6:35, John 8:12, John 10:7, 9, John 14:6, and John 15:1, 5, respectively

Scripture

"The Lord is my shepherd. I will always have everything I need. He gives me green pastures to lie in. He leads me by calm pools of water. He restores my strength. He leads me on right paths to show that he is good. Even if I walk through a valley as dark as the grave, I will not be afraid of any danger, because you are with me. Your rod and staff comfort me. You prepared a meal for me in front of my enemies. You welcomed me as an honored guest. My cup is full and spilling over. Your goodness and mercy will be with me all my life, and I will live in the Lord's house a long, long time."—Psalm 23:1–6 (ERV)

Grace

Heavenly Father, we are so grateful for your promise to always love and care for us. Help us grow in our understanding of all that you are so that we can trust you more and more as we grow. Remind us that you created us to love you and that all you want is a meaningful relationship with us. We pray for a life of goodness and for the sure knowledge that our cup will be full if we put our faith in you. We thank you for this food, Father, and ask your blessings on us all. Amen.

Grace notes

This is a famous psalm, and for good reason. Everyone, the world over (research has shown that this even includes many unbelievers), seems to love it. It speaks of God's great love for us and of the way in which he protects us. The green pastures picture nourishment and plenty, and the calm pools of water speak of rest. If we stay on the right path God assures us of his protection. The psalmist recognizes that life will not always be easy but declares that God will walk with us through every experience. The image of God's rod and staff comforting us is a reminder that he will take care of justice for his own. W. Phillip Keller, the author of *A Shepherd Looks at Psalm 23*, said this about this psalm: " . . . there is a thrilling awareness of God all around me. I live surrounded by His presence. . . . Bless His name." This beautiful psalm provides a wonderful picture of God and of the way he loves us. With the Lord as your protector, you can handle anything with confidence.

thyme

Scripture

"The Spirit God gave us does not make us afraid. His Spirit is a source of power and love and self-control." 2 Timothy 1:7 (ERV)

Grace

Almighty Father, we give you thanks for this wonderful day and for this great food. Please bless us and keep us safe and healthy. Lord, we know that you are our source of everything good. We pray for an awareness of the spiritual gifts you give to each of us so that we may be strong and courageous in our faith. Instill in us the knowledge that your gifts are a source for us of power and love and even of self-control. Inspire us to use your gifts well, knowing that with them we can be brave in our efforts to follow your will. We love you, God, and want you always with us. Amen.

Grace notes

Spiritual gifts are abilities and qualities given to each believer by the Holy Spirit. There are several lists in the New Testament, and they include wisdom, faith, spiritual knowledge, healing, serving, teaching, encouraging, giving, leadership, and mercy. The author Jim George offered some good advice on the subject: "Start where you are—do anything you can do, and do everything you can do, until you find something you must do! That something is probably your spiritual gift."

bay

Scripture

"Be strong. Take courage. Don't be intimidated. Don't give [threatening enemies] a second thought because God, your God, is striding ahead of you. He's right there with you. He won't let you down; he won't leave you."—Deuteronomy 31:6 (MSG)

Grace

Almighty Father, we're encouraged by your grace and mercy. We pray that we may feel your protection, knowing that you're with us at all times. Thank you, Father, for your promises; instill in us an eagerness to lean upon your Word for guidance in all things. Help us remember that even though our circumstances may change you are unchanging. Lord, we ask your blessing on this food and on our family; may we always be together. Amen.

Grace notes

Have you ever wondered why the Israelites had to wander in the desert for 40 years before reaching the promised land? After all, it was only 240 miles away. Before beginning their planned journey into Canaan they learned, from their spies, about ferocious and cruel giants who were living there, and they were too scared to go on. As we read in this verse, Moses and Joshua reminded the people of God's promise to protect them. Yet instead of believing God, all of them—except Joshua and Caleb—rebelled, saying in essence: "No, no we won't go." That made God seriously unhappy (let's make that angry), especially after all they'd been through together—the plagues, the Red Sea business, the manna, and all that. The people told Moses they'd rather take a chance in the wilderness—they'd rather die than face the dangers in Canaan. "Okay then," God agreed. "Have it your way: wander in that desert until all the men (except Joshua and Caleb) of your generation have died—that will take 40 years." The Israelites learned the hard way that when God makes a promise he keeps it. Pastor Charles R. Swindoll pointed out the fact they missed (even though it should have been obvious!): "God never calls His people to accomplish anything without promising to supply their every need." How has that worked for you? Don't you think Deuteronomy 31:6 would be a great verse to memorize?

SUNDAY
graces

Balaam Had a Talking Donkey!

Scripture

Balaam was a greedy, wicked man who was paid to tell fortunes to rich men and kings. Balaam got up in the morning. He put a saddle on his donkey. Then he went with the Moabite officials. But God was very angry when Balaam went. So the angel of the LORD stood in the road to oppose him. Balaam was riding on his donkey. His two servants were with him. The donkey saw the angel of the LORD standing in the road. The angel was holding a sword. He was ready for battle. So the donkey left the road and went into a field. Balaam hit the donkey. He wanted to get it back on the road.

Three times the angel of the LORD stood in the donkey's way, preventing him from moving forward. Three times Balaam hit him, hard. Then the LORD opened the donkey's mouth. It said to Balaam, "What have I done to you? Why did you hit me these three times?" Balaam answered the donkey. He said, "You have made me look foolish! I wish I had a sword in my hand. If I did, I'd kill you right now."

The donkey said to Balaam, "I'm your own donkey. I'm the one you have always ridden. Haven't you been riding me to this very day? Have I ever made you look foolish before?" "No," he said.

Then the LORD opened Balaam's eyes. He saw the angel of the LORD standing in the road. He saw that the angel was holding a sword. The angel was ready for battle. So Balaam bowed down. He fell with his face to the ground. The angel of the LORD spoke to him. He asked him, "Why have you hit your donkey three times? I have come here to oppose you. What you are doing is foolish. The donkey saw me. It turned away from me three times. Suppose it had not turned away. Then I would certainly have killed you by now. But I would have spared the donkey."

Balaam said to the angel of the LORD, "I have sinned. I didn't realize you were standing in the road to oppose me. Tell me whether you are pleased with me. If you aren't, I'll go back." The angel of the LORD said to Balaam, "Go with the men. But say only what I tell you to say." So Balaam went with Balak's officials.

Balak heard that Balaam was coming. So he went out to meet him. They met at a Moabite town near the Arnon River. The town was on the border of Balak's territory. Balak said to Balaam, "Didn't I send messengers to you? I wanted you to come quickly. So why didn't you come? I can make you very rich." "Well, I've come to you now," Balaam replied. "But I can't say whatever I please. I can only speak the words God puts in my mouth."—Paraphrased from Numbers 22:21–38 (NIrV)

Grace

Heavenly Father, we thank you for the blessings of this day and of this meal; please bless our time together, too. Lord, help us understand that the unusual ways you used to get people's attention in Old Testament days were necessary because Jesus had not yet come, in person, to deliver your message of greater things. Remind us, too, that after Jesus went to heaven you sent the Holy Spirit to live within each of us—to serve as our internal guides. Remind us that you also speak to us through your Word, the Bible. Teach us that you are as close to us as we invite you to be. Lord, your ways are so mysterious; we know that you are in control, and we are grateful to be in your care. Amen.

Grace notes

This is a very strange story. And crazy, isn't it, that Balaam was so angry with the donkey that he didn't even stop to think that he was talking to—a donkey! Even in Old Testament times that would have been eye-popping. But the strangest thing here was not so much that God made a donkey talk—after all, God created the universe. Here's the back story: Balaam was a very wicked man who cared only about power and money. He was on his way to Canaan as a hired gun to put a curse on the people of Israel, and he was to be paid a great reward for doing so. That was the wrong thing to do. Because Balaam thought himself so high and mighty, God decided to use a donkey—a lowly beast of burden—to get his attention, put him in his place, and force him to obey. (And who says God doesn't have a sense of humor!?)

This event left Balaam with no doubt about who was—and is—really in charge: God. God no longer uses strange means to communicate with us because we now have something they didn't have back then: the Bible. "Miracles," said C. S. Lewis, "are a retelling in small letters of the very same story which is written across the whole world in letters too large for some of us to see." God knows the big picture—the really big picture—and he used a little donkey to show Balaam a very big reality: who is actually in charge. Can you think of a time when you couldn't see the forest for the trees, so to speak—when something you needed to see or understand was right there in front of you, even though you totally missed it? Sometimes that's how important thoughts show up; you grow into them.

We Have Lift Off!
Jesus Soars to Heaven and the Great Commission

Scripture

Dear Theophilus, the first book I wrote was about everything Jesus did and taught from the beginning until the day he was carried up into heaven. The apostles saw Jesus many times during the 40 days after he was raised from death. He spoke to them about God's kingdom.

The apostles were all together. Jesus said to them, "The Holy Spirit will come on you and give you power. You will be my witnesses. You will tell people everywhere about me—in Jerusalem, in the rest of Judea, in Samaria, and in every part of the world."

After Jesus said this, he was lifted up into the sky. While they were watching, he went into a cloud, and they could not see him. They were staring into the sky where he had gone. Suddenly two men wearing white clothes were standing beside them. They said, "Men from Galilee, why are you standing here looking into the sky? You saw Jesus carried away from you into heaven. He will come back in the same way you saw him go."—Paraphrased from Acts 1:1–11 (ERV)

Grace

Wonderful Jesus, we can only imagine being there with you—after you had died and returned to life—talking and laughing together! To be in your presence, Lord, would have been incredible! You tell us, though, that we *can* be in your presence, both now and for eternity. We ask you to open the way for the Holy Spirit to empower us, to guide us to our purpose. Jesus, may we always remember that just as you once lived with us on earth, so you will one day return, for this is your promise. May we always remember that you love us and guide us to do everything in your name and for your sake. Thank you, Jesus, for this meal and for our family. We pray that your Word will fill us up. Amen.

Grace notes

The Scripture about Jesus' last words (Acts 1:8) is called "The Great Commission." It's not called "The Great Suggestion," is it? Praying and learning God's words cause amazing things to happen in your life, things you can't help but want to share. How could you spread the Good News? Help a neighbor? Help someone in another part of the world through prayer, letters, or donations? Invite someone to a church event? Set a good example by . . . ? "If God calls you to be a missionary, don't stoop to be a king," said the English writer and theologian G. K. Chesterton. It's all about priorities!

The Tower of Babel
Bla-Bla, Bla-Bla, Bla-Bla

Scripture

"At one time, the whole Earth spoke the same language. It so happened that as they moved out of the east, they came upon a plain in the land of Shinar [Babylonia] and settled down.

"They said to one another, 'Come, let's make bricks and fire them well.' They used brick for stone and tar for mortar. Then they said, 'Come, let's build ourselves a city and a tower that reaches Heaven. Let's make ourselves famous so we won't be scattered here and there across the Earth.'

"God came down to look over the city and the tower those people had built.

"God took one look and said, 'One people, one language; why, this is only a first step. No telling what they'll come up with next—they'll stop at nothing! Come, we'll* go down and garble their speech so they won't understand each other.' Then God scattered them from there all over the world. And they had to quit building the city. That's how it came to be called Babel, because their God turned their language into 'babble.' From there God scattered them all over the world."—Genesis 11:1–9 (MSG)

*This hints at the mystery of the Trinity: Father, Son, and Holy Spirit.

Grace

Father, Son, and Holy Spirit, we pray for understanding that we will come to learn more and more of your ways as we grow and mature. Give us the wisdom to accept that your plans for us are far better than anything we could come up with on our own. Stop us in our tracks when you see us doing foolish things, like thinking we know better than you. Help us see the excitement in reaching for the heavens with you, knowing that your hand is reaching down to give us a lift to the very top. We thank you for our food and ask you to bless our family. Please bless our church family, too, and thank you for the closeness we can share with our brothers and sister in Christ as we together praise and honor your name. "Lord, your love is as high as the heavens. Your faithful love reaches up to the skies."* Amen.

*Psalm 36:5 (ERV)

Grace notes

At first God wanted everyone on the whole planet to speak the same language, but the people began to think they were better than God and wanted to spread their own fame around. To keep them from making a mess of things (destroying themselves and their relationship with him) God confused their language to keep them from talking to each other about those foolish ideas.

Later, much later, Jesus came along with a message to spread the news—to the ends of the earth—about God's plan to save them and make them whole and united again. But there were so many languages by then; how could people understand each other? Ah, we need to keep in mind here that God's ways are not our ways. In fact, we learn in Acts 2 that some people began to speak words they had never learned, and others began to understand words they had never been taught! Everyone understood each other, and the Good News spread. "How will we understand each other in Heaven?" said the philosophy professor Peter Kreeft. "Will we all speak English or Dutch or Latin? No, we will speak music." (Don't worry, heaven isn't a Broadway musical where we'll sing all our words. That's just Dr. Kreeft's way of saying we'll make beautiful music together.)

Noah's VERY BIG Adventure

Scripture

This is the story of Noah. He had three sons, Shem, Ham, and Japheth. Noah had no faults. He lived in fellowship with God, but everyone else was evil in God's sight, and violence was everywhere. God looked at the world and saw that it was evil, for the people were all living evil lives.

God said to Noah, "I have decided to put an end to all people. I will destroy them completely, because the world is full of their violent deeds. Build a boat out of good timber; make rooms in it and cover it with tar inside and out. Make it 450 feet long, 75 feet wide, and 45 feet high. I am going to send a flood on the earth to destroy every living being. Everything on the earth will die, but I will make a covenant [deal] with you. Go into the boat with your wife, your sons, and their wives. Take into the boat with you a male and a female of every kind of animal and of every kind of bird, in order to keep them alive. Take along all kinds of food for you and for them." Noah did everything God commanded.

God then caused it to rain for 40 days and nights; the water rose 25 feet above the tops of the mountains. God then caused a great wind to blow and the water started going down gradually for 150 days. On the seventeenth day of the seventh month the boat came to rest on a mountain in the Ararat range. The water kept going down, and on the first day of the tenth month the tops of the mountains appeared. Noah sent out first a raven, and then a dove to see if the water had gone down, knowing that if they found land they would not come back. After 14 days of this, the dove did not come back and the earth was dry enough for survival. God told everyone it was safe to get out of the boat. Noah was 601 years old.

Noah built an altar and offered a sacrifice to God, who said, "Never again will I put the earth under a curse because of what people do; I know that from the time they are young their thoughts are evil. Never again will I destroy all living beings, as I have done this time. As long as the world exists, there will be a time for planting and a time for harvest. There will always be cold and heat, summer and winter, day and night."

God blessed Noah and his sons and said, "Have many children, so that your descendants will live all over the earth. I promise that never again will all living beings be destroyed by a flood; never again will a flood destroy the earth. Whenever I cover the sky with clouds and the rainbow appears, I will remember my promise to you and to all the animals that a flood will never again destroy all living beings. When the rainbow appears in the clouds, I will see it and remember the everlasting covenant between me and all living beings on earth. That is the sign of the promise which I am making to all living beings."—Paraphrased from Genesis 6, 7, 8, 9 (GNT)

Grace

Almighty, everlasting God, please bless our family. We thank you for the food that nourishes us. Teach us that just as you noticed and rewarded Noah's goodness, you will do the same for us. Remind us to think of this and of you whenever we spot a rainbow. Help us remember to send a prayer of thanksgiving up the rainbow's path, for at your end are surely the riches of the universe. Remind us that you sent Jesus to take on the sins of the world for us. Lord, how can you be so high and mighty and yet love us so much? This is a deep mystery to us, but then you already know that. We praise you for your goodness and grace. Lord, you amaze us. Amen.

Grace notes

What are the big ideas for us from the story of Noah's ark? God's purpose in bringing the flood was not to destroy people but to destroy sin; the flood was God's judgment on humanity's out-of-control wickedness and rebellion. But the story also tells of God's love and protection for those who follow him. In this story God was restoring the balance of good in the world for future generations. Remember God's promise that a flood will never again destroy the earth as you read this Cherokee (Native American) blessing: "May the warm winds of heaven blow softly upon your house. May the Great Spirit bless all who enter there. May your moccasins make happy tracks in many snows, and may the rainbow always touch your shoulder."

Here's an interesting fact: the ark was six times longer than it was wide. According to shipbuilders this ratio demonstrates an advanced knowledge of shipbuilding—the best possible design for stability on the high seas.

The Lost Son Who Found Himself (the Prodigal Son)

Scripture

"Then Jesus said, 'There was a man who had two sons. The younger son said to his father, "Give me now the part of your property that I am supposed to receive someday." So the father divided his wealth between his two sons.

"A few days later the younger son gathered up all that he had and left. He traveled far away to another country, and there he wasted his money living like a fool. After he spent everything he had, there was a terrible famine throughout the country. He was hungry and needed money. So he went and got a job with one of the people who lived there. The man sent him into the fields to feed pigs. He was so hungry that he wanted to eat the food the pigs were eating. But no one gave him anything. The son realized that he had been very foolish.

"Almost dead for lack of food, the son decided to go home to his father, hoping he would take him back. He realized he had committed a grave sin against God and wronged his father. Also realizing he was no longer worthy to be called 'son,' he would be grateful if he could be nothing more than a hired worker.

"While the son was still a long way off, his father saw him coming and felt sorry for him. So he ran to him and hugged and kissed him. The son said, 'Father, I have sinned against God and have done wrong to you. I am no longer worthy to be called your son.' But the father said to his servants, 'Hurry! Bring the best clothes and put them on him. Also, put a ring on his finger and good sandals on his feet. And bring our best calf and kill it so that we can celebrate with plenty to eat. My son was dead, but now he is alive again! He was lost, but now he is found!' So they began to have a party.

"When the older son came in from the field, he heard music and dancing. 'What does all this mean?' he asked a servant boy. The boy said, 'Your brother has come back, and your father killed the best calf to eat. He is happy because his son is back safe and sound.'

"The older son was angry and would not go in to the party. So his father went out and begged him to come in. But he said to his father, 'Look, for all these years I have worked like a slave for you. I have always done what you told me to do, and you never gave me even a young goat for a party with my friends. But then this son of yours comes home after wasting your money . . . and you kill the best calf for him!'

"His father said to him, 'Oh, my son, you are always with me, and everything I have is yours. But this was a day to be happy and celebrate.

Your brother was dead, but now he is alive. He was lost, but now he is found.'"—Luke 15:11–32 (ERV)

Grace

Heavenly Father, thank you for our family and for this food; we remember you in gratitude for our blessings. Thank you for teaching us how happy it makes you when we ask for forgiveness. Teach us that your compassion knows no limits and that you eagerly watch over each of us when we stray, ready to welcome us back with open arms. God, you are greater than any of our problems, and we are grateful for your love and protection. You are tremendous, remarkable, and awesome. We praise you, Lord; you are a merciful and just God, whose very nature is love. Amen.

Grace notes

This is a well-known story, but sometimes the father's and the older brother's parts get overlooked. The older son had some growing up to do—he was jealous because he didn't realize his father had more than enough love for both of his sons. Somehow, he thought his father loved him less because of his dad's reaction to the return of his brother. Nonsense! His dad had never given him reason to feel insecure or unloved. Maybe he thought that way because in Jesus' time the response of the father to the return of his wandering son would have been unheard of. The younger son had shamed his father by wasting his money and living like a fool. *Forgive him? Never!*

But that's not how it is with God; he will always delight in taking you back. In this story the father represents God, the come-back son represents you, the sinner, and the older son represents the unforgiving law of the day. God's amazing grace is there for you; he will always welcome you back. Take the theme of this story—forgiveness—to heart and let it show you how to act in your own life. Need an example? Here's a good one that comes from the Army chaplain Charles Mallory: "The father's reaction to the prodigal son and his elder son mirrors the answer Abraham Lincoln gave to a question he was asked about how he would treat all the confederate soldiers once the Civil War was over. Expecting vengeance and even thoughts of execution because of treason, Lincoln surprised all of them by saying, 'I will treat them as if they had never been away.'" We know that Mr. Lincoln knew the Bible. Not only did he know it, but he acted it out. Can you think of a time when you might need to remember this?

How Did He Do That? David and the Giant Goliath

Scripture

The Philistines [bad guys] gathered their armies for war. They had a champion fighter named Goliath. He was over nine feet tall. He wore a bronze helmet and a coat of bronze armor that weighed 125 pounds. He wore bronze protectors on his legs and he had a bronze spear on his back; the blade itself weighed fifteen pounds.

Goliath walked out of the Philistine camp and shouted to the Israelite soldiers, "Choose a man and send him to fight me. If he can fight and kill me, we will be your servants. But if I can kill him, you will be our servants." When Saul and the Israelites heard this, they were really scared. Goliath yelled at them like this every day for 40 days.

Now David, Jesse's son, took care of his father's sheep. Jesse told him to take food to his seven brothers fighting at the battlefront. While there he heard Goliath's daily rant. David said to Saul, "Don't let anyone be discouraged. I, your servant, will go and fight this Philistine!" Saul said, "You can't go out and fight him; you're a boy and Goliath has been a warrior since he was a young man.' But David said to Saul, "I have been keeping my father's sheep. When a lion or bear came and took a sheep from the flock, I would chase it and attack it and save the sheep from its mouth. When it attacked me, I caught it by its fur and hit it and killed it. I have killed both a lion and a bear! Goliath will be like them, because he has spoken against the armies of the living God. The Lord who saved me from a lion and a bear will save me from Goliath."

Saul agreed to the plan and put his own clothes on David. He put a bronze helmet on his head and dressed him in armor. David put on Saul's sword and tried to walk around, but he was not used to all the armor. David said, "I can't fight in this," and took it all off. He took his stick and chose five smooth stones from a stream. He put them in his shepherd's bag and grabbed his sling. Then he went to meet Goliath.

When Goliath saw that David was only a boy, tanned and handsome, he looked down on him with disgust. He said, "Do you think I am a dog that you come at me with a stick?" He said to David, "Come here. I'll feed your body to the birds of the air and the wild animals!"

But David said to him, "You come to me using a sword and two spears. But I come to you in the name of the Lord All-Powerful!" As Goliath came near to attack him, David took a stone from his bag, put it into his sling, and slung it. The stone hit the Philistine and went deep into his forehead, and Goliath fell face down on the ground—dead. David defeated the Philistine with only a sling and a stone.—Paraphrased from 1 Samuel 17 (NCV)

Grace

Heavenly Father, please bless our family and our food; may it nourish our bodies and sustain us. May we always praise you for who you are—Almighty God—and may we never forget that you can overcome any obstacle. Lord, teach us that we must be willing to defend your name, too. Remind us that you are the reason any good happens and that we must be willing to trust you completely—just as David did. May your strength be our armor, Lord and your love our shield. Dear God, you answer our prayers! Thank you for this day when we can take a little extra time from our busy lives to focus on you. Halleluiah! Amen.

Grace notes

Many people of courage have shared their perspective on the subject of bravery. Here are a few:

"A hero is no braver than an ordinary man, but he is braver five minutes longer."—Poet Ralph Waldo Emerson

"There is no need to be ashamed of tears, for tears bear witness that a man has the greatest of courage, the courage to suffer."—Victor Frankl, Holocaust (Nazi death camp) survivor

Perhaps the first-century Roman philosopher Marcus Tullius Cicero came closest to the truth: "A man of courage is also full of faith."

If you need courage, you need look no further than the Holy Spirit, who is already living within you. Picture the Creator of the universe as your protector. Then see with your mind's eye legions of angels with him, swords raised at the ready, surrounding you. Jesus said, "If you love me, you will do what I command. I will ask the Father, and he will give you another Helper [the Holy Spirit] to be with you forever. . . . You will know that you are in me and I am in you."* Now *that's* a reason for courage!

*John 14:15–16, 20(b) (ERV)

Jesus Walks on Water (Don't Try This at Home)

Scripture

"Immediately Jesus told his followers to get into the boat and go ahead of him across the lake. He stayed there to send the people home. After he had sent them away, he went by himself up into the hills to pray. It was late, and Jesus was there alone. By this time, the boat was already far away from land. It was being hit by waves, because the wind was blowing against it.

"Between three and six o'clock in the morning, Jesus came to them, walking on the water. When his followers saw him walking on the water, they were afraid. They said, 'It's a ghost!' and cried out in fear. But Jesus quickly spoke to them, 'Have courage! It is I. Do not be afraid.' Peter said, 'Lord, if it is really you, then command me to come to you on the water.' Jesus said, 'Come.'

"And Peter left the boat and walked on the water to Jesus. But when Peter saw the wind and the waves, he became afraid and began to sink. He shouted, 'Lord, save me!' Immediately Jesus reached out his hand and caught Peter. Jesus said, 'Your faith is small. Why did you doubt?'

"After they got into the boat, the wind became calm. Then those who were in the boat worshiped Jesus and said, 'Truly you are the Son of God!'"—Matthew 14:22–33 (NCV)

Grace

Dear Jesus, we may have been frightened too, seeing you walk on top of deep water. But we now know to look to you for miracles in our life. We pray for guidance and strength to live with purpose and to fulfill the plans you have for us. We have so much to be grateful for, and we are truly thankful that you are in our life. Teach us about your grace and mercy for us. Please bless our food, our family, our church, and your bigger church all around the world. Our Lord God Almighty, how we praise you. Amen.

Grace notes

Look at the other New Testament accounts of this story. In Mark's and John's Gospels (check out Mark 6:45–51 and John 6:16–21) Peter's walk on the water isn't even mentioned—probably because Mark and John didn't want to make Peter the center of the story, preferring to keep the focus on Jesus. Here's another interesting point: in the original Greek language, when Jesus says "It is I," he's using the exact words God the Father spoke to Moses at the burning bush: "I AM WHO I AM"* (*Eh-heh-yeh ashair Ehheh-yeh*). Something else to think about: when Jesus called to Peter to join him on the water Peter jumped right out of the boat—no hesitation—and began to walk. But then Peter took his eyes off Jesus, . . . and what happened? He started to sink. There's a message here for you, isn't there? Take your eyes off Jesus and you might just find yourself in deep water, too. But take heart: Jesus grabbed Peter immediately, before he could sink. Someone once asked, "What good is having someone who can walk on water if you don't follow in his footsteps?" Good question. A very good question.

*Exodus 3:14

Grumpy Workers

Scripture

Jesus said, "Many who are first now will be last in the future. And many who are last now will be first in the future.

"The kingdom of heaven is like a person who owned some land. One morning, he went out very early to hire some people to work in his vineyard. The man agreed to pay the workers one coin for working that day. Then he sent them into the vineyard to work. About nine o'clock the man went to the marketplace and saw some other people standing there, doing nothing. So he said to them, 'If you go and work in my vineyard, I will pay you what your work is worth.' So they went to work in the vineyard. The man went out again about twelve o'clock and three o'clock and did the same thing. About five o'clock the man went to the marketplace again and saw others standing there. He asked them, 'Why did you stand here all day doing nothing?' They answered, 'No one gave us a job.' The man said to them, 'Then you can go and work in my vineyard.'

"At the end of the day, the owner of the vineyard said to the boss of all the workers, 'Call the workers and pay them. Start with the last people I hired and end with those I hired first.'

"When the workers who were hired at five o'clock came to get their pay, each received one coin. When the workers who were hired first came to get their pay, they thought they would be paid more than the others. But each one of them also received one coin. When they got their coin, they complained to the man who owned the land. They said, 'Those people were hired last and worked only one hour. But you paid them the same as you paid us who worked hard all day in the hot sun.' But the man who owned the vineyard said to one of those workers, 'Friend, I am being fair to you. You agreed to work for one coin. So take your pay and go. I want to give the man who was hired last the same pay that I gave you. I can do what I want with my own money. Are you jealous because I am good to those people?'

"So those who are last now will someday be first, and those who are first now will someday be last"—Matthew 19:30—20:16 (NCV)

Grace

Gracious Lord, we thank you for this food, for our family, and for the gifts you have given each of us. Encourage us not to be jealous of what others get or to worry our heads about what is fair. Knowing that your love for us isn't based on what we do, teach us to treat others the same way. Encourage us to leave the fairness thing to you, the one who is perfectly just. Help us to remember that you will take care of everything in your perfect timing. Help us also to remember that your grace and mercy extend to us all and that the kingdom of heaven is open to all of us. Thank you, Jesus, for helping us straighten things out. May your love for us be all that matters. Amen.

Grace notes

This parable is about getting more than you deserve—just because God loves you. From the human side of things, it's about gratitude. Do you obey God because you expect to be rewarded (that attitude will get you in last place fast)? Or do you serve him out of gratefulness for what you have (hello, first place)? It's easy to fall into the trap of doing the right things for the wrong reasons. Can you think of examples? How about being nice in order to get something you want? Or giving someone a gift to keep them from getting angry at you? Gratitude and service: these are the two right motives for your good deeds.

To avoid falling into the pit of anger or resentment, don't pay attention to what others have done to you or whether they may have received a better break than you. Focus on what Jesus has done for you. Even more importantly, let Jesus himself, not the things he gives you, keep you faithful. "When it comes to life the critical thing is whether you take things for granted or take them with gratitude," said the British mystery writer G. K. Chesterton. Taking things for granted will soon take you out of the running. Taking things with gratitude wins the prize. Every time.

The Parable of the Really Nice Guy (the Good Samaritan)

Scripture

"A teacher of the Law came up and tried to trap Jesus. 'Teacher,' he asked, 'what must I do to receive eternal life?' Jesus answered him, 'What do the Scriptures say? How do you interpret them?'

"The man answered, 'Love the Lord your God with all your heart, with all your soul, with all your strength, and with all your mind'; and 'Love your neighbor as you love yourself.'

"'You are right,' Jesus replied; 'do this and you will live.'

"But the teacher of the Law wanted to justify himself, so he asked Jesus, 'Who is my neighbor?'

"Jesus answered, 'There was once a man who was going down from Jerusalem to Jericho when robbers attacked him, stripped him, and beat him up, leaving him half dead. It so happened that a priest was going down that road; but when he saw the man, he walked on by on the other side. In the same way a Levite also came there, went over and looked at the man, and then walked on by on the other side. But a Samaritan who was traveling that way came upon the man, and when he saw him, his heart was filled with pity. He went over to him, poured oil and wine on his wounds and bandaged them; then he put the man on his own animal and took him to an inn, where he took care of him. The next day he took out two silver coins and gave them to the innkeeper. 'Take care of him,' he told the innkeeper, 'and when I come back this way, I will pay you whatever else you spend on him.'

"And Jesus concluded, 'In your opinion, which one of these three acted like a neighbor toward the man attacked by the robbers?'

"The teacher of the Law answered, 'The one who was kind to him.' Jesus replied, 'You go, then, and do the same.'"—Luke 10:25–37 (GNT)

Grace

Dear Jesus, thank you for bringing us together and for blessing us with food, family, and good neighbors. Help us see that helping others is the way you want us to act. Give us a desire to do just that. Guide us to someone who needs help, knowing that we ourselves might just be changed for the better because of it. Remind us too, that it's not a matter of helping only those who are like us but helping anyone who needs it. And Lord, we pray not to become like deer in the headlights—frozen by so much need. Teach us to think of ourselves as pieces of a puzzle—without our piece, small as it may be, the picture can never be complete. Lord, you are the great Provider, and we put our trust in you. Amen.

Grace notes

A few background notes: the road from Jerusalem to Jericho was a known trouble spot, with bandits hiding in the brush around the mountainous twists and turns. It also helps to understand that Jews and Samaritans didn't get along—at all. The Jewish lawyer would have considered a Samaritan a "non-neighbor"—someone to turn away from, not to turn toward with a helping hand. Keep in mind, too, that the priest and the Levite were considered to be especially devoted to God.

The lawyer in this parable wanted to determine the scope of this "call to love your neighbor" thing. In other words, he wanted to pick and choose those he considered worthy of his help while still being right with God. "Not so fast, young man," Jesus warned. "*Anyone* in need is your neighbor." The actor and film director Tyler Perry had it right when he said: "I love to give. I've been a giver all my life."

But you singlehandedly can't help everyone (there are the hungry, the poor, the sick, the uneducated . . . , and the list goes on). Go down that road and you'll soon be overwhelmed and want to give up. A better attitude is to help where you can, wherever and whenever an opportunity presents itself. "If you can't feed a hundred people, feed just one," said the Catholic Nun Mother Teresa. She was right. You can also expand your reach, though, through your church. Many people working together in various programs can assist many more, in many ways. Just by being a member of your church you help make all the programs work well, because your presence is supportive, encouraging, and productive.

The Farmer's Greediness Was His Undoing

Scripture

"Someone out of the crowd said, 'Teacher, order my brother to give me a fair share of the family inheritance.' [Jesus] replied, 'Mister, what makes you think it's any of my business to be a judge or mediator for you?'

"Speaking to the people, he went on, 'Take care! Protect yourself against the least bit of greed. Life is not defined by what you have, even when you have a lot.'

"Then he told them this story: 'The farm of a certain rich man produced a terrific crop. He talked to himself: "What can I do? My barn isn't big enough for this harvest." Then he said, "Here's what I'll do: I'll tear down my barns and build bigger ones. Then I'll gather in all my grain and goods, and I'll say to myself, Self, you've done well! You've got it made and can now retire. Take it easy and have the time of your life!"

"'Just then God showed up and said, "Fool! Tonight you die. And your barnful of goods—who gets it?" That's what happens when you fill your barn with Self and not with God.'"—Luke 12:13–21 (MSG)

Grace

Gracious Jesus, we thank you for this food and for our family. Please bless those who are hungry, poor, hurting, or in any kind of trouble. Remind us, Lord, how important it is to love you first and then to love and help others just as we would like to be loved and helped. Show us that this doesn't mean we're off the hook when it comes to working hard or saving and planning for the future. Help us see that good, honest work is different from greed—a barn of a different color. Steer our thoughts toward you—the source of the only real, eternal wealth. Jesus, we put our trust in you. Amen.

Grace notes

In the first part of this story someone was trying to get Jesus to take sides—one brother against another. Jesus used that opportunity to tell a parable about greed and how it can ruin your life. The rich man in this story was someone who kept everything for himself. His wealth wasn't bad in itself, but his attitude about it sure was. His mindset kept him from pursuing God because his great riches had become his idol and his source of security. He might not have said so out loud, but the truth was that he worshiped his stuff, and Jesus knew it. Don't share what you have with others just because you are expected to; do it because you want to. Bless others because you have been blessed, and your blessings will continue. Hoard your wealth, and your greed will be your undoing. "Greed is not a financial issue. It's a heart issue," said the pastor and author Andy Stanley.

Jesus Calms the Storm: The Wind Ran Out of Breath

Scripture

"On the evening of that same day Jesus said to his disciples, 'Let us go across to the other side of the lake.' So they left the crowd; the disciples got into the boat in which Jesus was already sitting, and they took him with them. Other boats were there too. Suddenly a strong wind blew up, and the waves began to spill over into the boat, so that it was about to fill with water. Jesus was in the back of the boat, sleeping with his head on a pillow. The disciples woke him up and said, 'Teacher, don't you care that we are about to die?'

"Jesus stood up and commanded the wind, 'Be quiet!' and he said to the waves, 'Be still!' The wind died down, and there was a great calm. Then Jesus said to his disciples, 'Why are you frightened? Do you still have no faith?'

"But they were terribly afraid and began to say to one another, 'Who is this man? Even the wind and the waves obey him!'"—Mark 4:35–41 (GNT)

Grace

Dear Jesus, how awesome is your power—even the mighty wind cowers before you. Oh, it would have been something to see the astonishment in the disciples' eyes as they realized who you really, really were! Remind us to keep growing in our trust in you, Lord, so that when we face storms in our lives we will know you're there to help us through them. Thank you, Lord, for your awesome love, for our family, for our church, and for this meal. Jesus, you are truly God Almighty—the one who was, and is, and is to come.* Amen!

*Revelation 1:8

Grace notes

A sea, by its nature, isn't always calm. Life is like that, too. There will be times when you think your faith in Jesus is strong. But then something terrible happens. You become frightened that your faith is not delivering, and you wonder where God is. But Jesus has saved you from ultimate destruction, and your trust in him will help you face even the worst storms. Jesus may not deliver you from the storm, but he will get you through it. "I just want to grow spiritually with the Lord. I'm keeping strong at it, just trying to make my walk with faith a little better," said the NBA player Kevin Durant.

Lazarus Gets a Real Live Sequel

Scripture

Lazarus was sick. His sisters, Mary and Martha, with whom he lived, sent a message to Jesus. "Lord," they told him, "the one you love is sick." When Jesus heard this, he said, "This sickness will not end in death. No, it is for God's glory. God's Son will receive glory because of it."

Two days later, Jesus said to his disciples, "Our friend Lazarus has fallen asleep back in Judea, and I am going there to wake him up." His disciples replied, "Lord, if he's sleeping, he will get better." Jesus had been talking about the death of Lazarus. But his disciples thought he meant natural sleep. So then he told them plainly, "Lazarus is dead. For your benefit, I am glad I was not there. Now you will believe. But let us go to him."

When Jesus and the disciples arrived, they learned that Lazarus had been in the tomb for four days. When Martha heard that Jesus was coming, she went out to meet him. "Lord," she said to Jesus, "I wish you had been here earlier! Then my brother would not have died. But I know that even now God will give you anything you ask for." Jesus said to her, "Your brother will rise again." Martha answered, "I know he will rise again someday. This will happen when people are raised from the dead on the last day."

Jesus said to her, "I am the resurrection and the life. Anyone who believes in me will live, even if he dies. And those who live and believe in me will never die. Do you believe this" "Yes, Lord," she told him. "I believe that you are the Christ, the Son of God. I believe that you are the One who was supposed to come into the world."

Mary went home and got her sister Martha who also said she wished Jesus had been there to save her brother. "Where have you put him?" [Jesus] asked. "Come and see, Lord," they replied. He went to the tomb, a cave with a stone in front of the entrance. "Take away the stone," he said. "But, Lord," said Martha, "by this time there is a bad smell. Lazarus has been in the tomb for four days." Then Jesus said, "Didn't I tell you that if you believed, you would see God's glory?" They took away the stone.

Then Jesus looked up. He said, "Father, I thank you for hearing me. I know that you always hear me. But I say this for the benefit of the people standing here. I said it so they will believe that you sent me." Then Jesus called in a loud voice. He said, "Lazarus, come out!" The dead man came out. His hands and feet were wrapped with strips of linen. A cloth was around his face. Jesus said to them, "Take off the clothes he was buried in and let him go."—Paraphrased from John 11 (NIrV)

Grace

Dear Jesus, we bow our heads in wonder and ask for your blessing on our family and our food. Jesus, we thank you that you are with us. You are God, the one who created us, the one who loves us more than we know how to imagine, the one who is perfectly just and merciful, and the one who is powerful enough to solve any problem. Instill is us a craving to seek you always, to call out your name, and to allow you to fill our hearts with yourself. Jesus, point us toward the Spirit's eagerness to help strengthen our faith; sharpen our ears, too, so we can hear you calling us. May our souls find rest in you, dear Jesus. We pray now that you will speak to our hearts and help us understand your will for our lives. We pray for a faith that endures. We praise you, Lord. Amen.

Grace notes

Technically speaking, Lazarus was not resurrected from the dead. Jesus is the only one who can claim that. Jesus gave himself a new, glorified body and became immortal. The right word for what happened to Lazarus and several others is *revivication*, or *reanimation*. It means being brought back to life in the same body—a body that will eventually die all over again. In addition to Lazarus, Jesus raised Jairus's daughter and the son of the widow from Naim. Elijah raised the son of the widow from Zarapheth, Peter raised Tabitha, and Paul raised Eutychus.* But Jesus, and only Jesus, rose from the dead by the power of God. He rose with a new, glorified, perfect body, and he now lives forever. "The resurrection of Jesus," said Clarence W. Hall, "changes the face of death for all His people. Death is no longer a prison, but a passage into God's presence." (According to St. Thomas Aquinas, Jesus chose to keep his wounds on his resurrected body, mainly as proof of who he was to believers and non-believers alike. They were a sign of his love for us, not of his loss.)

*Matthew 9:18–26; Luke 7:11–17; 1 Kings 17:7–24; Acts 9:40; 20:7–12

"I'm Blind as a Bat!"

Scripture

All this time Saul was breathing down the necks of [Jesus'] disciples, out for the kill. From the Chief Priest he got blank arrest warrants to take to Damascus so that he could arrest anyone he found talking about Jesus and bring them to Jerusalem. At the outskirts of Damascus, he was suddenly dazed by a blinding flash of light. As he fell to the ground, he heard a voice: "Saul, Saul, why are you out to get me?" He said, "Who are you, Master?"

"I am Jesus, the One you're hunting down. I want you to get up and enter the city. In the city you'll be told what to do next." His companions stood there dumbstruck—they could hear the sound, but couldn't see anyone—while Saul, picking himself up off the ground, found himself stone-blind. They had to hold his hand and lead him into Damascus. He was blind for three days. He ate nothing, drank nothing.

There was a disciple in Damascus by the name of Ananias. Jesus spoke to him in a vision: "Ananias." "Yes, Master?" he answered. "Get up and go over to Straight Avenue. Ask at the house of Judas for a man from Tarsus. His name is Saul. He's there praying. He has just had a dream in which he saw a man named Ananias enter the house and lay hands on him so he could see again." Ananias protested, "Master, you can't be serious. Everybody's talking about this man and the terrible things he's been doing against your people in Jerusalem! And now he's shown up here with papers from the Chief Priest that give him license to do the same to us."

But Jesus said, "Don't argue. Go!" So Ananias went and found the house, placed his hands on blind Saul, and said, "Brother Saul, the Master sent me, the same Jesus you saw on your way here. He sent me so you could see again and be filled with the Holy Spirit." No sooner were the words out of his mouth than something like scales fell from Saul's eyes—he could see again! He got to his feet, was baptized, and sat down with them to a hearty meal.

Saul spent a few days getting acquainted with the Damascus disciples, but then went right to work, wasting no time, preaching in the meeting places that this Jesus was truly the Son of God. They were caught off guard by this and, not at all sure they could trust him, they kept saying, "Isn't this the man who wreaked havoc in Jerusalem among the believers? And didn't he come here to do the same thing—arrest us and drag us off to jail in Jerusalem for sentencing by the high priests?"—Paraphrased from Acts 9:1–22 (MSG)

Grace

Dear Jesus, you certainly have a way of getting our attention! May we experience the wonder and joy of that moment in which we discover the role you want us to play in this world. May we take heart in knowing that you can bring even the most stubborn unbeliever to salvation. Praise to you, Oh God, for your majesty. We worship you because you are Lord, and because there is no other God."* Praise be to your holy name. Amen.

*Isaiah 45:5

Grace notes

Does God choose you or do you choose God? The answer is yes—to both. Saul's "meeting" with Jesus in this dramatic story changed his life (as well it should have). Followers of Jesus saw the *new* Saul. Confused, they began asking questions, like "Who is this man who looks like the Saul who hated us but talks like he's one of us?" Saul's conversion—believing in Jesus—was reflected in his new name: Paul, the Gentile version of his Jewish name. Paul had a lot of work to do convincing people of the change in his life: "We live by what we believe, not by what we can see," he said (2 Corinthians 5:7). He managed to convince them, though, for that was God's plan. This Jesus-hater became the apostle Paul, who wrote many of the books of the New Testament (most of them, in fact). The preacher Charles Spurgeon said that "conversion is a turning onto the right road. The next thing to do is to walk on it." Take that first step in choosing God if you haven't yet. If you have, just keep walking. Either way, keep walking. As long as you're moving in the right direction, keep walking.

Gideon and the Very, Very Small Army

Scripture

Once again the people of Israel sinned against the Lord, so God let the people of Midian rule over them for seven years. The Midianites were strong, and the Israelites had to hide in caves and hills. The Midianites came and devastated the land, and Israel was helpless against them.

The people cried out to the Lord for help. The Lord's angel came and sat under the oak tree that belonged to Joash. The angel said to Joash's son Gideon: "The Lord is with you, brave and mighty man!" Then the angel (who was really the Lord) ordered him, "Go with all your great strength and rescue Israel from the Midianites. I myself am sending you." Gideon replied, "But Lord, how can I rescue Israel? My clan is the weakest in the tribe of Manasseh, and I am the least important member of my family." The Lord answered, "You can do it because I will help you. You will crush the Midianites as easily as if they were only one man."

Then Gideon tested God by asking for a sign! "You say that you have decided to use me to rescue Israel. Well, I am putting some wool on the ground where we thresh the wheat. If in the morning there is dew only on the wool but not on the ground, then I will know that you are going to use me to rescue Israel." That is exactly what happened. When Gideon got up early the next morning, he squeezed the wool and wrung enough dew out of it to fill a bowl with water. Then Gideon said to God, "Don't be angry with me; let me speak just once more. Please let me make one more test with the wool. This time let the wool be dry, and the ground be wet." That night God did that very thing. The next morning the wool was dry, but the ground was wet with dew.

The Lord then said: "There are too many fighters; they'll think they won by themselves, and give me no credit. Tell the people, 'Anyone who is afraid should go back home.'" So 22,000 went back, and 10,000 stayed. Then the Lord said, "Still have too many. Take them down to the water and separate everyone who laps up the water with his tongue like a dog from everyone who gets down on his knees to drink." 300 men scooped up water in their hands; all the others got down on their knees to drink. The Lord said, "I will rescue you and give you victory over the Midianites with these 300 men. Tell everyone else to go home." That night the Lord commanded Gideon to wake his men up. "Get up! The Lord is giving you victory!" he said. He gave each man a trumpet and a jar with a torch inside it and said, "When I get to the edge of the camp, watch me, do what I do. When I blow the trumpet, you blow yours all around the camp and shout, 'For the LORD!'" Gideon and his men came to the edge of the camp a while before midnight, just after the guard changed. They blew the trumpets, broke the jars, lit the torches and shouted, "A sword for the LORD and for Gideon!" Every man stood in his place around the camp, and the whole enemy army ran away yelling. So Midian was defeated by the Israelites and was no longer a threat. The land was at peace for 40 years, until Gideon died.—Paraphrased from Judges 6, 7, 8 (GNT)

Grace

Lord God, thank you for showing us how much you love us, even with all our faults and with our often stumbling faith. Remind us that you know every situation we get ourselves into, just as you knew Gideon's circumstances and his fears. Thank you so much for your encouragement when we're scared. Remind us you are always with us—as surely as the trumpets blew and Gideon tested you with the wool. May you give us courage and guidance each day. Thank you for your teachings, for this oh-so-great-smelling food, and for our family. Thanks be to you, God; you always lead us in victory through Christ.* In Jesus' name we pray. Amen.

*2 Corinthians 2:14

Grace notes

Be faithful to God, as Gideon was, and he will see you through even the toughest times, no matter how poor the odds for success may seem. Nothing is too difficult for God. And though God is incredibly patient with your growing faith, this story doesn't mean you too can *lay out the fleece* as Gideon did, before God in prayer. (God can't be manipulated.) And know that you have two things going for you that Gideon didn't. First, you have the whole of God's Word in the Bible. Seek your answers there. And second, you have the Holy Spirit—God himself—living in you to guide and encourage you. And here's something else to keep in mind: God knows that sometimes you must work things out while he stands by and watches; that's how your character grows. "Remember," as someone has said, "the teacher is always quiet during a test."

Here's an interesting aspect to the story, as told by Pastor Ken Ingold: Why do you think God chose men who drank from their cupped hands instead of bending down with their faces toward the water? Those who crouched down on all fours could see nothing around them while they were drinking; they had their heads down. Those who drank by bringing the water up to their mouths were able to stay on guard, safe and aware of their surroundings. Ah, what a golden opportunity to fast-forward this idea into the twenty-first century: Why would anyone walk or drive and text at the same time?

Moses and the Bush of Fire, Or Burn, Baby, Burn

Scripture

Moses was shepherding the flock of Jethro, his father-in-law. He came to the mountain of God, called Horeb. God appeared to him in flames of fire blazing out of the middle of a bush. The bush was blazing away but it didn't burn up. Moses said, "What's going on here? I can't believe this! Amazing! Why doesn't the bush burn up?" God called to him from out of the bush, "Moses! Moses!" He said, "Yes? I'm right here!" God said, "I am the God of your father: The God of Abraham, the God of Isaac, the God of Jacob." Moses hid his face, afraid to look at God.

God then told Moses that he had come to save his people, to pry them loose from the grip of Egypt, get them out of that country, and bring them to a good land with wide-open spaces, a land lush with milk and honey [the promised land]. God told Moses he was sending him to Pharaoh to bring the People of Israel out of Egypt. Moses said, "But why me? What makes you think that I could ever go to Pharaoh and lead the children of Israel out of Egypt?" "I'll be with you," God said.

Then Moses said, "Suppose I go to the People of Israel and I tell them, 'The God of your fathers sent me to you'; and they ask me, 'What is his name'? What do I tell them?" God said, "I-AM-WHO-I-AM. Tell the People, 'I-AM sent me to you.'" God said, "Now be on your way. Gather the leaders of Israel and go." Moses objected, "They won't trust me. They won't listen to a word I say. They'll say, 'God? Appear to him? Hardly!'" So God said, "What's that in your hand?" "A staff." "Throw it on the ground." He threw it. It became a snake. Moses jumped back—fast! God said to Moses, "Reach out and grab it by the tail." He reached out and grabbed it—and he was holding his staff again. "That's so they will trust that God appeared to you, the God of their fathers, the God of Abraham, the God of Isaac, and the God of Jacob," God replied.

Moses raised another objection to God: "Master, please, I don't talk well. I've never been good with words, neither before nor after you spoke to me. I stutter and stammer." God said, "And who do you think made the human mouth? And who makes some mute, some deaf, some sighted, some blind? Isn't it I, God? So, get going. I'll be right there with you—with your mouth! I'll be right there to teach you what to say."—Paraphrased from Exodus 3 and 4 (MSG)

Grace

Almighty God, we thank you that your grace and mercy are so plentiful and that you love us so much. We thank you for this food and for the many blessings of each day. Fix our thoughts and our eyes on you, God—on your unlimited power and your presence everywhere—for that is how blessings come to us. Remind us that, as mighty as you are, you focus on the smallest details in our lives, just as you did with Moses when you empowered him, a stutterer, to change the world. Today you speak to us—not through a burning bush but through the Holy Spirit in us and your Word right here in front of us. Teach us that you will make us ready for whatever tasks you call us to do. Lord, we call your name. There is no one else like you. Amen.

Grace notes

Have you noticed that one of the hardest things to believe in is your own ability? Is your first response to an invitation to do something sometimes "Not me—I could never do that"? But wait, you know that with God nothing is impossible. If you haven't heard that before, you will many times from now on. Concentrate on that, and then realize that success doesn't happen overnight. Reaching your goal is a journey, and God designed life that way. Break the task down, master each step, no matter how tiny, and then move on to the next. That's how anything is built. "If God is your partner, make your plans BIG," said the preacher and evangelist D. L. Moody. You can say that again!

Lay it On, Lord: The Ten Commandments

Scripture

Three months after leaving Egypt the Israelites entered the Wilderness of Sinai. Israel camped there, facing the mountain. As Moses went up to meet God, God called down to him from the mountain: "Speak to the House of Jacob, tell the People of Israel: 'You have seen what I did to Egypt and how I carried you on eagles' wings and brought you to me.'"

On the third day at daybreak, there were loud claps of thunder, flashes of lightning, a thick cloud covering the mountain, and an ear-piercing trumpet blast. Everyone in the camp shuddered in fear. Moses led the people out of the camp to meet God. They stood at attention at the base of the mountain. Mount Sinai was all smoke because God had come down on it as fire. Smoke poured from it like smoke from a furnace. The whole mountain shuddered in huge spasms. The trumpet blasts grew louder and louder. Moses spoke and God answered in thunder. God descended to the peak of Mount Sinai. God called Moses up to the peak and Moses climbed up.

So Moses went down to the people. He said to them: "God spoke all these words: 'I am God, your God, who brought you out of the land of Egypt, out of a life of slavery. No other gods, only me. No carved gods of any size, shape, or form of anything whatever, whether of things that fly or walk or swim. Don't bow down to them and don't serve them because *I* am God. No using the name of God, your God, in curses or silly banter; God won't put up with the irreverent use of his name. Observe the Sabbath day, to keep it holy. Work six days and do everything you need to do. But the seventh day is a Sabbath to God, your God. Don't do any work. For in six days God made Heaven, Earth, and sea, and everything in them; he rested on the seventh day. Therefore God blessed the Sabbath day; he set it apart as a holy day. Honor your father and mother so that you'll live a long time in the land that God is giving you. No murder. No adultery. No stealing. No lies about your neighbor. No lusting after your neighbor's house. Don't set your heart on anything that is your neighbor's."

Moses spoke to the people: "Don't be afraid. God has come to test you and instill a deep and reverent awe within you so that you won't sin."—Paraphrased from Exodus 19, 20 (MSG)

Grace

Heavenly Father, we thank you for taking care of us, for the food and for the family we love. Bless those who do not yet know you. Teach us that you gave us these commandments to show us how to act toward you and toward each other. Help us to see, too, that getting into heaven is not so much about following rules but about being in a right relationship with you. Remind us that it's your grace, and your grace alone, that gets us past the pearly gates into heaven. Lord, we are reminded that you pay attention to us, just like those who care for us, because you love us. We honor your holiness and pray for your guidance in living our lives according to your purpose. You are a forgiving God, kind and full of mercy, patient and full of love.* Amen.

*Nehemiah 9:17 (ERV)

Grace notes

"If God would have wanted us to live in a permissive society He would have given us Ten Suggestions and not Ten Commandments," said the American author Zig Ziglar. The Ten Commandments, also known as the Decalogue, were given by God to the people of Israel shortly after their escape (their exodus) from Egypt. Many people mistakenly think that all they need to do is to obey these laws and that entrance into heaven will then be guaranteed. But only a perfect person can live life without ever making a mistake. You're not perfect, neither is anyone else, which is why God's grace and mercy are so important.

And the Next King Is . . .

Scripture

"God addressed Samuel: 'So, how long are you going to mope over Saul? You know I've rejected him as king over Israel. Fill your flask with anointing oil and get going. I'm sending you to Jesse of Bethlehem. I've spotted the very king I want among his sons.'

" . . . God said to Samuel: 'Take a heifer with you and announce, "I've come to lead you in worship of God, with this heifer as a sacrifice." Make sure Jesse gets invited. I'll let you know what to do next. I'll point out the one you are to anoint.'

"Samuel did what God told him. When he arrived at Bethlehem, the town fathers greeted him. . . . 'Prepare yourselves, be consecrated, and join me in worship,' said Saul. He made sure Jesse and his sons were also consecrated and called to worship. When they arrived, Samuel took one look at Eliab [one of Jesse's sons] and thought, 'He must be the one! God's anointed!'

"But God told Samuel, 'Looks aren't everything. Don't be impressed with his looks and stature. I've already eliminated him. God judges persons differently than humans do. Men and women look at the face; God looks into the heart.'

"Jesse then called up Abinadab and presented him to Samuel. Samuel said, 'This man isn't God's choice either.' Next Jesse presented Shammah. Samuel said, 'No, this man isn't either.' Jesse presented his seven sons to Samuel. Samuel was blunt with Jesse, 'God hasn't chosen any of these.'

"Then he asked Jesse, 'Is this it? Are there no more sons?' 'Well, yes, there's the runt. But he's out tending the sheep.' Samuel ordered Jesse, 'Go get him. We're not moving from this spot until he's here.'

"Jesse sent for him. He was brought in, the very picture of health—bright-eyed, good-looking. God said, 'Up on your feet! Anoint him! This is the one.' Samuel took his flask of oil and anointed him, with his brothers standing around watching. The Spirit of God entered David like a rush of wind, God vitally empowering him for the rest of his life."—1 Samuel 16:1–13 (MSG)

Grace

Almighty God, we thank you for being here with us and for providing us with this good food. Encourage us to open our hearts to become people after your heart. Fill us with a desire to learn what you want and not to worry so much about what others think. We hear what you're saying: "Believe in me, make yourselves right with me, and I'll take care of everything else." Remind us how easy it can be to be fooled by appearances; we don't really know someone else's story, and they don't know ours. Teach us never to underestimate what you can accomplish through us—even through the least of us. Praise be to your holy name. Amen.

Grace notes

Challenges don't always come in big packages. David was the humble shepherd of his father's sheep, but the challenges of that job were preparing him for a really big one in the future. Here are some little things you can do every day that will prepare you for the time when you'll need greater courage and strength of character. (Challenges and courage often go together.) Make eye contact with five kids at school you don't know and smile at them like you mean it. Ask a question in class, especially if you don't get something and are afraid other kids might laugh at you. Talk to your parents about their day and show real interest in what they do. Audition for something. If being in a school play terrifies you, try out for a small part or volunteer to be part of the stage crew. Volunteer for something. Take a really cold shower! (Do that last one for three minutes and you'll feel like you can do anything!) Cook a real breakfast—from a recipe! What other ideas can you think of? "God does not necessarily call upon only those who are ready, but he will make ready those he calls," said Hattie Elizabeth Turner, a widow who spent her time caring for injured soldiers during the American Civil war. (Hattie is the main character in a play called *Witness to Gettysburg* by Annette Hubbell). Could it just be that God is preparing you in those little things for big things later?

Solomon, a Real Wise Guy

Scripture

"One day two women . . . came to Solomon. As they stood before him, one of the women said, 'My master, this woman and I live in the same house. I gave birth to a baby while she was there with me. Three days later this woman also gave birth. No one else was in the house with us; it was just the two of us. One night this woman rolled over on her baby, and he died. She then took my son from my bed during the night while I was asleep, and carried him to her bed. Then she moved her dead baby to my bed. The next morning when I got up to feed my baby, I saw that he was dead! When I looked at him more closely, I realized he was not my son.'

"'No!' the other woman cried. 'The living baby is my son, and the dead baby is yours!' But the first woman said, 'No! The dead baby is yours, and the living one is mine!' So the two women argued before the king.

"Then King Solomon said, 'One of you says, "My son is alive and your son is dead." Then the other says, "No! Your son is dead and my son is alive."'

"The king sent his servants to get a sword. When they brought it to him, he said, 'Cut the living baby into two pieces, and give each woman half.'

"The real mother of the living child was full of love for her son and said to the king, 'Please, my master, don't kill him! Give the baby to her!' But the other woman said, 'Neither of us will have him. Cut him into two pieces!'

"Then King Solomon said, 'Don't kill him. Give the baby to the first woman, because she is the real mother.'

"When the people of Israel heard about King Solomon's decision, they respected him very much. They saw he had wisdom from God to make the right decisions."—1 Kings 3:16–28 (NCV)

Grace

Father God, while we thank you for your blessings, including this food, we also pray for those who are facing sad or hard times. May they come to know you, if they don't already, and seek wisdom and understanding from you. And may your grace and goodness cover them. Remind us that people who have had bad things happen in their lives will sometimes do or say desperate things. Teach us that Solomon knew exactly what he was doing; that his test to figure out the identity of the baby would keep the little one safe. Give us guidance and wisdom as we seek to understand the actions and motives of others. Foster in us a desire to study your Word, for that is where wisdom begins. Amen.

Grace notes

"Always keep an open mind and a compassionate heart," said the Chicago Bulls basketball coach Phil Jackson. That's good advice for any time but especially great when you're faced with making a decision. Here are some other things you can do when that decision will be tough: Pray about it. Put that first on your list—not last. Think about what it is you really want and evaluate the pros and cons both ways. Are you considering a choice that will make you look good, whether or not it's the right thing to do? *Hmmm*, better think again. Finally, doing *something* is usually better than doing nothing. What if it's time to choose a college and you can't make a choice? Which will be better, even if the decision is only temporary: going to a community college near you until you have a better idea, or doing nothing at all?

Elijah Challenges King Ahab to a Contest of Fire

Scripture

The famine in Samaria was severe; no rain for a long time. Elijah the Prophet set out to prove that God was the one true God and that all pagan gods were nothing. He wanted non-believers to realize how much they've dumped God's ways, and he challenged the king to a contest. He already knew how the contest would end, and that it would also end the drought, for God had spoken to him.

The King agreed to this contest and summoned the people and their 850 prophets of the god and goddess Baal and Asherah to Mount Carmel. Elijah challenged them: "How long are you going to sit on the fence? If God is the real God, follow him; if it's Baal, follow him. Make up your minds!" Elijah set the terms: "You petition your gods and I will petition the one true God for rain. Your prophets will sacrifice an ox and I will sacrifice an ox. But no one will ignite the firewood on the altar. Then we will pray. The god who answers with fire will prove to be, in fact, God." All the people agreed: "A good plan—do it!"

Elijah told the Baal prophets, "Choose your ox and prepare it. You go first, you're the majority. Then pray to your god, but don't light the fire." They prayed all morning long, "O Baal, answer us!" But nothing happened—not so much as a whisper of breeze. Desperate, they jumped and stomped on their altar. By noon, Elijah had started making fun of them, taunting, "Call a little louder—he is a god, after all. Maybe he's off meditating somewhere or other, or maybe he's gotten involved in a project, or maybe he's on vacation. You don't suppose he's overslept, do you, and needs to be waked up?"

Then Elijah said, "Enough of that—it's my turn. Gather around." He put the altar back together for by now it was in ruins. Elijah took twelve stones, one for each of the tribes of Jacob. He built the stones into the altar in honor of God. Then Elijah dug a fairly wide trench around the altar. He laid firewood on the altar, cut up the ox, put it on the wood, and said, "Fill four buckets with water and drench both the ox and the firewood."' Then he said, "'Do it again," and they did it. Then he said, "Do it a third time," and they did it a third time. The altar was drenched and the trench was filled with water. Elijah prayed, "God; O answer me and reveal to this people that you are God, the true God, and that you are giving these people another chance at repentance." Immediately the fire of God fell and burned up the offering, the wood, the stones, the dirt, and even the water in the trench. All the people saw it happen and fell on their faces in awed worship, exclaiming, "God is the true God! God is the true God!"

Later, Elijah climbed to the top of Carmel and bowed deeply in prayer. Then he said to his servant, "On your feet now! Look toward the sea." He said, "I don't see a thing." "Keep looking," said Elijah, "seven times if necessary." Sure enough, the seventh time he said, "Oh yes, a cloud! But so small, no bigger than someone's hand, rising out of the sea." "Quickly, then, on your way. Tell Ahab, "saddle up and get down from the mountain before the rain stops you."' Things happened fast. The sky grew black with wind-driven clouds, and then a huge cloudburst of rain, with Ahab hightailing it in his chariot for Jezreel. And God strengthened Elijah mightily. Pulling up his robe and tying it around his waist, Elijah ran in front of Ahab's chariot until they reached Jezreel.—Paraphrased from 1 Kings 18 (MSG)

Grace

Lord, you are the supreme God; we know there is no other. May we always remember that you are powerful enough to control the weather and make the fields abundant with crops. We trust that you will provide for us. Teach us to trust you even more, remembering to come to you in prayer, as Elijah did. Thank you for the food at this table and for those who love and teach us. Hallelujah, Hallelujah, forever. Amen.

Grace notes

Elijah had a great relationship with God. You can too. Jeremiah 29:13 tells you that "you will seek me and find me when you seek me with all your heart." But what is the best way to tap in to God's divine guidance? First—there's no getting around this one—you have to do it God's way. (He does know better than you, after all.) And he says you must come to him through his Son, Jesus. So make Jesus your role model. To do that you will need to know what he teaches. God also speaks through the Holy Spirit, who softens and changes your heart. Ask for his guidance and be willing to follow. That's all there is to it. "God made a way out of no way," said the actress and film director Angela Bassett.

Wee Little Zacchaeus

Scripture

"Jesus was going through the city of Jericho. A man was there named Zacchaeus, who was an important tax collector, and very wealthy. He wanted to see who Jesus was, but he was too short to see above the crowd. He ran ahead to a place where Jesus would come, and he climbed a sycamore tree so he could see him. When Jesus came to that place, he looked up and said to him, 'Zacchaeus, hurry and come down! I must stay at your house today.'

"Zacchaeus came down quickly and welcomed him gladly. All the people saw this and began to complain, 'Jesus is staying with a sinner!' But Zacchaeus stood and said to the Lord, 'I will give half of my possessions to the poor. And if I have cheated anyone, I will pay back four times more.'

"Jesus said to him, 'Salvation has come to this house today, because this man also belongs to the family of Abraham. The Son of Man came to find lost people and save them.'"—Luke 19:1–10 (NCV)

Grace

Gracious Jesus, we love you and see that you want us to be kind to all your children, including those who don't yet know you. Remind us that Zacchaeus, even though he was rich, couldn't buy his way into heaven (no one can) but showed his change of heart through his generous actions and eager willingness to follow you. Inspire us, Lord, to live a life that shows how good a relationship with you can be. Lord, give us that wonderful feeling of gratitude for everything we have, and especially for who you are in our lives. We pray that we will never get lost but that even if we temporarily stray from your right path you will be right there, looking for us and calling our names, as you called Zacchaeus's name. Thank you too, Lord, for our family here around this table, for all our blessings, for this food, and for loving us so much. Amen.

Grace notes

In Jesus' time tax collectors had a bad reputation—and deserved it. They were hated by nearly everyone because of their underhanded ways, and the religious leaders criticized Jesus for even associating with them. But Jesus came into the world to save sinners. There is a fine line, too, between not wanting to spend time with people who might be a bad influence on you and serving as a good example, hoping that your actions will rub off on them—not the other way around.

It's also important to guard against feeling superior to others who have trouble in their lives. Outreach activities at church are good ways to put yourself in places where Christ's good example can shine through you. There are so many opportunities to represent Jesus at school, on sports teams, and in other areas that are already a part of your life, too. "Example is not the main thing in influencing others," said the author, musician, and Nobel Prize winner Albert Schweitzer. "It is the only thing."

The Story of Two Sons or What Say You?

Scripture

"Jesus said, 'Tell me what you think of this story: A man had two sons. He went up to the first and said, "Son, go out for the day and work in the vineyard." The son answered, "I don't want to." Later on he thought better of it and went.

"'The father gave the same command to the second son. He answered, "Sure, glad to." But he never went. Which of the two sons did what the father asked?' They said, 'The first.'

"Jesus said, 'Yes, and I tell you that crooks are going to precede you into God's kingdom. John came to you showing you the right road. You turned up your noses at him, but the crooks believed him. Even when you saw their changed lives, you didn't care enough to change and believe him.'"—Matthew 21:28–32 (MSG)

Grace

Loving Jesus, we thank you for bringing us together to eat and talk—first *to* you and then *about* you. Please bless our food and family. Thanks for reminding us of your generous love, grace, and mercy for all of us. Teach us that what we do speaks so much louder than what we say (or say we'll do!). And remind us that we are called to love you and to treat everyone else the way we want to be treated. This is the way of your kingdom, Lord. Amen.

Grace notes

God loves sinners. He must—he loves *you*, after all (smile!). What he doesn't like are people who say one thing but do another—on purpose. In today's story Jesus was telling the religious leaders (they were called Sadducees and Pharisees) that "crooks" (bad guys in general) would get to heaven before the supposedly good and moral people. That's because many of those bad guys would recognize their sins, come to Jesus, and mend their ways long before those leaders would ever even admit their faults. Those who only talk a good game, without living it, are playing a dangerous game. The playwright Tennessee Williams said it well: "The only thing worse than a liar is a liar that's also a hypocrite!" A hypocrite is someone who believes in double standards of behavior. Can you think of some examples of hypocritical behavior?

mint

Jesus Mobilizes the Immobile (Let Me Move You!)

Scripture

"A few days later, Jesus came back to Capernaum. The news spread that he was back and a large crowd gathered to hear him speak. The house was standing room only, people spilling out the door. While Jesus was teaching, some people brought a paralyzed man to see him, but they couldn't get the man inside because of the crowds. So four men went to the roof, made a hole in it, and lowered the mat with the paralyzed man on it down to Jesus. When Jesus saw how much faith they had, he said to the paralyzed man, 'Young man, your sins are forgiven.'

"Some of the teachers of the law were sitting there. They saw what Jesus did, and they said to themselves, 'Why does this man say things like that? What an insult to God! No one but God can forgive sins.' Jesus knew immediately what these teachers of the law were thinking. So he said to them, 'Why do you have these questions in your minds? The Son of Man has power on earth to forgive sins. But how can I prove this to you? Maybe you are thinking it was easy for me to say to the crippled man, "Your sins are forgiven." There's no proof it really happened. But what if I say to the man, "Stand up. Take your mat and walk"? Then you will be able to see if I really have this power or not.' So Jesus said to the paralyzed man, 'I tell you, stand up. Take your mat and go home.'

"Immediately the paralyzed man stood up. He picked up his mat and walked out of the room. Everyone could see him. They were amazed and praised God. They said, 'This is the most amazing thing we have ever seen!'"—Mark 2:1–12 (ERV)

Grace

Jesus, we are amazed at how well you know us and how much you care. We are amazed by your wisdom, your love, and your ability to heal, forgive us, and save us. Jesus, you are a force no one can deny. Encourage us to never forget that your kingdom isn't one of anger and punishment but of love and healing. Encourage us to picture you with a smile in your eyes, reaching out for us to walk—or run—to you! Thank you for giving us wonderful thoughts, wonderful food, and wonderful people in our lives who love us. Amen.

Grace notes

Since God created the universe and everything in it, why would anyone doubt that he could work a miracle, as he did with the crippled man? As Eric Metaxas put it, not believing in miracles would be like saying "Oh yes, I certainly believe that Tolstoy could write *War and Peace*, and did, but I could never believe he'd be able to move a comma in the manuscript. That would be too much." How silly! The creator of a great novel could surely change the punctuation in a sentence. Expect amazing things from God, for they will surely come.

Would You Want Jesus to Wash Your Feet?

Scripture

"Just before the Passover Feast, Jesus knew that the time had come to leave this world to go to the Father. Having loved his dear companions, he continued to love them right to the end. It was suppertime. The Devil by now had Judas, son of Simon the Iscariot, firmly in his grip, all set for the betrayal.

"Jesus knew that the Father had put him in complete charge of everything; that he came from God and was on his way back to God. So he got up from the supper table, set aside his robe, and put on an apron. Then he poured water into a basin and began to wash the feet of the disciples, drying them with his apron. When he got to Simon Peter, Peter said, 'Master, you wash my feet?' Jesus answered, 'You don't understand now what I'm doing, but it will be clear enough to you later.'

"Peter persisted, 'You're not going to wash my feet—ever!' Jesus said, 'If I don't wash you, you can't be part of what I'm doing.' 'Master!' said Peter. 'Not only my feet, then. Wash my hands! Wash my head!'

"Jesus said, 'If you've had a bath in the morning, you only need your feet washed now and you're clean from head to toe. My concern, you understand, is holiness, not hygiene. So now you're clean. But not every one of you.' (He knew who was betraying him. That's why he said, 'Not every one of you.') After he had finished washing their feet, he took his robe, put it back on, and went back to his place at the table.

"Then he said, 'Do you understand what I have done to you? You address me as "Teacher" and "Master," and rightly so. That is what I am. So if I, the Master and Teacher, washed your feet, you must now wash each other's feet. I've laid down a pattern for you. What I've done, you do. I'm only pointing out the obvious. . . . If you understand what I'm telling you, act like it—and live a blessed life.'"—John 13:1–17 (MSG)

Grace

Loving Jesus, thank you for this food and for this day full of blessings. Thank you for weekdays and weekends, special days—all days! What a gift they are! Thank you for the way Mom and Dad and others take care of us. Help us think of ways to surprise them by doing something kind for them. Give us eyes, Lord to see the importance of cheerfully doing things for others. Help us see that that those who serve also need to be served. Inspire us to think of little and big ways to help—maybe eventually even change-the-world-ways. Amen.

Grace notes

The washing of visitors' feet in Jesus' time was good manners—a regular practice done as a sign of hospitality. The catch: this job was performed only by the lowest of servants or slaves. Imagine the president of the United States showing up (with no cameras rolling) at your house to weed your garden or clean your toilet! Jesus' point in washing his disciples' feet wasn't about the chore itself but about who was doing it. Jesus' example showed his disciples—and reminds you—how much he wants his followers to help and serve others. Think of some good ways you can be a help—not someday but today, maybe even right this minute. "You feel alive to the degree that you feel you can help others," said the actor John Travolta. Think about a time when helping someone else made you feel terrific?

How Does Your Garden Grow?

Scripture

"Jesus went out of the house and sat by the lake. Large crowds gathered around him, so he got into a boat and sat down, while the people stood on the shore. Then Jesus used stories to teach them many things.

"He said: 'A farmer went out to plant his seed. While he was planting, some seed fell by the road, and the birds came and ate it all up. Some seed fell on rocky ground, where there wasn't much dirt. That seed grew very fast, because the ground was not deep. But when the sun rose, the plants dried up, because they did not have deep roots. Some other seed fell among thorny weeds, which grew and choked the good plants. Some other seed fell on good ground where it grew and produced a crop. Some plants made a hundred times more, some made sixty times more, and some made thirty times more. Let those with ears use them and listen.'"—Matthew 13:1–9 (NCV)

Grace

Dear Jesus, shine on us your ever-present light so we may grow strong and fruitful. May this food nourish our body, just as rain and rich soil work together to grow plants that are strong and plentiful. Give us wisdom and a desire to hear—really hear—what you have to say to us. May our hearts never become hard, shallow, or thorny; keep them open and caring, and keep our reasoning sharp. May your force be with us. The glory of God, the Messiah, is in your words. Amen.

Grace notes

Here's how it goes: Jesus throws out the seed on the ground; he's the sower. The seed is the Word of God, and the soil is you. What will be your response to the seed—to God's Word? What kind of soil will he find in your life? Will you live a fruitful life, producing healthy growth with luscious fruit because you not only hear God's Word but work hard to listen and understand it, too? Or, when the sun beats down and the going gets tough, will you stumble and fall in a rough patch?

It's good to think about these things, but Jesus' parable is just as much about him. Jesus sows God's Word—the seed—in every kind of soil, with no regard to its "potential" (there's a difference between thick black topsoil and desert sand dunes, isn't there?). He won't decide to skip the field that is your heart—he wants to be in your life. It's up to you what to do with the seed he sends your way. "You get faith by studying the Word. Study that Word until something in you 'knows that you know' and that you do not just hope that you know," said the editor and generous giver Carrie Judd Montgomery. Do you know what she meant?

Why Does Jesus Tell So Many Stories?

Scripture

"The disciples came up and asked, 'Why do you tell stories?' [Jesus] replied, 'You've been given insight into God's kingdom. You know how it works. Not everybody has this gift, this insight; it hasn't been given to them. Whenever someone has a ready heart for this, the insights and understandings flow freely. But if there is no readiness, any trace of receptivity soon disappears. That's why I tell stories: to create readiness, to nudge the people toward receptive insight. In their present state they can stare till doomsday and not see it, listen till they're blue in the face and not get it. I don't want Isaiah's forecast repeated all over again:

"'Your ears are open but you don't hear a thing. Your eyes are awake but you don't see a thing. The people are blockheads! They stick their fingers in their ears so they won't have to listen; They screw their eyes shut so they won't have to look, so they won't have to deal with me face-to-face and let me heal them.

"'But you have God-blessed eyes—eyes that see! And God-blessed ears—ears that hear! A lot of people, prophets and humble believers among them, would have given anything to see what you are seeing, to hear what you are hearing, but never had the chance.'"—Matthew 13:10–17 (MSG)

Grace

Dear Jesus, we thank you for the food you give us, for our family, for hearts that are open, for your Word to fill them, and for a readiness within us to understand and learn. We pray for insight, so that every time we hear your Word we may learn something new. May no one have reason to call us blockheads, Lord. Amen.

Grace notes

For different reasons these crowds could not or did not want to understand Jesus' message, and Jesus knew that. Some were stubborn and others suspicious. Jesus' ideas were revolutionary in his day and culture. God blessed the disciples' eyes and ears so they could understand; more importantly, he blessed their hearts so they would want to receive his Word. Jesus wants to share the Good News with everyone, so until such time as they want to hear he chooses to speak in such a way that they may *someday* be ready to understand. This is God's grace at work. "To one who has faith, no explanation is necessary. To one without faith, no explanation is possible," said Saint Thomas Aquinas.

Eight—Count 'Em—Eight Kinds of Blessing

Scripture

"When Jesus saw the crowds, he went up on a mountainside and sat down. His disciples came to him, and he began to teach them. He said: 'Blessed are the poor in spirit, for theirs is the kingdom of heaven. Blessed are those who mourn, for they will be comforted. Blessed are the meek, for they will inherit the earth. Blessed are those who hunger and thirst for righteousness, for they will be filled. Blessed are the merciful, for they will be shown mercy. Blessed are the pure in heart, for they will see God. Blessed are the peacemakers, for they will be called children of God. Blessed are those who are persecuted because of righteousness, for theirs is the kingdom of heaven. Blessed are you when people insult you, persecute you and falsely say all kinds of evil against you because of me.'"*—Matthew 5:1–11 (NIV)

*It may look like there are nine blessings (Beatitudes), but the last blessing is really a clarification of the eighth.

Grace

Heavenly Father, thank you for being with us and for blessing our food and fellowship—and even our fun. We pray for our family and friends, and especially for those in need. Thank you, Jesus, for wrapping your arms around those who are poor, sick, hungry, sad, or live in a place where following you isn't a safe choice. Encourage us to keep our eyes in the Bible and our ears tuned in, too, until the words of your Word become a part of us. Inspire us to take these blessings to heart, to believe in and take comfort from them, and to live by these words as we pass along our comfort to others. We all need you, Lord. Amen.

Grace notes

The people in Jesus' day had no trouble understanding these "blessings." (They are called the Beatitudes or "Supreme" Blessings.) It may help to remember as we think about Jesus' blessings here that the meanings of words can change over time. For instance, the phrase "poor in spirit" may have made more sense to Jesus' early listeners than it does to us. Think of a spirit as "poor" because it needs the richness of God's grace and mercy. Following is a paraphrase (a restatement in different words) of the Beatitudes:

Blessings flow and your life unfolds in amazing, wonderful ways when you recognize your need for Christ. You are *Blessed* when you're sorry for your sins and surrender yourself to him because he knows what's best for you. You're *Blessed* when you are sad, for you will be comforted. You're *Blessed* when you long to do the right thing (this requires studying God's Word). You're *Blessed* when you forgive others. You're *Blessed* when you long to know Jesus more and more and are loyal to him. You're *Blessed* when you act with love, compassion, and mercy toward others. You're *Blessed* when you want to be holy inside and out. You're *Blessed* when you believe in Jesus and feel good about sharing that, no matter what. "No God, no peace; Know God, know Peace," said an unknown author. Is that language easier to understand?

What's the Big Deal about Forgiveness?

Scripture

"At that point, Peter got up the nerve to ask, 'Master, how many times do I forgive a brother or sister who hurts me? Seven?' Jesus replied, 'Seven! Hardly. Try seventy times seven.

"'The kingdom of God is like a king who decided to square accounts with his servants. As he got under way, one servant was brought before him who had run up a debt of a hundred thousand dollars. He couldn't pay up, so the king ordered the man, along with his wife, children, and goods, to be auctioned off at the slave market.

"'The poor wretch threw himself at the king's feet and begged, "Give me a chance and I'll pay it all back." Touched by his plea, the king let him off, erasing the debt.

"'The servant was no sooner out of the room when he came upon one of his fellow servants who owed him ten dollars. He seized him by the throat and demanded, "Pay up. Now!" The poor wretch threw himself down and begged, "Give me a chance and I'll pay it all back." But he wouldn't do it. He had him arrested and put in jail until the debt was paid. When the other servants saw this going on, they were outraged and brought a detailed report to the king.

"'The king summoned the man and said, "You evil servant! I forgave your entire debt when you begged me for mercy. Shouldn't you be compelled to be merciful to your fellow servant who asked for mercy?" The king was furious and put the screws to the man until he paid back his entire debt. And that's exactly what my Father in heaven is going to do to each one of you who doesn't forgive unconditionally anyone who asks for mercy.'"—Matthew 18:21–35 (MSG)

Grace

Heavenly Father, there's so much for us to be thankful for. May we always—not just on church days—take time, like now, to say thank you. Thank you for this food and for all that we have. Thank you for the way you use events in our life, both the good and the not-so-good, to teach us so that we can become strong, mature, loving adults. May we always honor in words and actions your two greatest commandments: to love you and to treat others the way we ourselves want to be treated. May we remember that this love includes forgiving others, even when we don't feel like it. Keep us open to your whispered reminder in our ear: "*How many times* have I forgiven you?" Praise you, Jesus, for your right-living words. Amen.

Grace notes

The Jewish religion taught that a person needed to be forgiven only three times for the same offense; any more than that, and you could assume they really weren't sorry. But Jesus' rule is so different we could call it opposite: forgive always—as in again and again, without keeping count. That would have been an astonishing idea in Jesus' day. The phrase "seventy times seven" is all about God's eternal forgiveness. "Consider yourself the chief of sinners," said the Scottish-American preacher Peter Marshall, "not the chief of the sinned-against."

King Nebuchadnezzar's Incredible Dream

Scripture

Nebuchadnezzar had a dream. He demanded of his fortunetellers, magicians, sorcerers, and wizards: "Explain it!" They said, "Tell us the dream and we'll tell you what it means." "Not so fast," the king said. "You will first tell me my dream and then tell me what it means. If you can't, I'll have you torn limb from limb." They said that was impossible—no one can do that. The king got so mad he ordered their execution—all of them, including Daniel! Daniel prayed and asked his friends to pray. That night, God showed him the dream and what it meant. Daniel praised God, saying: "God is wise and powerful! Praise him forever. He controls the times and the seasons; he makes and unmakes kings; it is he who gives wisdom and understanding. He reveals things that are deep and secret; he knows what is hidden in darkness, and he himself is surrounded by light. I praise you and honor you, God of my ancestors. You have given me wisdom and strength; you have answered my prayer and shown us what to tell the king"

Daniel said to the king: "Your Majesty, there is no human who can tell the dream, but God in heaven reveals mysteries. Your dream was revealed to me, not because I am wiser than anyone else, but so you may learn the meaning of your dream. Your Majesty," Daniel went on, "in your vision you saw standing before you a giant statue, bright, shining, and terrifying to look at. Its head was made of the finest gold; its chest and arms of silver; its waist and hips of bronze, its legs of iron, and its feet mixed of iron and clay. While you were looking at it, a great stone broke loose from a cliff, without anyone touching it, struck the iron and clay feet of the statue, and shattered them. At once the rest of the statue crumbled and became like the dust on a threshing place in summer. The wind carried it away, leaving not a trace. But the stone grew to be a mountain that covered the whole earth.

"Now for what it means: You are the golden head. After you die another empire will rise, but not as strong—that is the chest and arms of silver. After that, an empire lesser still (the waist and hips of bronze), and after that an empire lesser still, like the iron which is strong but shatters and breaks everything. The clay and iron feet mean it will be a divided empire. It will have some strength of iron, because iron was mixed with the clay. That means the rulers of that empire will try to unite their families by intermarriage, but they will not be able to, any more than iron can mix with clay. Then, just as the stone struck the statue made of iron, bronze, clay, silver, and gold (without anyone touching it), completely destroying all those empires, the God of heaven will establish a kingdom that will never end. It will never be conquered, and will last forever. The great God is telling Your Majesty what will happen in the future. I have told you exactly what you dreamed, and have given you its true meaning."

Then the King said, "Your God is the greatest of all gods, the Lord over kings, and the one who reveals mysteries. I know this because you have been able to explain this mystery."—Paraphrased from Daniel 2 (GNT)

Grace

Almighty Creator, we're thankful for your reminder through Daniel to focus on your kingdom rather than on the kingdoms of the world. Assure us that you will fulfill your pledge to replace earthly kingdoms with your everlasting rein in glory and that your power is immeasurably greater than that of any earthly empire or ruler. You have a plan for history, a perfect plan that includes each of us. Encourage us to seek the kind of wisdom and courage Daniel showed by getting close to you, Jesus, for you are the key that opens all the hidden treasures of your wisdom and knowledge.* Lord, you're in charge! Amen.

*Colossians 2:3

Grace notes

This story is about the danger of pride and preoccupation (that means obsession or fascination) with earthly things. God is in control, no matter how powerful the world thinks someone else might be. Nebuchadnezzar had an important lesson to learn. It's a great one for you, too. Wouldn't you rather read about it, and learn from it, then experience something like it firsthand? Take your direction from the Bible and save yourself a lot of pain and trouble. "Earthlings have the worst sense of direction!" commented the Looney Tunes character Marvin the Martian. Ah, let's make this Martian eat his words!

Hear Ye, Hear Ye: VIPs Visit Baby Jesus

Scripture

"Jesus was born in the town of Bethlehem in Judea during the time when Herod was king. After Jesus was born, some wise men from the east came to Jerusalem. They asked people, 'Where is the child who has been born to be the king of the Jews? We saw the star that shows he was born. We saw it rise in the sky in the east and have come to worship him.'

"When King Herod heard about this, it upset him as well as everyone else in Jerusalem. Herod called a meeting of all the leading Jewish priests and teachers of the law. He asked them where the Messiah would be born. They answered, 'In the town of Bethlehem in Judea, just as the prophet [Micah] wrote:

"'"Bethlehem, in the land of Judah, you are important among the rulers of Judah. Yes, a ruler will come from you, and that ruler will lead Israel, my people."'

"Then Herod had a private meeting with the wise men from the east. He learned from them the exact time they first saw the star. Then he sent them to Bethlehem. He said, 'Go and look carefully for the child. When you find him, come tell me. Then I can go worship him too.'

"After the wise men heard the king, they left. They saw the same star they had seen in the east, and they followed it. The star went before them until it stopped above the place where the child was. They were very happy and excited to see the star.

"The wise men came to the house where the child was with his mother Mary. They bowed down and worshiped him. Then they opened the boxes of gifts they had brought for him. They gave him treasures of gold, frankincense, and myrrh. But God warned the wise men in a dream not to go back to Herod. So they went home to their own country a different way.

"After the wise men left, an angel from the Lord came to Joseph in a dream. The angel said, 'Get up! Take the child with his mother and escape to Egypt. Herod wants to kill the child and will soon start looking for him. Stay in Egypt until I tell you to come back.'

"So Joseph got ready and left for Egypt with the child and the mother. They left during the night. Joseph stayed in Egypt until Herod died. This gave full meaning to what the Lord said through the prophet: 'I called my son to come out of Egypt.'"—Matthew 2:1–15 (ERV)

Grace

Heavenly Father, we thank you for being with us, for this food, and that we are together this day. We can look up at the stars—remembering that you made them—and think back to that night when you changed the world. What faith the magi must have had! May your mercy and grace lead us, just as the star led the wise men—right straight to you. Open our hearts to the reality that you can speak to us in so many ways. We love you, Jesus, and worship you together. We pray for those in need. We honor you with our hearts. We praise you by generously giving to you and others those things that are really important: goodness, helpfulness, gentleness, and faithfulness. Amen.

Grace notes

The Magi, wise men or kings, brought gifts to the baby Jesus fit for a king. These kings bowed down and worshiped him as though he were the Messiah—which, we know, he was! What is the message, though, for you, here and now in the twenty-first century? Think of this as an illustration of how to give. The Magi gave expensive, lavish gifts, yes, but Jesus gave so much more—himself—setting for us an example of the kind of giving he expects of us. Jesus wants you to give it all, but don't worry—it's not as hard as you think. For example, think of what your other family members need or want, not of what you need or want, and then fulfill their desires as best as you can. (It's important to keep in mind, though, that when you let others know what you want you don't demand it or "place an order"). If every one of you would go out of your way to do something kind for each other, the tone of family life would be so different. Instead of the tug of war that comes with an "I want that" or "That's not fair" kind of attitude, you'd be giving to each other without first having to demand. This is what Jesus teaches: when you give, you receive. Here's an example: your brother is late for practice, but it's his turn to clean up after dinner. Don't wait for him to ask—offer to do it for him. You'll look like a hero, and chances are he'll pledge to return the favor. Smooth. What if you folded the laundry, giving your mom more time to spend with you? Together you could make up a long list of "gives" that would be truly appreciated, couldn't you? "Family is not an important thing," said the Canadian-American actor and producer Michael J. Fox. "It's everything."

John the Baptist Says, "It Ain't Me You're Lookin' For!"

Scripture

"The Jewish authorities in Jerusalem sent some priests and Levites to John to ask him, 'Who are you?' John did not refuse to answer, but spoke out openly and clearly, saying: 'I am not the Messiah.' 'Who are you, then?' they asked. 'Are you Elijah?' 'No, I am not,' John answered. 'Are you the Prophet?' they asked. 'No,' he replied.' 'Then tell us who you are,' they said. 'We have to take an answer back to those who sent us. What do you say about yourself?' John answered by quoting the prophet Isaiah: 'I am "the voice of someone shouting in the desert: Make a straight path for the Lord to travel!"'

"The messengers, who had been sent by the Pharisees, then asked John, 'If you are not the Messiah nor Elijah nor the Prophet, why do you baptize?' John answered, 'I baptize with water, but among you stands the one you do not know. He is coming after me, but I am not good enough even to untie his sandals.' All this happened in Bethany on the east side of the Jordan River, where John was baptizing. The next day John saw Jesus coming to him, and said, 'There is the Lamb of God, who takes away the sin of the world! This is the one I was talking about when I said, a man is coming after me, but he is greater than I am, because he existed before I was born. I did not know who he would be, but I came baptizing with water in order to make him known to the people of Israel.'

"And John gave this testimony: 'I saw the Spirit come down like a dove from heaven and stay on him. I still did not know that he was the one, but God, who sent me to baptize with water, had said to me, "You will see the Spirit come down and stay on a man; he is the one who baptizes with the Holy Spirit." I have seen it,' said John, 'and I tell you that he is the Son of God.'"—John 1:19–34 (GNT)

Grace

Dear Jesus, we are thankful for the food we have; please bless our meal. Please bless our time together as a family. Teach us the importance of knowing and loving you. Encourage us to learn about you, to understand the whys of what you say, and to think about these things. Teach us that as we come to know you better it will be easier for us to imitate the way you lived and to see the value in that quality of life. We pray for wisdom to understand that the Holy Spirit is in us, as surely as John the Baptist saw it descend upon you. In your wonderful name we pray. Amen.

Grace notes

Do you know why Jesus is called the Lamb of God? In Old Testament times people used to sacrifice animals (like sheep, goats, and birds) as a way to pay for their sins. But these sacrifices were only temporary and when the person sinned again (which, as you know, happens pretty regularly), another animal sacrifice had to be made. But God had a plan: send Jesus to be the ultimate and permanent sacrifice for our sins. Jesus willingly died for our sins; he became our permanent sacrificial lamb. "Dear church," pointed out the pastor Carlos A. Rodrigues, "John the Baptist died for exposing the sins of others. Jesus died to actually pay for the sins of others." Jesus became the Lamb of God, so that we could one day stand in God's presence. What a perfect plan!

Breaking News: 10,000+ Fed from a Lunch Box It's a Miracle!

Scripture

"Jesus went across Lake Galilee. Many people followed him because they saw the miracles he did to heal the sick. Jesus went up on a hill and sat down there with his followers. It was almost the time for the Jewish Passover Feast.

"When Jesus looked up and saw a large crowd coming toward him, he said to Philip, 'Where can we buy enough bread for all these people to eat?' (Jesus asked Philip this question to test him, because Jesus already knew what he planned to do.) Philip answered, 'Someone would have to work almost a year to buy enough bread for each person to have only a little piece.'

"Another one of his followers, Andrew, Simon Peter's brother, said, 'Here is a boy with five loaves of barley bread and two little fish, but that is not enough for so many people.'

"Jesus said, 'Tell the people to sit down.' There was plenty of grass there, and about five thousand men sat down there. Then Jesus took the loaves of bread, thanked God for them, and gave them to the people who were sitting there. He did the same with the fish, giving as much as the people wanted.

"When they had all had enough to eat, Jesus said to his followers, 'Gather the leftover pieces of fish and bread so that nothing is wasted.' So they gathered up the pieces and filled twelve baskets with the pieces left from the five barley loaves.

"When the people saw this miracle that Jesus did, they said, 'He must truly be the Prophet who is coming into the world.'

"Jesus knew that the people planned to come and take him by force and make him their king, so he left and went into the hills alone." —John 6:1–15 (NCV)

Grace

Lord Jesus, you are the one who provides food for us—for our bodies and for our spirits. You are the source of life, and for that we honor you. Thank you for being here with us, too. Teach us that feeding a hungry person quiets the "roar" of a growling tummy so they can concentrate on other thoughts—like the wonder of you. Encourage us to center our thoughts on the importance of your words, Jesus, including the words you spoke that day on the hill. We wonder how we would react if we realized we were being fed through a miracle like that one! How focused we would be, how in awe of you! Teach us now that the best food is food for thought—but only if the nourishment is coming from you. Amen.

Grace notes

Can you think about anything else besides food when you're stomach-growling famished? Yes, but it's pretty hard, isn't it? Food is like a universal peace sign, right? Offer a very hungry person some food, and their gloom is replaced with appreciation. God offers everyone the bread of life—himself.* "There are people in the world so hungry, that God cannot appear to them except in the form of bread," noted the Indian leader Mahatma Gandhi. Missionaries know and practice the same strategy Jesus did: fill the tummy first, so the mind can concentrate on the Spirit meal.

*John 6:35

Which Is Better, What You Say or What You Do?

Scripture

Jesus said, "A good tree does not produce bad fruit. And a bad tree does not produce good fruit. Every tree is known by the kind of fruit it produces. You won't find figs on thorny weeds. And you can't pick grapes from thornbushes! Good people have good things saved in their hearts. That's why they say good things. But those who are evil have hearts full of evil, and that's why they say things that are evil. What people say with their mouths comes from what fills their hearts.

"Why do you call me, 'Lord, Lord,' but you don't do what I say? The people who come to me, who listen to my teachings and obey them—I will show you what they are like: They are like a man building a house. He digs deep and builds his house on rock. The floods come, and the water crashes against the house. But the flood cannot move the house, because it was built well.

"But the people who hear my words and do not obey are like a man who builds a house without preparing a foundation. When the floods come, the house falls down easily and is completely destroyed."—Luke 6:43–49 (ERV)

Grace

We praise your name, Lord Jesus. Hear now our prayer of thanksgiving. We are happy to be together, and we ask for your blessing. Watch over our hearts and give us wisdom, for we surely need it. Thanks for reminding us that acting one way while thinking another does no good; you know what's really going on. We ask for your help in keeping our hearts and minds full of you. When we do blow it, help us to remember that we can rely on your promise to forgive us—a special thanks for that. You are an amazing God, and we couldn't live without you. Thank you for this food, for this most special day of the week, and for all of your other countless blessings. Amen.

Grace notes

You can't earn your way into heaven. It's a gift. No other faith (no other religion) in the world makes that claim. You do good works not because you have to but because you want to. Having Jesus in your life totally changes your heart—spins you around and starts you moving in the opposite direction, toward a life that pleases your Lord and Savior. The fruit you bear—the good things you do—are evidence of Jesus at work in your life. God's love and forgiveness are mind-blowing realities, when you stop to think about it (it's so easy to take them for granted, isn't it?). "I'm not perfect," said the football star Tim Tebow. "And who knows how many times I've fallen short. We all fall short. That's the amazing thing about the grace of God." Tim is right. God's grace is unlimited, his forgiveness eternal. By the way, do you know what the difference is between grace and mercy? Grace is getting something you don't deserve. Mercy is not getting something you do deserve. Get it?

Glory Be!
(the Transfiguration)

Scripture

"About eight days after saying this, [that someone with him would see the kingdom of God before he died] [Jesus] climbed the mountain to pray, taking Peter, John, and James along. While he was in prayer, the appearance of his face changed and his clothes became blinding white. At once two men were there talking with him. They turned out to be Moses and Elijah—and what a glorious appearance they made! They talked over his exodus, the one Jesus was about to complete in Jerusalem.

"Meanwhile, Peter and those with him were slumped over in sleep. When they came to, rubbing their eyes, they saw Jesus in his glory and the two men standing with him. When Moses and Elijah had left, Peter said to Jesus, 'Master, this is a great moment! Let's build three memorials: one for you, one for Moses, and one for Elijah.' He blurted this out without thinking.

"While he was babbling on like this, a light-radiant cloud enveloped them. As they found themselves buried in the cloud, they became deeply aware of God. Then there was a voice out of the cloud: 'This is my Son, the Chosen! Listen to him.'

"When the sound of the voice died away, they saw Jesus there alone. They were speechless. And they continued speechless, said not one thing to anyone during those days of what they had seen."—Luke 9:28–36 (MSG)

Grace

Heavenly Father, we are amazed by you and by how much you love each of us. We are speechless at the very thought of who you are and what you mean in and to this world. May your glory shine for all to see. We thank you for our food and for your favor and ask you to bless us, watch over us, protect us, guide us, and give us the wisdom to even begin to understand who you are. We don't know the right words to say, but you know what's in our hearts, for you know everything. Thank you, Lord, for loving us. Jesus truly is your Son. Help us listen to him! Amen.

Grace notes

As anyone would have been, Peter, James, and John were stunned into silence at the sight they beheld: Jesus as God. God spoke directly to them, telling them to listen to Jesus. These mere mortals (humans) were incredibly privileged to catch a glimpse of the glory of God. Someone once said, "The real voyage of discovery consists not in seeking new landscapes, but in having new eyes." The growth of the apostles' faith was a discovery unlike any other. Now it's up to you to choose your own voyage. "There are only two kinds of people in the end: those who say to God, 'Thy will be done,' and those to whom God says, in the end, 'Thy will be done.' All that are in Hell, choose it. Without that self-choice there could be no Hell," said C. S. Lewis, the author of *The Lion, The Witch, and the Wardrobe.*

Don't You Just Love Finding Lost Things?

Scripture

Jesus said, "Suppose one of you has a hundred sheep and loses one of them—what do you do? You leave the other ninety-nine sheep in the pasture and go looking for the one that got lost until you find it. When you find it, you are so happy that you put it on your shoulders and carry it back home. Then you call your friends and neighbors together and say to them, 'I am so happy I found my lost sheep. Let us celebrate!' In the same way, I tell you, there will be more joy in heaven over one sinner who repents than over ninety-nine respectable people who do not need to repent.

"Or suppose a woman who has ten silver coins loses one of them—what does she do? She lights a lamp, sweeps her house, and looks carefully everywhere until she finds it. When she finds it, she calls her friends and neighbors together, and says to them, 'I am so happy I found the coin I lost. Let us celebrate!' In the same way, I tell you, the angels of God rejoice over one sinner who repents."—Luke 15:4–10 (GNT)

Grace

Heavenly Father, thank you for teaching us that we are a big deal to you—a really big deal—no matter who we are or where we come from. Thank you for telling us about the joy in being forgiven; that you run after us to find us and bring us back home, tucked safely in your arms. Remind us too, how much you want us to tell others about you—by doing good things, talking about you, or giving credit to you out loud! Teach us to say "I am blessed" when others ask "How are you?" Give us guidance and wisdom, Lord, and instill in us a desire to read your Word so that we may be ready and eager to represent you in thought, word, and action. Thank you, Lord for the food you provide and for the privilege of being together with you. Amen.

Grace notes

It's important to know a parable's background. In this one, everyone knew that shepherds worked in groups, so one shepherd could leave the other 99 sheep in the care of the other shepherds if he needed to. The silver coin in the shorter parable was probably part of a wedding necklace and most likely held a good deal of sentimental and monetary value. (Depending on its size, one silver coin may have been worth about a day's wages.) Like that earthly shepherd, Jesus searches for those who have strayed from him. And like the woman who rejoiced when she found the ring, all of heaven rejoices when a lost one is found. Jesus refused to isolate himself from unbelievers, and he doesn't want you to hide away in your own safe little world, either. These stories Jesus told are a call to action. Let others see the point of Jesus' teachings in the way you live. Can you think of an example or two? "Be happy when Jesus answers your prayer but be happier when you are an answer to others' prayers," said an unknown author.

The Widow Gives Her All

Scripture

"As Jesus taught [his disciples], he said, 'Watch out for the teachers of the Law, who like to walk around in their long robes and be greeted with respect in the marketplace, who choose the reserved seats in the synagogues and the best places at feasts. They take advantage of widows and rob them of their homes, and then make a show of saying long prayers. Their punishment will be all the worse!'

"As Jesus sat near the Temple treasury, he watched the people as they dropped in their money. Many rich men dropped in a lot of money; then a poor widow came along and dropped in two little copper coins, worth about a penny.

"He called his disciples together and said to them, 'I tell you that this poor widow put more in the offering box than all the others. For the others put in what they had to spare of their riches; but she, poor as she is, put in all she had—she gave all she had to live on.'"—Mark 12:38–44 (GNT)

Grace

Lord, we thank you for this food and ask your blessing this day. Encourage us to understand that this story isn't about the money but about the giver's heart. Help us see that the point of giving isn't about "Look at me, I'm giving" but about a heart that gives simply for the love of you. Thank you for showing us that anyone can make an offering worthy of your attention. Help us see that our grateful and generous heart, not the size of our contribution, is the real gift. Amen.

Grace notes

Jesus isn't telling you to give away everything. The widow gave humbly, with all her heart, because she loved God. In contrast, in Jesus' day many of the rich would give their gift with a loud ring of a bell, self-announcing the importance of themselves and of their offering. "Look at me and how important I am," the bell would clang out, over and over again. After they gave their money they would still be rich—no big deal. A gift that doesn't cost you much in terms of effort, cost, or time involved isn't really much of a gift, is it? (A background detail to this story is that some crooked high priests would take that money given at the temple and live in high style rather than using it to help others. A very two-faced thing to do, don't you think?) Which gift do you think meant more to God: the penny from the widow or the thousand dollars from the rich man? Have you ever thought that your giving helps you as much as it does the person who benefits from your gift? "It's not how much we give," said Mother Teresa, who devoted all of her adult life to helping the homeless poor in India, "but how much love we put into giving."

340

The More You Have, the More You'll Get: The Story of Three Servants

Scripture

Jesus said, "The kingdom of heaven is like a man who was going to another place for a visit. Before he left, he called for his servants and told them to take care of his things while he was gone. He gave one servant five bags of gold, another servant two bags of gold, and a third servant one bag of gold, to each one as much as he could handle. Then he left. The servant who got five bags went quickly to invest the money and earned five more bags. In the same way, the servant who had two bags invested them and earned two more. But the servant who got one bag went out and dug a hole in the ground and hid the master's money.

"After a long time the master came home and asked the servants what they did with his money. The servant who was given five bags of gold brought five more bags to the master and said, 'Master, you trusted me to care for five bags of gold, so I used your five bags to earn five more.' The master answered, 'You did well. You are a good and loyal servant. Because you were loyal with small things, I will let you care for much greater things. Come and share my joy with me.'

"Then the servant who had been given one bag of gold came to the master and said, 'Master, I knew that you were a hard man. . . .So I was afraid and went and hid your money in the ground. Here is your bag of gold.' The master answered, 'You are a wicked and lazy servant! You say you knew that I harvest things I did not plant and that I gather crops where I did not sow any seed. So you should have put my gold in the bank. Then, when I came home, I would have received my gold back with interest.'

"So the master told his other servants, 'Take the bag of gold from that servant and give it to the servant who has ten bags of gold. Those who have much will get more, and they will have much more than they need. But those who do not have much will have everything taken away from them.' Then the master said, 'Throw that useless servant outside, into the darkness where people will cry and grind their teeth with pain.'"—Matthew 25:14–30 (NCV)

Grace

Dear Jesus, thank you for the food we eat, the air we breathe, and the smiles of our parents. Teach us that the carefully chosen talents and abilities you've given to each of us are meant to be developed and wisely used. Thank you for reminding us that these wonderful gifts from your hand grow when we demonstrate our willingness to use them well. Inspire us to get excited about following instructions and to devote our attention and energy to doing the little things well, because that's the path to the blessed, full life. Jesus, we accept your invitation to share your joy. Amen.

Grace notes

The servants in this story were trustworthy, smart, and faithful businessmen. In today's dollars the amount this wealthy man entrusted to them would have been almost two million dollars! The third servant attempted to blame someone else—his boss—for his failure rather than to admit his lazy attitude. That didn't work very well for him, did it? Jesus is telling you that it's important for you, too, to use your talents to help others. This has nothing to do with the size of your talent or of its importance in the world's eyes. You may, if your abilities and opportunities allow for it, choose a life of service as a scientist or doctor. Or you may choose to volunteer part of your time serving the poor at a soup kitchen or mowing a disabled neighbor's lawn. Jesus will lead you to the right opportunity if you will just let him. "The purpose of life," said Senator Robert F. Kennedy, "is to contribute in some way to making things better."

King Belshazzar's Banquet: The Mysterious Handwriting on the Wall

Scripture

One night Belshazzar invited a thousand noblemen to a banquet. He gave orders to bring the gold and silver cups and bowls taken from the Temple in Jerusalem by his father, Nebuchadnezzar, so everyone could drink from them. They did, and all praised gods made of gold, silver, bronze, iron, wood, and stone.

Suddenly a human hand appeared and began writing on the plaster wall of the palace, where the light from the lamps was shining most brightly. The king saw the hand as it was writing. He turned pale and was so frightened his knees began to shake. He shouted for someone to bring in the magicians, wizards, and astrologers. When they came in, the king said, "Anyone who tells me what it means will be dressed in royal purple robes, wear a gold chain of honor around his neck, and be the third in power in the kingdom." The royal advisers came forward, but none of them could read the writing or tell the king what it meant. In his distress King Belshazzar grew even paler, and his noblemen had no idea what to do.

The queen mother heard the noise and entered the banquet hall. She said, "When your father was king, there was a man who showed good sense, knowledge, and wisdom like the wisdom of the gods. He has unusual ability and is wise and skillful in interpreting dreams, solving riddles, and explaining mysteries; send for this man Daniel, and he will tell you what all this means."

Daniel was brought at once into the king's presence. Daniel told him he could keep the gifts for himself, but he would read what had been written: "The Supreme God made your father Nebuchadnezzar a great king and gave him dignity and majesty. He was so great that people of all nations, races, and languages were afraid of him and trembled. If he wanted to kill someone, he did; if he wanted to keep someone alive, he did. He honored or disgraced anyone he wanted to. But because he became proud, stubborn, and cruel, he was removed from his royal throne and lost his place of honor. He was driven away from human society, and his mind became like that of an animal. He lived with wild donkeys, ate grass like an ox, and slept in the open air with nothing to protect him from the dew. Finally he admitted that the Supreme God controls all human kingdoms and can give them to anyone he chooses.

"But you, his son, have not humbled yourself, even though you knew all this. You acted against the Lord and brought in the cups and bowls taken from his Temple. You praised gods made of gold, silver, bronze, iron, wood, and stone—gods that cannot see or hear and that do not know anything. But you did not honor the God who determines whether you live or die and who controls everything you do. That is why God has sent the hand to write these words.

"This is what was written: 'Number, number, weight, divisions,' and it means: *number*, God has numbered the days of your kingdom and brought it to an end; *weight*, you have been weighed on the scales and found to be too light; *divisions*, your kingdom is divided up and given to the Medes and Persians."

That same night Belshazzar, the king of Babylonia, was killed; and Darius the Mede, who was then sixty-two years old, seized the royal power.—Paraphrased from Daniel 5 (GNT)

Grace

Almighty Father, all of the blessings we have in life come from you. We are thankful right now for this food and for being here with our family. Give us the wisdom to understand that you hold supreme power and authority over everyone, even those in high earthly positions. Give us the wisdom to understand that you gave up your life for all of us. Help us realize that you hate disrespect and wickedness. Give us wisdom to hear you, to seek your guidance, and to rely on your strength. We praise your holy name with reverence and wonder. Amen.

Grace notes

This story is about the sovereignty—the supreme power and authority—of God. Simply put, God will bless those who believe in him and punish those who don't—maybe not in this life but most certainly in the next. From this story rose the expression to "read the handwriting on the wall," which means that the person "gets it"—understands the point and what is likely to happen next if they don't listen up. "Most of us can read the writing on the wall; we just assume it's addressed to someone else," said the Pulitzer Prize-winning American historian William S. McFeely. There's a word for the idea of not believing what's right in front of you—the handwriting on the wall. It's *denial*. It's the refusal to believe that the consequences that happen to everyone else for a certain kind of action won't happen to you. We've all done it at times—like taking the test cold and still expecting to pass; thinking that extra piece of pie won't show up on your thighs; telling just that one lie; doing that *thing*—that no-no thing, whatever it is—just once. Can you think of other examples of denial? Let this story remind of you bad consequences so that you can put yourself in a course correction mode—before the handwriting . . .

God Drives Back the Mighty Red Sea

Scripture

When the king of Egypt let the people go, God did not take them by the shortest route. God thought, "I do not want the people to change their minds and return to Egypt when they see they are going to have to fight." Instead, he led them in a roundabout way through the desert toward the Red Sea. [The Israelites were armed for battle.] During the day the Lord went in front of them in a pillar of cloud to show them the way, and during the night he went in front of them in a pillar of fire to give them light, so that they could travel night and day. The pillar of cloud was always in front of the people during the day, and the pillar of fire at night.

Realizing that the Israelites had really gone, the king of Egypt and his officials said, "What have we done? We let the Israelites escape, and we have lost our slaves!" The king set out with all his war chariots, including the six hundred finest, commanded by their officers. The Lord made the king stubborn, and he pursued the Israelites. The Egyptian army, with all the horses, chariots, and drivers, pursued them and caught up with them where they were camped by the Red Sea.

When the Israelites saw the king and his army marching against them, they were terrified and cried out to the Lord for help. Moses answered, "Don't be afraid! Stand your ground, and you will see what the Lord will do to save you today; you will never see these Egyptians again. The Lord will fight for you." The Lord said to Moses, "Why are you crying out for help? Tell the people to move forward. Lift up your walking stick and hold it out over the sea. The water will divide, and the Israelites will be able to walk through the sea on dry ground. I will make the Egyptians so stubborn that they will go in after them, and I will gain honor by my victory over the king, his army, his chariots, and his drivers. When I defeat them, the Egyptians will know that I am the Lord." The angel of God, who had been in front of the army of Israel, moved and went to the rear. The pillar of cloud also moved until it was between the Egyptians and the Israelites. The cloud made it dark for the Egyptians, but gave light to the people of Israel, and so the armies could not come near each other all night.

Moses held out his hand over the sea, and the Lord drove the sea back with a strong east wind. It blew all night and turned the sea into dry land. The water was divided, and the Israelites went through the sea on dry ground, with walls of water on both sides. The Egyptians pursued them and went after them into the sea with all their horses, chariots, and drivers. Just before dawn the LORD looked down from the pillar of fire and cloud at the Egyptian army and threw them into a panic. He made the wheels of their chariots get stuck, so that they moved with great difficulty. The Egyptians said, "The LORD is fighting for the Israelites against us. Let's get out of here!"

The LORD said to Moses, "Hold out your hand over the sea, and the water will come back over the Egyptians and their chariots and drivers." So Moses held out his hand over the sea, and at daybreak the water returned to its normal level. The Egyptians tried to escape from the water, but the LORD threw them into the sea. The water returned and covered the chariots, the drivers, and all the Egyptian army that had followed the Israelites into the sea; not one of them was left. But the Israelites walked through the sea on dry ground, with walls of water on both sides.

On that day the LORD saved the people of Israel from the Egyptians, and the Israelites saw them lying dead on the seashore. When the Israelites saw the great power with which the LORD had defeated the Egyptians, they stood in awe of the LORD; and they had faith in the LORD and in his servant Moses.—Paraphrased from Exodus 13–22, 14 (GNT)

Grace

Lord, you've shown us in so many ways who is in charge. Thank you for showing us that you have more than enough power to control nature, protect us from problems or obstacles in our lives, and seek and find us when we feel lost and afraid. Guide us to trust your power and wisdom; after all, Lord, we know we're a part of your perfect plan. Remind us that you respond personally to each situation in our life in order to accomplish your purpose. Remind us, too, that while we do not know the details of your plan, all we really need to understand is that you are perfectly good, perfectly fair, and perfectly just—and that you always will be. Teach us always to depend on you, the source of our strength. Thank you, Lord, for this day, for bringing us together, for our family, and for our food. Amen.

Grace notes

The book of Exodus says that there were about two million Israelites who crossed the Red Sea with Moses. Mathematicians say that this feat was physically and logistically possible. *Of course it was!* (The parting of the Red Sea was the miracle part.) Have faith in God's power, believing that he can do anything. Have faith in his wisdom, too, believing that he knows everything. Nothing is too hard for God, and he will fight for you. "Safety comes in our nearness to God, not in our distance from our enemies," pointed out the author Dillon Burroughs. How close is God to you? Your choice—totally.

So the Bad Guy Is Really the Good Guy? (Being Right with God)

Scripture

"There were some people who thought they were very good and looked down on everyone else. Jesus used this story to teach them: 'One time there was a Pharisee and a tax collector. One day they both went to the Temple to pray. The Pharisee stood alone, away from the tax collector. When the Pharisee prayed, he said, "O God, I thank you that I am not as bad as other people. I am not like men who steal, cheat, or commit adultery. I thank you that I am better than this tax collector. I fast twice a week, and I give a tenth of everything I get!"

"'The tax collector stood alone too. But when he prayed, he would not even look up to heaven. He felt very humble before God. He said, "O God, have mercy on me. I am a sinner!" I tell you, when this man finished his prayer and went home, he was right with God. But the Pharisee, who felt that he was better than others, was not right with God. People who make themselves important will be made humble. But those who make themselves humble will be made important.'"—Luke 18:9–14 (ERV)

Grace

Heavenly Father, we are humbled and amazed by your willingness to forgive us and to always remain faithful to us, even when we are unfaithful to you. Develop in us a sense of big-time gratefulness for your gifts. Remind us that you look with favor upon the one who truly seeks forgiveness. Thank you for reminding us that when we think we're better than others, we're not. Thank you, Jesus, for your words that nourish our minds and for the food that nourishes our bodies. Amen.

Grace notes

It was common at the temple for people to pray out loud, so the Pharisee wasn't drawing unusual attention to himself just by praying. What Jesus wants is for you to see the difference in the attitudes of the Pharisee and the tax collector. The tax collector was humble. He didn't look down on others and was truly seeking God's mercy and forgiveness. The tax collector knew better than to think he could impress God. But the Pharisee was too busy congratulating himself on his own importance to think about what he truly needed from God. "Talent is God given," said the UCLA basketball coach John Wooden. "Be humble. Fame is man-given. Be grateful. Conceit is self-given. Be careful."

The Crowd Roars with Excitement

Scripture

"As Jesus and his disciples approached Jerusalem, they came to Bethphage at the Mount of Olives. There Jesus sent two of the disciples on ahead with these instructions: 'Go to the village there ahead of you, and at once you will find a donkey tied up with her colt beside her. Untie them and bring them to me. And if anyone says anything, tell him, "The Master needs them"; and then he will let them go at once.'

"This happened in order to make come true what the prophet [Zechariah] had said: 'Tell the city of Zion, look, your king is coming to you! He is humble and rides on a donkey and on a colt, the foal of a donkey.'

"So the disciples went and did what Jesus had told them to do: they brought the donkey and the colt, threw their cloaks over them, and Jesus got on. A large crowd of people spread their cloaks on the road while others cut branches from the trees and spread them on the road. The crowds walking in front of Jesus and those walking behind began to shout, 'Praise to David's Son! God bless him who comes in the name of the Lord! Praise be to God!'

"When Jesus entered Jerusalem, the whole city was thrown into an uproar. 'Who is he?' the people asked. 'This is the prophet Jesus, from Nazareth in Galilee,' the crowds answered."—Matthew 21:1–11 (GNT)

Grace

Dearest Jesus, we praise your holy name, loving you for who you are. We thank you that you come to us with God's message of faith. Teach us to become more like you every day and in every way. Teach us, too, that our actions tell the world who we are—no titles, riches, or fame are necessary because you know us inside and out. Inspire us to think always about you and about others and to remember that all our blessings come from you. We thank you for this time together, Jesus. We thank you for this food. You are the King. You are the Messiah. Amen.

Grace notes

Five days after Jesus' crowd-pleasing entrance into Jerusalem, the people went from shouting "Messiah" to shouting "Crucify him!" What happened? The people had heard of his miracles and his power, but they had their own ideas about what power and glory are supposed to look like—of what their king should be like—and Jesus wasn't it. He didn't ride in on a chariot or flash a sword. He didn't have thousands of warriors. He was humble and meek, not proud or bold. Jesus brought new ways of thinking that would take time for many to understand. "As I read [the New Testament]," said the Messianic Jew Jay Alan Sekulow, "[my] suspicion that Jesus might really be the Messiah was confirmed," he said. (A Messianic Jew is a person of the Jewish faith who also believes that Jesus is the Messiah. The symbol, or seal, pictured here, representing the Messianic Jew, was found on pottery found at Mt. Zion, dating back to about A.D. 135.)

You'll Never Believe What Happened on the Road to Emmaus

Scripture

"That same day two of them were walking to the village Emmaus, about seven miles out of Jerusalem. They were deep in conversation, going over all these things that had happened. In the middle of their talk and questions, Jesus came up and walked along with them. But they were not able to recognize who he was.

"He asked, 'What's this you're discussing so intently as you walk along?' They just stood there, long-faced, like they had lost their best friend. Then one of them, his name was Cleopas, said, 'Are you the only one in Jerusalem who hasn't heard what's happened during the last few days?'

"He said, 'What has happened?' They said, 'The things that happened to Jesus the Nazarene. He was a man of God, a prophet, dynamic in work and word, blessed by both God and all the people. Then our high priests and leaders betrayed him, got him sentenced to death, and crucified him. And we had our hopes up that he was the One, the One about to deliver Israel. And it is now the third day since it happened. But now some of our women have completely confused us. Early this morning they were at the tomb and couldn't find his body. They came back with the story that they had seen a vision of angels who said he was alive. Some of our friends went off to the tomb to check and found it empty just as the women said, but they didn't see Jesus.'

"Then he said to them, 'So thick-headed! So slow-hearted! Why can't you simply believe all that the prophets said? Don't you see that these things had to happen, that the Messiah had to suffer and only then enter into his glory?' Then he started at the beginning, with the Books of Moses, and went on through all the Prophets, pointing out everything in the Scriptures that referred to him.

"They came to the edge of the village where they were headed. He acted as if he were going on but they pressed him: 'Stay and have supper with us. It's nearly evening; the day is done.' So he went in with them. And here is what happened: He sat down at the table with them. Taking the bread, he blessed and broke and gave it to them. At that moment, open-eyed, wide-eyed, they recognized him. And then he disappeared.

"Back and forth they talked. 'Didn't we feel on fire as he conversed with us on the road, as he opened up the Scriptures for us?' They didn't waste a minute. They were up and on their way back to Jerusalem. They found the Eleven and their friends gathered together, talking away: 'It's really happened! The Master has been raised up—Simon saw him!' Then the two went over everything that happened on the road and how they recognized him when he broke the bread."—Luke 24:13–35 (MSG)

Grace

Dear Jesus, you have risen! You are alive! Hallelujah! We believe in you, our Almighty God. Strengthen our faith, Lord. Our hearts yearn within us to grow and learn more about you. Remind us that even though we weren't one of the hundreds and hundreds who got to physically see you after you had died and come back to life, we can "see" you all around us: in your Word, in creation, in the lives of others, and especially in our own hearts. Thank you, Jesus, that you want to be a part of our lives—and each of us to be a part of yours. Thank you for blessing us, for blessing this food, and for blessing us every day. Hosanna in the highest! We praise your name! Amen.

Grace notes

Jesus rose from the dead and presented himself to people so they might believe. The Bible recounts at least 12 different times he did this. In this particular instance Jesus did more than show up; he explained, in great detail, how the Old Testament pointed to himself as the Messiah (the Savior). Look and you, too, will find Jesus very much alive, waiting to be part of your life. "What we see depends mainly on what we look for," said Sir John Lubbock. "Seek and you shall find" is a common theme in the Bible. What do you think that means, and why do you think that works?

Read All about It!
A Widow's Faith Turns Food into Money

Scripture

"A man from the group of prophets had a wife. This man died, and his wife cried out to Elisha, 'My husband was like a servant to you. Now he is dead! You know he honored the LORD. But he owed money to a man. Now that man is coming to take my two boys and make them his slaves!'

"Elisha answered, 'How can I help you? Tell me, what do you have in your house?' The woman said, 'I don't have anything in the house except a jar of olive oil.'

"Then Elisha said, 'Go and borrow bowls from all your neighbors. They must be empty. Borrow plenty of bowls. Then go to your house and close the doors. Only you and your sons will be in the house. Then pour the oil into all the bowls. Fill them, and put them in a separate place.'

"So the woman left Elisha, went into her house, and shut the door. Only she and her sons were in the house. Her sons brought the bowls to her and she poured oil. She filled many bowls. Finally, she said to her son, 'Bring me another bowl.' But all the bowls were full. One of the sons said to her, 'There aren't any more bowls.' Then the oil in the jar was finished!

"When she told the man of God what had happened, Elisha said to her, 'Go, sell the oil and pay your debt. You and your sons can live on the money that is left.'"—2 Kings 4:1–7 (ERV)

Grace

Almighty Father, thank you for teaching us again about how important it is for us to trust in you with all our hearts. We might as well forget about trying to figure out or explain your mysterious ways; it's enough for us to put our trust in you. Give us wisdom to understand your Word, and encourage us to stand firm in our love for you. Teach us to expect the unexpected in our lives, knowing that you love us more than we can possibly imagine—the Bible tells us so. May we show our gratefulness in all we do. Thank you for our food, Lord. May the spiritually hungry be fed through their faith. Amen.

Grace notes

A king should take care of his people, but in this case the king was not following God, so Elisha the prophet stepped in. God cares about the poor and needy, and he worked in the widow's heart to motivate her to follow Elisha's strange instructions. God is always able to work in unexpected ways—don't ever worry about whether or not something is possible, because that isn't an issue for him. "Miracles are not contrary to nature," said Saint Augustine, "but only contrary to what we know about nature."

The Outsider Is the Insider: The Story of Ten Lepers

Scripture

"It happened that as Jesus made his way toward Jerusalem, he crossed over the border between Samaria and Galilee. As he entered a village, ten men, all lepers, met him. They kept their distance but raised their voices, calling out, 'Jesus, Master, have mercy on us!'

"Taking a good look at them, he said, 'Go, show yourselves to the priests.' They went, and while still on their way, became clean. One of them, when he realized that he was healed, turned around and came back, shouting his gratitude, glorifying God. He kneeled at Jesus' feet, so grateful. He couldn't thank him enough—and he was a Samaritan.

"Jesus said, 'Were not ten healed? Where are the nine? Can none be found to come back and give glory to God except this outsider?' Then he said to him, 'Get up. On your way. Your faith has healed and saved you.'"—Luke 17:11–19 (MSG)

Grace

Loving Jesus, may we see how much your compassion and grace can change our lives. More importantly, may we always be grateful and eager to show our thankfulness in our daily prayers and actions. May we understand that you are loving and kind even to those who do not believe in you and that you want us always to follow your example. Teach us that through faith we can catch glimpses of you showing up in many places, surprising us all. Thank you for Mom and Dad, our grandparents, the rest of our family, and our friends. We are grateful to be in their lives and to have them in ours. Thank you for our food and for this time together. Amen.

Grace notes

Being thankful expands your soul; you can almost feel it taking up more space in your body, and that really feels good. Watch for this, because it will surely happen; being grateful triggers an awareness in you that your life is a gift—a wonderful gift that puts you on the fast track to joy. It makes you feel more alive. The two-time Olympic gold medalist Kristen Armstrong understands the value of gratitude: "I think I run my strongest when I run with joy, with gratitude, with focus, with grace," she said.

Gods or Men—Who Were They?

Scripture

"There was a man in Lystra who couldn't walk. He sat there, crippled since the day of his birth. He heard Paul talking, and Paul, looking him in the eye, saw that he was ripe for God's work, ready to believe. So he said, loud enough for everyone to hear, 'Up on your feet!' The man was up in a flash—jumped up and walked around as if he'd been walking all his life.

"When the crowd saw what Paul had done, they went wild, calling out in their Lyconian dialect, 'The gods have come down! These men are gods!' They called Barnabas 'Zeus' and Paul 'Hermes' (since Paul did most of the speaking). The priest of the local Zeus shrine got up a parade—bulls and banners and people lined right up to the gates, ready for the ritual of sacrifice.

"When Barnabas and Paul finally realized what was going on, they stopped them. Waving their arms, they interrupted the parade, calling out, 'What do you think you're doing! We're not gods! We are men just like you, and we're here to bring you the Message, to persuade you to abandon these silly god-superstitions and embrace God himself, the living God. We don't make God; he makes us, and all of this—sky, earth, sea, and everything in them.

"'In the generations before us, God let all the different nations go their own way. But even then he didn't leave them without a clue, for he made a good creation, poured down rain and gave bumper crops. When your bellies were full and your hearts happy, there was evidence of good beyond your doing.' Talking fast and hard like this, they prevented them from carrying out the sacrifice that would have honored them as gods—but just barely."—Acts 14:8–18 (MSG)

Grace

Gracious Father, thank you for the many blessings of this, your day; we are so grateful. Thank you for this food and for our family. Please bless us, one and all. Thank you for reminding us that you may call us in ways that do not necessarily make our job easy but that will make us stronger. Thank you for reminding us that success may not be what we imagined it to be. Remind us that our job is to trust you; you see the bigger picture, and obeying what you call us to do gets the results you want. Please watch over us. Amen.

Grace notes

Paul and Barnabas had just come from Iconium, where some riled up people had wanted to stone them. Now they were experiencing the opposite: being hailed as gods. Back in Iconium, as bad as things had gotten, they could have felt defeated enough to give up. Now, in Lystra, they faced the temptation of letting the people's undeserved adoration go to their heads. They didn't do either; instead, they stayed faithful and true to Jesus, knowing that God would work things out, even if in the most unexpected ways. If you find yourself in a place like Iconium, remember the words of the Civil War veteran Robert Green Ingersoll: "The greatest test of courage on earth is to bear defeat without losing heart." If you find yourself in a place like Lystra, remember the words of the major league baseball fielder Ichiro Suziki: "People striving for approval from others become phony."

Paul Has Some Choice Words for the Greeks

Scripture

"Paul stood up before the meeting of the Areopagus council and said, 'Men of Athens, everything I see here tells me you are very religious. I was going through your city and I saw the things you worship. I found an altar that had these words written on it: "to an unknown god." You worship a god that you don't know. This is the God I want to tell you about.

"'He is the God who made the whole world and everything in it. He is the Lord of the land and the sky. He does not live in temples built by human hands. He is the one who gives people life, breath, and everything else they need. He does not need any help from them. He has everything he needs. God began by making one man, and from him he made all the different people who live everywhere in the world. He decided exactly when and where they would live.

"'God wanted people to look for him, and perhaps in searching all around for him, they would find him. But he is not far from any of us. It is through him that we are able to live, to do what we do, and to be who we are. As your own poets have said, "We all come from him."

"'That's right. We all come from God. So you must not think that he is like something people imagine or make. He is not made of gold, silver, or stone. In the past people did not understand God, and he overlooked this. But now he is telling everyone in the world to change and turn to him.

"'He has decided on a day when he will judge all the people in the world in a way that is fair. To do this he will use a man he chose long ago. And he has proved to everyone that this is the man to do it. He proved it by raising him from death!'

"When the people heard about Jesus being raised from death, some of them laughed. But others said, 'We will hear more about this from you later.' So Paul left the council meeting. But some of the people joined with Paul and became believers. Among these were Dionysius, a member of the Areopagus council, a woman named Damaris, and some others."—Acts 17:22–34 (ERV)

Grace

Lord, you made the heavens and earth, and it is in you that we put our faith and trust. Guide us to a life that is filled up with knowing, loving, and thanking you. Thank you for the Spirit who lives within us; may we hear you, listen to you, and speak to you as the friend and Father you are. Guide us to make the right choices in life—guide us as though our life depends on it. May we fully realize that life with you provides joy and reassurance now, to be followed for all eternity by life in heaven with you. Remind us in the meantime, Father, that we ain't seen nothin' yet! Please bless our food and our family. Amen.

Grace notes

Paul used this Greek altar to an unknown god to tell the people of Athens about the one true God, the God who has no needs, the only God who gives life. God wants you to seek him and find him; he is waiting for you to open your heart's door. "When you realize that every breath is a gift from God. When you realize how small you are, but how much he loved you. That he, Jesus, would die, the son of God himself on earth, then you . . . you just weep," said the American actress and film director Angela Bassett. Do you realize—really realize—that when you turn to God you are turning to the Creator of the universe?

Daniel Versus the Lions: And the Winner Is . . .

Scripture

King Darius liked Daniel so much that he made him a supervisor and planned to eventually let him rule over the entire empire. Others became jealous and began searching for fault in Daniel. Finding no wrong, they hatched a plot to take him down, first tricking the king into making a law they knew Daniel could not obey: saying a pray to anyone but the king would get you thrown into the lions' den.

Then they said to the king, "Daniel, one of the captives from Judah, is not paying attention to you, O king, or to the law you signed. Daniel still prays to his God three times every day."

So King Darius gave the order, and Daniel was thrown into the lions' den. The king said to Daniel, "May the God you serve all the time save you!" [So there!] A big stone was placed over the opening of the lions' den. Then the king used his signet ring and the rings of his royal officers to put special seals on the rock. This ensured that no one would move the rock and bring Daniel out.

The next morning King Darius got up at dawn [after not eating or sleeping] and hurried to the lions' den. As he came near the den, he was worried. He called out to Daniel, "Daniel, servant of the living God! Has your God that you always worship been able to save you from the lions?" Daniel answered, "O king, live forever! My God sent his angel to close the lions' mouths. They have not hurt me, because my God knows I am innocent. I never did anything wrong to you, O king."

King Darius was very happy and told his servants to lift Daniel out of the lions' den. They did not find any injury on him, because Daniel had trusted in his God. Then the king commanded that the men who had accused Daniel be brought to the lions' den and thrown into it. The lions grabbed them before they hit the floor of the den and crushed their bones.

Then King Darius wrote a letter to all people and all nations, to those who spoke every language in the world: "I wish you great peace and wealth. I am making a new law for people in every part of my kingdom. All of you must fear and respect the God of Daniel. Daniel's God is the living God; he lives forever. His kingdom will never be destroyed, and his rule will never end. God rescues and saves people and does mighty miracles in heaven and on earth. He is the one who saved Daniel from the power of the lions."—Paraphrased from Daniel 6 (NCV)

Grace

Almighty God, we are in awe of your great power, knowing that you always have been and always will be. We trust you, Lord, to take care of us. We trust you, Lord, to always be faithful. We trust you, Lord, to keep every promise, even if it takes a mighty miracle. Encourage us to look to you in times of trouble. Encourage us to build our faith so we can boldly proclaim your goodness. Encourage us to recognize and announce your greatness, as King Darius did. We thank you for our family, for our friends, for this food, and for teaching us your ways. We praise you, Almighty God. Amen.

Grace notes

God says: "I am the Alpha and the Omega, the First and the Last. I am the One who is, and who was, and who will come. I am the Mighty One."* Daniel had no doubt about this, but King Darius had to see God's work for himself before he was willing to be convinced. As Jesus said, "Blessed are those who have not seen and yet have believed."** Look for the mighty miracles in life, the small miracles, and even those "miracles" that masquerade as "coincidences." How many can you name that have happened just in the last few days? God is there, with all of you, all the time. "Faith," said the Welsh preacher Dr. Martyn Lloyd-Jones, "is the refusal to panic."

*Revelation 1:8; **John 20:29

Jonah and the Super Huge Fish

Scripture

One day long ago God told Jonah to travel to Nineveh and tell the people there about Him and that he loves them. But Jonah didn't like those bad people and didn't want them to have a second chance, so he boarded a ship bound for another place, Tarshish. Jonah was running away from God.

God sent a huge storm at sea, the waves towering. The ship was about to break into pieces. The sailors were terrified. They took Jonah and threw him overboard. Immediately the sea was quieted down.

Then God assigned a huge fish to swallow Jonah. Jonah was in the fish's belly for three days and nights. Then Jonah prayed to his God from the belly of the fish. Jonah prayed to God with gratefulness that he had not drowned, acknowledging that only God could save him: "I'm worshiping you God, calling out in thanksgiving!" he said.

Then God spoke to the fish, and it vomited up Jonah on the seashore. Next, God spoke to Jonah a second time: "Up on your feet and on your way to the big city of Nineveh! Preach to them. They're in a bad way and I can't ignore it any longer." This time Jonah started off straight for Nineveh, obeying God's orders to the letter.—Paraphrased from Jonah 1, 2, 3 (MSG)

Grace

Heavenly Father, you certainly got our attention with this one! We see that even your prophets like Jonah sometimes had to learn things the hard way. Remind our hearts that growing in your Word is a process. Give us the wisdom to learn from Jonah's experience, to know and believe that you are the God of Second Chances. Help us to realize how much you love us, how much you want everyone to know you, and how a journey to heaven happens only through you, Lord. May these words strengthen our minds, hearts, and spirits. Thank you for the food, and may it make our bodies, minds, and wills strong. Amen.

Grace notes

Do you think Jonah was surprised at the miraculous way God saved him from drowning? God wants you to know that he will often respond with compassion (for you and others) when you show a willingness to move in the right direction. It doesn't matter where you start out; what does matter is what you do—where you go—from here on out. He wants you to respond to him. Here's another good thought: "Make no judgments where you have no compassion," said the American-born Irish writer Anne McCaffrey. How does this apply to the Jonah story? Have you ever looked down on some "Ninevites," only to find out that God didn't?

Shadrach, Meshach, and Abednego*

Scripture

King Nebuchadnezzar was furious with Shadrach, Meshach, and Abednego* for refusing to serve his gods and ordered them thrown into a huge, fiery furnace.

So Shadrach, Meshach, and Abednego were tied up and thrown into the blazing furnace while still wearing their robes, trousers, turbans, and other clothes. The huge flames were so hot that the soldiers throwing them in couldn't escape the heat and burned to death.

After a while King Nebuchadnezzar was so surprised at what he saw that he jumped to his feet. He asked the men who advised him, "Didn't we tie up only three men and throw them into the fire?" They answered, "Yes, O king." The king said, "Look! I see four men walking around in the fire. They are not tied up, and they are not burned. The fourth man looks like a son of the gods."

Nebuchadnezzar called them out of the fire. "When they came out, the governors, assistant governors, captains of the soldiers, and royal advisers crowded around them and saw that the fire had not harmed their bodies. Their hair was not burned, their robes were not burned, and they didn't even smell like smoke!"

Nebuchadnezzar said, "Praise the God of Shadrach, Meshach, and Abednego. Their God has sent his angel and saved his servants from the fire! These three men trusted their God and refused to obey my command. They were willing to die rather than serve or worship any god other than their own."—Paraphrased from Daniel 3 (NCV)

*Here's a funny way to remember their names: Shake the Bed, Make the Bed, and Off to Bed We Go!

Grace

Almighty Lord, we are amazed by the faith of these three young men. Inspire us to be strong in our faith, too; we want to act in your name. Show us that Shadrach, Meshach, and Abednego were reaching out to us with their story of complete faith in you. They knew that you would be there for them, and we do, too. May we come to have the same enduring faith in your presence and power. Thank you for this food and for this time to share your Word as a family. Amen.

Grace notes

Nebuchadnezzar, who ruled Babylonia, was the cruel and ruthless king who destroyed Jerusalem in 586 B.C. He saw the three young men from Judah walking around in the furnace—with another man, no less (someone who *hadn't* been thrown into the fire). Who do you think would have voluntarily stepped into that blazing furnace with them? Nebuchadnezzar said, whoever it was, looked like the son of gods. He was partly right; it was the Son of the only God: Jesus! (Sightings of Jesus recorded in the Old Testament have a special name: Christophany.) Nebuchadnezzar witnessed other miracles to, yet he never changed his ways. What does it take to convince some people? "A proud man is always looking down on things and people," said the writer C. S. Lewis. "And, of course, as long as you are looking down, you cannot see something that is above you."

If You Could Ask for Anything . . .

Scripture

"God appeared to Solomon and said he would grant Solomon anything he wanted. Solomon answered, 'I, your servant, am here among your chosen people, and there are too many of them to count. I ask that you give me a heart that understands, so I can rule the people in the right way and will know the difference between right and wrong. Otherwise, it is impossible to rule this great people of yours.'

"The Lord was pleased that Solomon had asked this. So God said to him, 'You did not ask for a long life, or riches for yourself, or the death of your enemies. Since you asked for wisdom to make the right decisions, I will do what you asked. I will give you wisdom and understanding that is greater than anyone has had in the past or will have in the future. I will also give you what you did not ask for: riches and honor. During your life no other king will be as great as you. If you follow me and obey my laws and commands, as your father David did, I will also give you a long life.'"—1 Kings 3:8–14 (NCV)

Grace

Almighty Father, we ask you to guide us with your wisdom and strength. Fill us with the desire to serve you by doing what is right and what is good for others, as Solomon did. Guide us to the right values in life, Lord. Give us the ability and the desire to go after wisdom and understanding; how we need them both. Lord, thank you for this day; please bless us, one and all. Amen.

Grace notes

God values wisdom, and you can be confident that he'll be the source of *your* wisdom if you'll only let him. He also wants others to see the wisdom in you so that they, too, will have the confidence to seek God and find him. "Your wishes and desires make clear who you are," said the Afghan journalist M. F. Moonzaier.

What's That Thing Wagging in Your Mouth?

Scripture

"A bit in the mouth of a horse controls the whole horse. A small rudder on a huge ship in the hands of a skilled captain sets a course in the face of the strongest winds. A word out of your mouth may seem of no account, but it can accomplish nearly anything—or destroy it! It only takes a spark, remember, to set off a forest fire. A careless or wrongly placed word out of your mouth can do that.

"By our speech we can ruin the world, turn harmony to chaos, throw mud on a reputation, send the whole world up in smoke and go up in smoke with it, smoke right from the pit of hell. This is scary: You can tame a tiger, but you can't tame a tongue—it's never been done. The tongue runs wild, a wanton killer. With our tongues we bless God our Father; with the same tongues we curse the very men and women he made in his image. Curses and blessings out of the same mouth!" —James 3:3–9 (MSG)

Grace

Heavenly Father, we thank you for food and family and ask your blessing. Instruct us in the long-lasting power of words, Lord. Keep us mindful of how hard it is to take back angry words—can anyone un-ring a bell? Help us see that it's the kind and inspiring words that change the world in the right way. Help us to think of you, Lord, and what *you* would have us say and do. May we live lives of love and joy that magnify your power—full of love and joy. Amen.

Grace notes

Maybe you can't un-ring a bell any more than you can take back angry, hurtful, nasty, or naughty words, but Jesus has shown us that he will forgive and forget those words you wish had never escaped your mouth. That's a blessing you can count on. Even so, it's better to think first and speak second, don't you think? "A fool is made more of a fool, when their mouth is more open than their mind," said the American poet and author Anthony Liccione.

Boaz and Ruth Get Married (A Doozy of a Family Tree!)

Scripture

"Naomi's widowed daughter-in-law Ruth respected her mother-in-law very much and moved away from her own family to care for the widowed Naomi, even though it meant sacrificing any opportunity of getting remarried in her home country of Moab and of raising a family there. God took note of this devotion. After a while he brought a man named Boaz into Ruth's life; they married and had a child. The town women said to Naomi, 'Blessed be God! He didn't leave you without family to carry on your life. May this baby grow up to be famous in Israel! He'll make you young again! He'll take care of you in old age. And this daughter-in-law who has brought him into the world and loves you so much, why, she's worth more to you than seven sons!' Naomi took the baby and held him in her arms, cuddling him, cooing over him, waiting on him hand and foot.

"The neighborhood women started calling him 'Naomi's baby boy!' [Even though it was her grandson.] But his real name was Obed. Obed was the father of Jesse, and Jesse the father of David."—Ruth 4:14–17 (MSG)

Grace

Heavenly Father, please bless and be with us today. Please bless also our family and friends. Thank you for bringing us together and for this meal. Remind us of how your purposes and plans are carried out to the smallest details. Give us the wisdom, Lord, to know you and to follow your path faithfully, so that we, too, can be a wonderful, willing part of your great plan. Lord, guide us in the little decisions as well as in the big ones. We want to be included in all the good stuff. Amen.

Grace notes

Obed became famous, all right—Jesus Christ was to become his distant grandson! Now that's some family tree! Ruth's act of devotion was one stone on the path God took to bring his Son, Jesus Christ, into the world. Do you think the people in this story had any idea of the role they were to play in the future of the world? Isn't it amazing how one ordinary act of faithfulness can change the world? Try to imagine what God might have in store for you! "Never be afraid to trust an unknown future to a known God," said the Nazi death camp survivor Corrie ten Boom.

The Amazing Tale of Esther and Mordecai

Scripture

King Xerxes reigned over 127 provinces stretching from India to Ethiopia. He gave a man named Haman the best job in the empire, and everyone, except a certain Jewish man named Mordecai, bowed down to him. This made Haman hate Jews, even leading the king to believe that all Jewish people should be destroyed. Xerxes let Haman do what he wanted. Mordecai, however, caught wind of this scheme and encouraged Esther, Xerxes' Jewish queen, to do something about it. Esther was very, very scared to approach the king.

Mordecai said to her: "Don't think for a moment that because you're in the palace you will escape when all other Jews are killed. If you keep quiet at a time like this, deliverance and relief for the Jews will arise from some other place, but you and your relatives will die. Who knows if perhaps you were made queen for just such a time as this?"

Esther formed a plan, asking the king to come to a banquet; there she would ask a favor. She invited Haman and Mordecai, too. Haman, thrilled with the invitation, began to lament that his great wealth and many children meant nothing with Mordecai hanging around. Haman planned to get rid of him by asking the king to spike Mordecai on a 75-foot tall sharpened pole.

On the banquet's eve King Xerxes could not sleep and so had the kingdom's history read to him. He discovered that Mordecai was the very man who had saved his life many years earlier. "What reward or recognition did we ever give Mordecai for this?" the king asked. His attendants replied, "Nothing has been done for him." Just then, Haman arrived to ask the king to kill Mordecai. The king, still lost in his own thoughts, didn't give him a chance and said to Haman, "What should I do to honor a man who truly pleases me?" Haman thought to himself, "Whom would the king wish to honor more than me?" So he replied, "If the king wishes to honor someone, he should bring out one of the king's own royal robes, as well as a horse that the king himself has ridden; one with a royal emblem on its head. Let the robes and the horse be handed over to one of the king's most noble officials. And let him see that the man whom the king wishes to honor is dressed in the king's robes and led through the city square on the king's horse. Have the official shout as they go, 'This is what the king does for someone he wishes to honor!'" "Excellent!" the king said, and ordered Haman to do that for Mordecai! Haman, humiliated, had to obey.

At the banquet, Esther asked her favor to spare the lives of her and her people who were about to be killed. "Who would do such a thing?" Xerxes demanded. "Who would be so presumptuous as to touch you?" Esther replied, "This wicked Haman is our adversary and our enemy." Haman grew pale with fright before the king and queen. Then Harbona, one of the king's eunuchs, said, "Haman has set up a sharpened pole that stands seventy-five feet tall in his own courtyard. He intended to use it to impale Mordecai, the man who saved the king from assassination." "Then impale Haman on it!" the king ordered. So they impaled Haman on the pole he had set up for Mordecai, and the king's anger subsided.

The order to kill the Jewish people was stopped. Mordecai the Jew became the prime minister, with authority next to that of King Xerxes himself. He was very great among the Jews, who held him in high esteem, because he continued to work for the good of his people and to speak up for the welfare of all their descendants.—Paraphrased from Esther 1,4, 6, 7, 9, 10 (NLT)

Grace

Heavenly Father, we thank you for this food and ask your blessing on all our family. We are grateful for your Word. Steer us from thoughts that might end up leading to actions that will lead to bad consequences. Give us the courage to stand up for what is right and just, just as Esther did. Make us determined to pursue goodness and stand fast in your ways, Lord. Thank you for this food. We are blessed to have you for our defender and provider. Amen.

Grace notes

God's ways are not our ways—that's for sure! Sometimes God works up front, out in the open, but in other situations, as in Esther's case, he chooses to do his work quietly from behind the scenes. Either way, God is in complete control, and you must never think of him as absent even when you can't see him at work. Why he chooses in one situation to help but allows disaster in another is beyond human knowledge. If you could just see the big picture you would better understand his ways; you would see that all his actions, or non-actions, are grounded in his love for us—nothing that he does is motivated by anger, moodiness, or any other reason. Did you know that one day in eternity he *will* clue you in on the whole big story?* Your job for now is to trust that his love for you is far greater than you could ever imagine and that he will always do what's right. That's a promise! "Whatever is at the center of our life will be the source of our security, guidance, wisdom, and power," said the writer Stephen Covey. Is God at the center of your life? What a difference that makes!

*Ephesians 2:6–7

SPECIAL
graces

New Year's Day

Scripture

"Commit your life to the Lord. Here is what he will do if you trust in him. He will make your godly ways shine like the dawn. He will make your honest life shine like the sun at noon. Be still. Be patient. Wait for the Lord to act."—Psalm 37:5–7 (NIrV)

Grace

Dear Jesus, this is the first day of new beginnings. Thank you for your blessing on this feast and for bringing us together to celebrate the year that lies ahead. Thank you, too, for the year behind us; its events have shaped our lives and made a difference in who we are today. We pray for wisdom and guidance all through this year. We pray for a year filled with adventure and excitement and curiosity. We ask your help that we may be better people—kinder, more compassionate, and more loving. May you fill our lives with the knowledge that you are with us every step of the way, and may this day and the days ahead hold many blessings for us. Amen.

Grace notes

The history of New Year celebrations is interesting. Did you know that we Westerners began celebrating the new year as a holiday only about four hundred years ago? Three thousand years ago, however, the ancient Babylonians (who lived in what is now modern Iraq) celebrated the New Year on March 23 (the date of the vernal equinox—the time in the spring when days and nights are of equal length) in a very different way. Their celebration lasted for 11 days, during which the king was stripped of his clothes and banished! "When the cat's away," as the saying goes, "the mice will play"—the people did as they pleased. After the 11 days the king would return in a grand procession, wearing splendid new robes, and everybody would get back to work. *Hmmm!* And all we do is watch fireworks and write resolutions! Sounds a little tame by comparison, doesn't it? By the way, New Year's resolutions should be a little less about breaking bad habits and a little more about positive goals and achievements, wouldn't you say? "Never be afraid to try something new," challenged an unknown author. "Remember [that] amateurs built the ark, professionals built the Titanic."

Easter

Scripture

In the words of Paul: "I passed on to you what was most important and what had also been passed on to me. Christ died for our sins, just as the Scriptures said. He was buried, and he was raised from the dead on the third day, just as the Scriptures said. He was seen by Peter and then by the Twelve. After that, he was seen by more than 500 of his followers at one time, most of whom are still alive, though some have died. Then he was seen by James and later by all the apostles. Last of all, as though I had been born at the wrong time, I also saw him. For I am the least of all the apostles. In fact, I'm not even worthy to be called an apostle after the way I persecuted God's church."—1 Corinthians 15:3–9 (NLT)

Grace

Dear Jesus, we thank you for our meal and for this joyful Easter day. We're thankful, too, that even if some of our loved ones may not be here with us, they're present in our hearts and minds, just as you are, Jesus. We love Easter because the day means lots of fun and surprises—maybe new shoes and Easter egg hunts. Help us to remember, though, that Easter is really all about new beginnings, that you alone conquered death, and that you are alive again today! Lord, remind us that Easter means you have made the "impossible" possible. Thank you for your love and protection, for you are way more powerful than anything else in the whole universe. We know that we never have to hunt for you, for you are always with us. Amen.

Grace notes

Jesus rose from the dead, just as he said he would. No one else in history has ever predicted his own death, resurrection, and then come back to fulfill the promise. (Had the writers who knew Jesus written anything but the truth, they would have been quickly discredited by the readers who also knew him.) Today about one-third of the world's population (about 2.2 billion people) call Jesus their Lord and Savior. Paul says that one act by Jesus—the resurrection—is the reason Christianity makes sense.* He's right. "If Jesus rose from the dead," said the pastor Timothy Keller, "then you have to accept all that he said; if he didn't rise from the dead, then why worry about any of what he said?" It's all or nothing, isn't it?

*1 Corinthians 15:1–20

Mother's Day

Scripture

"I thank God every time I remember you."—Philippians 1:3 (ERV)

Grace

Dear Jesus, we are so grateful for MOM. Whatever's going on—no matter how crazy things get—MOM is always there for us. Help us to be more understanding of all she has to go through for us. Teach us to say thank you more often, to mind her more often, and to pick up our clothes more often! We pray that MOM may be happy and that her work today may be fun. Most of all, we pray that whenever she thinks of us it will be with a big smile on her face! Lord, even though she loves us no matter what, teach us to want to make her happy—always!

We are so glad that Mom's our mother
We love her dearly; there is no other.
She makes us laugh, she kisses our tears
And quiets, with grace, our nighttime fears.
Our prayer is for a grateful heart,
So in spirit and mind we never will part.
As we bow our heads in thanks for this meal,
We want to say, "Mom, you're a really big deal!"
Lord, before we were born you knew our need;
With Mom you saw your plan would exceed
Our hopes and dreams of what we could do.
With her by our side, we'll be true, Lord, to you. Amen.

Grace notes

Billy Sunday was a straight-talking preacher who said, "I don't believe there are devils enough in hell that can pull a child out of the arms of a godly mother." Here's an idea: pick one word to describe something good about your mom. Okay, now pick two. Now three. Keep doing that and pretty soon you'll have a poem (poems don't have to rhyme, you know) to give her today. And that will probably be the gift she treasures most. Moms are like that . . .

Memorial Day

Scripture

"No one has greater love than the one who gives his life for his friends."—John 3:15 (NIrV)

Grace

Lord our God, we gather here together, asking your blessing on this food and on our family and friends. May we give thanks for America and for all the liberties and other blessings we enjoy. On this special day we give thanks to those who have served our country in its hour of need, and especially for those who have sacrificed their lives to preserve our freedom. May we never forget. Lord, watch over those who stand watch over America, ready still to uphold our liberties. Grant your divine care over all family members who are called upon to watch and wave goodbye—for a time—to their loved ones. We honor the devotion of our active service men and women away from home, and pray for the day of their joyous homecoming. Amen.

Grace notes

While it is true that the apostle John was talking about the enormous significance of Jesus' sacrifice for us, not only in this life but for all eternity, it's good for us to also keep in mind the sacrifices made by those who fight to protect our freedom and to rescue others from oppression. It's true that only Jesus can protect us for all eternity, but the men and women who give their lives make the greatest possible sacrifice they could make. For that we honor them. "Now the true soldiers of Christ must always be prepared to do battle for the truth." said the Greek scholar Origen Adamantius more than 1,800 years ago.

Father's Day

Scripture

"A father is tender and kind to his children. In the same way, the LORD is tender and kind to those who have respect for him." —Psalm 103:13 (NIrV)

Grace

Heavenly Father, our *Abba* (Daddy!), thank you for bringing us together on this special day. Your blessing means so much to us, and we give thanks for our food. We thank you for our earthly dad who loves us, cares for us, and holds us always in his thoughts. Encourage us to follow his ways, knowing that his rules are made out of love and a wish that we may grow up loving, kind, strong, and smart. Help us see that the greatest gift we could give Dad is not a *thing* we buy but a *thing* we do—for it's the heart that speaks the loudest. We pray that all kids may find in their lives the love of a "daddy." Happy Father's day, Daddy. Amen.

Grace notes

Did you know that most of us have at least two fathers? One of them is God himself. Some fathers, like God, can easily share their thoughts and feelings (many grandpas are like that, too). Others, though, don't quite know how to do that. Just as you do with your spiritual Father, maybe you can be the one to start a conversation with your earthly dad. Or maybe all you have to do is pay attention to the way he cares for you to know how much he loves you. You can be pretty sure that all godly daddies, whether or not they're physically present with the kids they love, dream of what the future will be like for them, praying that they'll grow up to be happy, loving, and kind. Sometimes the most loving thing they can do is to let their children make their own mistakes, knowing this will help their character grow strong. Anne Frank, a young Jewish girl who was forced to hide out from the Nazis, said this: "How true Daddy's words were when he said: 'All children must look after their own upbringing.' Parents can only give good advice or put them on the right paths, but the final forming of a person's character lies in their own hands."

Independence Day

Scripture

"Now the Lord is the Spirit, and where the Spirit of the Lord is, *there* is liberty."—2 Corinthians 3:17 (NASB)

Grace

Lord God Almighty, we give you thanks for the freedom and independence you have given us. May we honor you by never taking for granted your blessings, in particular the freedoms we cherish. We are grateful for everything you give us. As the fireworks light up the sky we say a prayer of thanksgiving for our forefathers and for the freedoms they fought for. Remind us of your goodness and love for all people of this earth. And—oh yes, Lord—thank you for this scrumptious holiday food fest! Amen.

Grace notes

The events that led to the founding of America were motivated in large part by a craving for religious freedom. Your own independence, however, is achieved through a complete dependence upon God. That sounds upside down and backward, doesn't it? How can dependence lead to independence? That is indeed one of life's mysteries. Relying on God means you'll have a fullness in life independent of how much stuff you have or don't have, or what you achieve or don't. The important thing is not to let your *things* or your status in life define you. Only then can you achieve real independence—and oh, what freedom that will give you. "God does not guide those who want to run their own life. He only guides those who admit their need of His direction and rely on His wisdom," said the New Zealand author Winkie Pratney.

Thanksgiving
A Song of Praise

Scripture

"Come, let us praise the Lord! Let us sing for joy to God, who protects us! Let us come before him with thanksgiving and sing joyful songs of praise. For the Lord is a mighty God, a mighty king over all the gods. He rules over the whole earth, from the deepest caves to the highest hills. He rules over the sea, which he made; the land also, which he himself formed. Come, let us bow down and worship him; let us kneel before the Lord, our Maker!"—Psalm 95:1–6 (GNT)

Grace

Heavenly Father, on this Thanksgiving Day we are so grateful and thankful for our family. We pray for those we love and for those we will come to love. We pray for those in need and for those who may never know you. We thank you for your loving grace and mercy. We thank you for life, for the food that sustains us, and for your Word that feeds our souls. We thank you, too, for our home, our country, our world—all your creation. We ask now for guidance, wisdom, and forgiveness. We offer you our grateful hearts in everything because we trust you and your perfect plan and purpose—for each of us. We give you thanks through Jesus Christ, our Lord and Savior. Amen.

Grace notes

Did you know that being thankful is the best gift you can give *yourself* (not to mention those who directly receive your thanks? Gratitude changes you. Look for those around you who always seem to be happy, and copy what they do. You'll be happier, and so will others. Here's a fun, easy Thanksgiving project: take one big linen napkin and have everyone at the table write something on it, in permanent ink, that they're thankful for. Date it and bring it out each Thanksgiving until it's filled up. Then start a new one. What memories you'll have! You'll be amazed at how your priorities change over the years, too. "Be thankful for what you have; you'll end up having more. If you concentrate on what you don't have, you will never, ever have enough," said Oprah Winfrey.

thyme

A Christmas Grace

Scripture

"You, O Bethlehem . . . are only a small village among all the people of Judah, yet a ruler of Israel will come from you, one whose origins are from the distant past."—Micah 5:2 (NLT)

"There were sheepherders camping in the neighborhood. They had set night watches over their sheep. Suddenly, God's angel stood among them and God's glory blazed around them. They were terrified. The angel said, 'Don't be afraid. I'm here to announce a great and joyful event that is meant for everybody, worldwide: A Savior has just been born in David's town, a Savior who is Messiah and Master. This is what you're to look for: a baby wrapped in a blanket and lying in a manger.' At once the angel was joined by a huge angelic choir singing God's praises: 'Glory to God in the heavenly heights, Peace to all men and women on earth who please him.'"—Luke 2:8–14 (MSG)

"For even the Son of Man did not come to be served; he came to serve and to give his life to redeem many people."—Mark 10:45 (GNT)

Grace

Lord Jesus, we ask your blessing upon this food as we celebrate your birth. Oh Lord, it's Christmas! A day of hope and cheer at the promise of peace and eternal life, a day that fills us with goodwill toward all. Christmas, a sign of hope for all in the world. Christmas, when your name is said in praise. We pray to you, Lord Jesus, that you will fill us with the Holy Spirit to spread the Good News and do what is right. We pray that you will motivate us to love one another, to help those in need, to support those who fight for our freedom, and to sustain those anywhere who are suffering persecution. We remember that life's path is not always easy. Jesus, you knew that Calvary—the cross—lay ahead, and still you kept walking. We carry you in our hearts, Jesus. Happy Birthday! Amen.

Grace notes

No one knows the actual date of Jesus' birthday, so why do we celebrate Christmas on December 25? Some say this date was borrowed from the celebration of the winter solstice (the shortest day and the longest night of the year). Others think that March 25 was the date on which the angel told Mary she would give birth to the Christ child, and nine months from that date is December 25. Some families today have a big birthday cake for Jesus and sing "Happy Birthday" to him. A birthday is a great day, though, isn't it? "The Son of God became a man to enable men to become sons of God," said C. S. Lewis.

A Birthday Grace for Her

Scripture

"Children are a gift from the Lord; they are a reward from him." —Psalm 127:3 (NLT)

Grace

Wonderful Jesus, we're so happy you're here with us to celebrate this special day. Thank you for food and family. Let your smile shine on all of us, but especially on our sister [or mother, grandma, aunt, etc., as appropriate]—it's her birthday today! Help her to do Christ-like things because your love glows within her soul. Cherish her, protect her, encourage her, and fill her with anticipation for the new things she'll learn and do this year. Light up her life with energy and passion. Let us sing now: "Happy Birthday to you, Happy Birthday to you, Happy Birthday, oh dear one, Happy Birthday to you." Yay, God! Amen.

Grace notes

Dr. Seuss delightfully said: "Today you are You, that is truer than true. There is no one alive who is Youer than You." If you're the birthday girl it's your day—all day. Does your family celebrate with birthday traditions? Do you get to blow out candles on a cake? Maybe a present, or several, have your name on them. Some families like to do other things, too, and these traditions make memory presents for years to come. Here are some ideas that might be new for your family: decorate her bedroom door with balloons and streamers. How fun for her to walk through it: *Surprise!* Give her a birthday donut—candle and everything—for breakfast! Let her pick the meal for her birthday dinner. It could be anything!—well, anything within reason (macaroni and marshmallows, anyone?). Decorate the cake together—all of you but her, that is. How about a treasure hunt? What fun!

A Birthday Grace for Him

Scripture

"May the Lord bless you and take good care of you. May the Lord smile on you and be gracious to you. May the Lord look on you with favor and give you his peace."—Numbers 6:24–26 (NIrV)

Grace

Dear Jesus, we are so happy for our brother [or father, grandfather, uncle, etc., as fitting]—it's his own special day! Yay! Thank you for your blessings on this red-letter, super-duper, supercalifragilisticexpialidocious day! Remind him that a person without a dream is in worse shape than a person without a penny. Give him high expectations for a life of walking by your side, for then joy will surely follow in his footsteps. Amen.

Grace notes

Ask the one celebrating his special day today to picture God saying his name with a big smile on his face and looking at him with delight, just waiting to see what choices he will make in life as time goes by. If that birthday boy is YOU, know that God wants you to know that he will be with you every step of the way. So be brave, adventurous, and bold! "If you can give your child only one gift, let it be enthusiasm," said Bruce Barton, a U.S. Congressman from New York. You can bet he said that with gusto!

parsley

Index

82. James 2:1–4 (MSG)
83. 2 Peter 3:8 (NIrV)
84. Romans 8:26–28 (MSG)*
85. Psalm 121:3(b) (NCV)
86. Romans 12:18 (ERV)
87. Proverbs 3:30–32 (MSG)
88. Romans 12:1–2 (MSG)
89. Hebrews 13:2 (NASB)
90. Proverbs 19:3 (GNT)
91. Isaiah 30:15, 18 (MSG)
92. Proverbs 19:19 (GNT)
93. Proverbs 27:19 (NIrV)
94. John 14:2–4 (MSG)
95. James 4:2–3 (NIrV)
96. Micah 6:8 (MSG)
97. Isaiah 40:28–31 (GNT)
98. Proverbs 4:5–7 (NLT)
99. Isaiah 55:8–9 (GNT)
100. Psalm 37:4 (GNT)
 Psalm 37:4 (KJV)
101. Proverbs 11:1 (MSG)
102. Proverbs 10:8; 12:15 (GNT)
103. Isaiah 43:25 (NCV)
104. Romans 12:17–19 (MSG)
105. Matthew 17:19–21 (NIrV)
106. Genesis 1:1–5 (NLT)
107. Proverbs 2:6–8 (GNT)
108. Psalm 40:8 (NCV)
109. Proverbs 9:7–9 (GNT)
110. Proverbs 10:18 (GNT);
 16:28 (NCV); 11:13 (GNT)
111. Proverbs 12:27 (GNT);
112. 1 Corinthians 10:31 (NCV)
113. Philippians 4:8–9 (GNT)
114. 1 Timothy 2:1 (NCV)
115. Acts 20:35 (NLT)
116. Isaiah 46:9–10 (NCV)
117. Psalm 116:1–2 (NLT)
 1 Thessalonians 5:17 (KJV)
118. 2 Corinthians 9:6–7 (MSG)
119. Isaiah 55:10–11 (NCV)
120. James 4:16 (NCV)
121. Mark 11:25 (NCV)
122. Philippians 4:12–13 (GNT)
123. Job 40:1–5 (NLT)
124. Psalm 46:1–3 (GNT)
125. Hebrews 11:6 (NCV)
126. Ephesians 2:10 (ERV)
127. Romans 8:31–32 (GNT)
128. 1 Peter 5:5 (NCV)
129. Psalm 46:10 (NCV);
 Psalm 3:4 (NCV)
130. Ephesians 1:4 (MSG)
131. Romans 12:10–12 (NIrV)
132. Romans 4:7–8 (NLT)
133. Colossians 4:2 (NCV)
134. Joshua 1:9 (GNT)*
135. Ecclesiastes 7:9 (MSG)
136. Romans 5:3–5 (NLT)
137. 1 Corinthians 12:7–9 (GNT)
138. Psalm 95:1–5 (NCV)
139. Luke 6:27–31(MSG)
140. Luke 18:14(b) (MSG)
141. John 10:14–15 (GNT)
142. Luke 19:26 (GNT)
143. Judges 21:25 (NIV)
144. Luke 12:48(b) (GNT)
145. Luke 16:10–12 (NCV)
146. Hebrews 4:13 (NCV)
147. Hebrews 11:3 (NCV)
148. Luke 8:18 (NLT)
149. 1 Thessalonians 5:16–18 (MSG)
150. Romans 2:1–2 (GNT)
151. Romans 8:26 (NLT)*
152. Psalm 18:1–2 (NLT)
153. 2 Corinthians 9:8 (NCV)
154. Proverbs 18:1–3 (ERV)
155. Philippians 2:3–4 (NCV)
156. Ecclesiastes 4:9 (MSG)
157. 1 John 3:18 (NCV);
 Hebrews 10:24 (NCV)
158. Psalm 145:8 (NCV)
159. Luke 6:47–48 (MSG)
160. Galatians 6:1 (GNT)
 Ephesians 4:32 (KJV)
161. Luke 18:1–8(a) (NLT)
162. Psalm 121:1–2 (MSG)
163. Ephesians 1:11–12 (MSG)
164. Colossians 1:15–17 (NCV)
165. John 15:16 (NCV)
166. James 4:7–8 (NCV)
167. Romans 13:9(b)–10 (GNT)

168. Psalm 141:3 (NLT)
169. Psalm 139:13–16 (NLT)
170. Deuteronomy 4:19 (NLT)
171. Proverbs 14:27 (MSG)
    Psalm 135:1 (KJV)
172. Proverbs 15:1 (GNT); 25:15 (NCV)
173. Romans 11:34–36 (MSG)*
174. Isaiah 42:5–6(a) (MSG)
175. Ephesians 2:10 (NLT)
176. John 15:4 (MSG)
177. 1 Corinthians 9:24–5 (MSG)
178. 2 Peter 3:18 (NIrV)
179. Proverbs 23:1–3 (GNT)
180. Psalm 103:1–3 (NIrV)*
181. Psalm 139:1–6 (NIrV)
182. Matthew 6:31–33 (NIrV)
183. 1 Corinthians 2:9–10 (NIV)
184. James 1:19–20 (NIV)
185. Ecclesiastes 7:5 (GNT)
186. Ecclesiastes 7:21–22 (MSG)
187. Proverbs 20:12 (GNT)
188. Nehemiah 8:10 (NCV)
189. Mark 4:24–27 (NLT)
190. Mark 4:21–23 (MSG)
191. James 1:27 (GNT);
    Isaiah 1:17 (NIV)
192. Exodus 4:10–12 (NCV)
193. Philippians 1:9–11 (NCV)
194. Proverbs 22:1 (NCV)
195. Luke 6:43–45 (GNT)
196. Proverbs 25:18 (NLT)
197. Luke 14:26 (NIV)
198. Proverbs 25:16–17 (MSG)
199. Matthew 23:11–12 (NCV)
200. Ephesians 1:3 (NCV)
201. Matthew 7:21 (NCV)
202. Psalm 103:1–5 (GNT)*
203. Proverbs 18:13 (GNT)
204. Joshua 1:9 (NLT)*
205. Philippians 4:19 (ERV)
206. Luke 6:12–16 (GNT)
207. Matthew 5:3* (NIV, MSG)
208. John 1:1–5 (NIV)
209. Revelation 1:8 (NLT);
    Hebrews 13:8 (NLT)
210. Colossians 3:20–21 (MSG)
211. Romans 2:10–11 (NLT)
212. Luke 6:38 (NCV)
213. Psalm 37:8–9 (MSG)
214. Psalm 91:9–11 (NLT)
215. Luke 12:15 (NLT)
216. Proverbs 21:2 (NCV)
217. Psalm 96:11–13 (MSG)
218. Psalm 118:24 (NIV)
219. Matthew 5:5* (HCSB, MSG)
220. John 1:29–30 (NLT)
221. Jude 1:24–25 (NCV)
222. 3 John 11 (NIV)
223. 2 John 1:5–6 (NLT)
224. Philemon 17–18 (NCV)
225. Titus 1:15–16 (MSG)
226. Jeremiah 9:23–24 (HCSB)
227. 2 Thessalonians 2:16–17 (MSG)
228. Zechariah 9:9 (NLT)
229. Haggai 1:3–6 (NLT)
230. Habakkuk 3:18–19 (MSG)
231. Obadiah 21(b) (NIV)
232. Psalm 51:10* (NLT, MSG)
233. Nahum 1:3 (GNT)
234. Obadiah 12 (MSG)
235. Psalm 116:12 (GNT);
    Proverbs 17:22 (GNT)
236. Hosea 14:8(b)–9 (ERV)
237. Romans 11:33–36 (NCV)*
238. Ezekiel 36:26 (MSG);
    Mark 9:23 (NIrV)
239. Lamentations 3:25–27 (NCV)
240. Song of Songs 8:7 (MSG)
241. 2 Chronicles 2:5–6 (GNT)
242. Psalm 18:29(b) (NCV)
243. Acts 2:32–34 (NCV)
244. Zephaniah 2:3; 3:17 (NIV)
245. Ezekiel 7:19–20 (NCV)
246. Psalm 34:12–14 (ERV)
247. Psalm 19:7–8 (ERV)
248. 1 Corinthians 10:13 (NLT)
249. 1 Corinthians 12:21 (NCV)
250. I John 3:18 (GNT)
251. 1 Peter 5:6–7 (MSG)
252. Matthew 25:21 (NCV)
253. Galatians 5:22–23(a) (NLT)
254. Mark 15:37–39 (GNT)

255. Proverbs 11:29 (ERV)
256. Mark 12:29–31 (NIV)
257. Psalm 34:12–15 (ERV)
258. 2 Peter 1:5–9 (CEV)
259. Romans 1:24–25 (MSG)
260. 1 Peter 3:8–9 (ERV)
261. Genesis 1:27–28 (NCV)
262. Proverbs 4:23–27 (NCV)*
263. John 6:35 (NIrV)
264. Ecclesiastes 3:11–13 (GNT)
265. Jeremiah 29:11–12 (NIV)
266. Isaiah 40:13–14 (MSG)
267. Joel 3:9-10 (NCV); Isaiah 2:4 (GNT)
268. John 10:10 (NLT)
269. 2 Kings 12:1–2 (NCV)
270. Numbers 6:22–26 (NLT)
271. Proverbs 16:7 (MSG)
272. 1 Peter 1:8 (NCV)
273. John 3:16–17 (MSG)
274. 1 John 3:1(a) (GNT)
275. Psalm 19:1-4 (NCV)
276. Psalm 69:30–31 (MSG)
277. Psalm 95:1–5 (MSG)
278. Galatians 6:1–3 (MSG)
279. Luke 12:3 (NLT)
280. Revelation 3:20 (NIrV)
281. Psalm 119:9–12(a) (NIrV)
282. Proverbs 27:2 (GNT)
283. Proverbs 27:3 (ERV)
284. Proverbs 27:11 (MSG)
285. Proverbs 27:12 (MSG)
286. Proverbs 27:14 (MSG)
287. 1 Corinthians 15:33 (NIrV)
288. 2 Corinthians 1:3–4 (NCV)
289. Luke 12:6–7 (ERV)
290. Deuteronomy 6:4–9 (NIV)
291. 2 Timothy 3:16–17 (NLT)
292. 2 Corinthians 13:11, 14 (NLT)
293. Ecclesiastes 3:11 (NLT)
294. 1 Samuel 17:45 (ERV)
295. Proverbs 4:23–27 (NIrV)
296. Romans 12:2 (NLT)
297. Proverbs 17:7 (GNT)
298. Jeremiah 29:13–14 (NIrV)
299. Leviticus 19:17–18 (NCV)
300. James 3:17 (NCV)
301. John 8:58 (NIrV)
302. Psalm 23:1–6 (ERV)
303. 2 Timothy 1:7 (ERV)
304. Deuteronomy 31:6 (MSG)
305. Balaam Had a Talking Donkey!
306. We Have Lift Off! Jesus Soars to Heaven and the Great Commission
307. The Tower of Babel: Bla-Bla, Bla-Bla, Bla-Bla
308. Noah's VERY BIG Adventure
309. The Lost Son Who Found Himself (the Prodigal Son)
310. How Did He Do That? David and the Giant Goliath
311. Jesus Walks on Water (Don't Try This at Home)
312. Grumpy Workers
313. The Parable of the Really Nice Guy (the Good Samaritan)
314. The Farmer's Greediness Was His Undoing
315. Jesus Calms the Storm: "The Wind Ran Out of Breath"
316. Lazarus Gets a Real Live Sequel
317. I'm Blind as a Bat!
318. Gideon and the Very, Very Small Army
319. Moses and the Bush of Fire, Or Burn, Baby, Burn
320. Lay it On, Lord: The Ten Commandments
321. And the Next King Is . . .
322. Solomon, a Real Wise Guy
323. Elijah Challenges King Ahab to a Contest of Fire
324. Wee Little Zacchaeus
325. The Story of Two Sons or What Say You?
326. Jesus Mobilizes the Immobile (Let Me Move You!)
327. Would You Want Jesus to Wash *Your* Feet?
328. How Does Your Garden Grow?
329. Why Does Jesus Tell So Many Stories?

330. Eight—Count 'Em—Eight Kinds of Blessing
331. What's the Big Deal about Forgiveness?
332. King Nebuchadnezzar's Incredible Dream
333. Hear Ye, Hear Ye: VIPs Visit Baby Jesus
334. John the Baptist Says, "It Ain't Me You're Lookin' For!"
335. Breaking News: 10,000+ Fed from a Lunch Box—It's a Miracle!
336. Which Is Better, What You Say or What You Do?
337. Glory Be! (the Transfiguration)
338. Don't You Just Love Finding Lost Things?
339. The Widow Gives Her All
340. The More You Have, the More You'll Get: The Story of Three Servants
341. King Belshazzar's Banquet: The Mysterious Handwriting on the Wall
342. God Drives Back the Mighty Red Sea
343. So the Bad Guy Is Really the Good Guy? (Being Right with God)
344. The Crowd Roars with Excitement
345. You'll Never Believe What Happened on the Road to Emmaus
346. Read All about It! A Widow's Faith Turns Food into Money
347. The Outsider Is the Insider: The Story of Ten Lepers
348. Gods or Men—Who Were They?
349. Paul Has Some Choice Words for the Greeks
350. Daniel Versus the Lions: And the Winner Is . . .
351. Jonah and the Super Huge Fish
352. Shadrach, Meshach, and Abednego
353. If You Could Ask for Anything . . .
354. What's That Thing Wagging in Your Mouth?
355. Boaz and Ruth Get Married (A Doozy of a Family Tree!)
356. The Amazing Tale of Esther and Mordecai
357. New Year's Day
    Psalm 37:5–7 (NIrV)
358. Easter
    1 Corinthians 15:3–9 (NLT)
359. Mother's Day
    Philippians 1:3 (ERV)
360. Memorial Day
    John 3:15 (NIrV)
361. Father's Day
    Psalm 103:13 (NIrV)
362. Independence Day
    2 Corinthians 3:17 (NASB)
363. Thanksgiving
    Psalm 95:1–6 (GNT)
364. A Christmas Grace
    Micah 5:2 (NLT); Luke 2:18–14 (MSG); Mark 10:45 (GNT)
365. A Birthday Grace for Her
    Psalm 127:3 (NLT)
366. A Birthday Grace for Him
    Numbers 6:24–26 NIrV)

*Intentional duplication or overlap of verses using different translations

Key to Bible Translations

CEV Contemporary English Version
ERV Easy-to-Read Version
GNT Good News Translation
HCSB Holman Christian Standard
KJV King James Version
LEB Lexham English Bible
NASB New American Standard Bible
NCV New Century Version
NIV New International Version
NLT New Living Translation
NLV New Life Version
MSG The Message Remix
NIrV New International Reader's Version

Acknowledgments

On May 11, 2007, I had lunch with Jack and Suzy Hinrichs. Jack began the meal with a blessing: "Come Lord Jesus." That was it! The idea for this book was born. It was an astonishing thought, too, because writing a book was the furthest thing from my mind. "But okay, God," I thought. "I can do this," little knowing where it would take me. It's ten years later, and the energy of that moment is in your hands. It wasn't an easy write; God had many things to teach me! I am profoundly grateful that he took me on this journey, for it nurtured my faith in ways I never would have imagined.

I am very grateful for my friends who helped me, encouraged me, and inspired me. Family pastors Pam and Ken Ingold (CRB, The Church at Rancho Bernardo) critically reviewed it, providing a welcome and necessary blanket of theological oversight.

What an inspiration and family my church (CRB) has been to me! Pastor Harry Kuehl taught me more than he realizes; the Holy Spirit just saturates his messages with the glory of God's Word, filled with *aha* moments for me. Dr. Mark Strauss and the other teaching pastors, Jeanette Moffett, Ken Ingold, and Bob Meissner, helped me more than they know. The binders full of notes taken furiously at every service attest to that. I am grateful beyond words.

I am indebted to the families who road-tested these graces and helped me find my voice: Trip, Miriam, and Waters Sliter; Tom, Julie, Dominic, and Vince Bendinelli; Pat, Michiko, Patrick II, and Catherine Johnson.

Thank you as well to Jane Allen (my accountability partner), Marilyn Wyman, Ruth Frost, David Slagle, Faye Bradley, Marcia Ramsland, Shelly Pinomaki, Teresa Bullock, Carol Anderson, Melissa Shoop, Marty Sesto, and the members of my Small Groups who provided me with comment, encouragement, and prayer.

I could not have done this without the expert help of my editor, Donna Huisjen—one of the best in the business. (She's also a great writer and thinker. Look for her books on Amazon.)

Thank you also to my agent, Karen Neumair of Credo Communications, for her persistence and encouragement.

And to my husband, Monte Hubbell; I could not have done this without him. He is my biggest supporter and fan, as I am his.

CPSIA information can be obtained
at www.ICGtesting.com
Printed in the USA
LVOW10s1520271017
554035LV00009B/442/P